EDGAR CAYCE,

the greatest healer of our age, was so shocked by his first vision of a "previous" life that he rejected its significance. But again and again "readings" of subjects by this great clairvoyant uncovered past lives—lives that would explain the subjects' present dilemmas and conflicts. The evidence in Cayce's files shows why he himself finally accepted the concept of reincarnation.

Dr. Cerminara's interpretation of Cayce's discoveries has been a classic for nearly two decades. She searches all levels of human experience in the light of karma and reincarnation, offering compelling proof that each soul lives not once but many times. And she substantiates again and again, with case histories, Cayce's astounding accuracy in prescribing cures for people he had never seen.

All About the Occult from SIGNET

GINA CERMINARA

MANY MANSIONS

With an Introduction by
Hugh Lynn Cayce

A SIGNET BOOK from
NEW AMERICAN LIBRARY
TIMES MIRROR

CONTENTS

Introduction

Many Mansions by Gina Cerminara, Ph.D., in my opinion, has been the best book in print on reincarnation and karma since its publication in 1950. Of course, as the son of Edgar Cayce, 2,500 of whose psychic "readings" are the basis for this book, I must admit at once that I am prejudiced. I find Dr. Cerminara's presentation the most stimulating and comprehensive that has come to my attention.

Although Edgar Cayce had been giving medical diagnoses by clairvoyance since 1901, it was not until 1923, in Dayton, Ohio, that the first reference to reincarnation appeared during one of his readings. After being asked by a man to give him an astrological chart, the first request of its kind posed to Edgar Cayce, he mentioned casually from his unconscious state that more important than the urges from the planetary influences were the drives, talents, and abilities which came to the man from previous lives on earth. He then went on to say about the subject, "For in the last incarnation he was a monk."

Following this reading, members of Edgar Cayce's family and his close friends secured what later began to be known as "life readings." In each of these Edgar Cayce described some details of previous incarnations on earth, apparently picking out only those that were most influential in the present. He then frequently gave names, dates, and places, as well as characteristic urges of talents, weaknesses, and abilities, and sometimes physical and psychological problems arising as a result, he explained, of memory carried over at a deep unconscious level from these previous lives.

Gina Cerminara brings to her analysis of these readings,

which she studied while living in Virginia Beach for a two-year period, a trained psychological point of view. Dr. Cerminara proved to be a skillful interviewer of many of the people who received readings, so that her book comes alive not only as a document dealing with case histories but also as a human-interest story about very live people wrestling with what apparently are unusual capacities or difficult problems from karmic memory.

Many Mansions begins with the story of Edgar Cayce, one of the most carefully documented and widely publicized psychics in the history of parapsychological research. Approaching the companion subjects of reincarnation and karma, two of the oldest beliefs in the history of man and more widely accepted than almost any religious concepts known to man, Dr. Cerminara examines the data in terms of depth psychology. Her analytical perception and her analyses of both of these concepts as possible explanations for well-known psychological problems move the whole subject from a consideration of religious beliefs of primitive and ignorant people to the respectability of a serious study.

The Edgar Cayce "readings" contain descriptions of many kinds of problems that seem to have no origin in the subject's present environment or heredity. For many readers the most exciting parts of Dr. Cerminara's book will be the chapters entitled "Karma and Problems of Health," "Parents and Children," "Marriage and the Destiny of Women," and "Past-Life Origin of Vocational Competence." It should be easy for the reader to find himself in these pages and hold up through these clear analyses a mirror which can be extremely helpful in pointing his life toward a richer and fuller experience.

With the acceptance of hypnosis as a means of medical therapy, more and more deep areas of the memory are being opened up, revealing what might well be memories of previous incarnations. Many of the hallucinogenic drugs apparently have broken down barriers and disclosed memories beyond the range of conscious perception. Outstanding is the work of Ian Stevenson, a psychiatrist and investigator of paranormal phenomena, in his study of more than six hundred cases of what seemed to be conscious memory of previous lives on earth. His *Twenty Cases Suggestive of Reincarnation* * is a most thought-provoking and scholarly essay.

All of the evidence for and against reincarnation and karma,

* Published in September, 1966, as Proceedings of the American Society for Psychical Research, New York.

subjects treated so challengingly in *Many Mansions*, is not yet complete. Dr. Cerminara suggests that "there is nothing so powerful as an idea whose time has come." *Many Mansions* certainly has opened the way for what seems to be one such idea. The reader has ahead of him an exciting, and indeed perhaps a disturbing experience.

HUGH LYNN CAYCE

Chapter I

The Magnificent Possibility

_____

MEN are born; they suffer; they die. In these seven words, according to a tale told by Anatole France, a wise man once summarized all the history of mankind.

There is another, more ancient, and more significant story told about the suffering of men. It is the legend related about young Prince Siddhartha who was later to be known as Buddha, the Enlightened One. Siddhartha's father was a wealthy Hindu potentate who was determined that his son should be protected from knowledge of the evils of the world. So the prince grew up to young manhood in pleasant seclusion and was given a beautiful princess in marriage without having once set foot beyond the palace walls. It was not until after the birth of his first child that young Prince Siddhartha—blissfully happy with his wife and child but curious about the outer world—managed to elude the palace guards and take his first trip through the teeming city.

On this fateful excursion, three sights on the streets impressed him deeply: an old man, a sick man, and a dead man. Shocked, the sensitive young prince asked his servant companion the meaning of such terrible distress. When he was told that these three afflictions were not uncommon, but fell to the lot of all mankind, the prince was so profoundly affected that he could not bring himself to return to his life of ease and pleasure. Renouncing all his worldly possessions, he set himself to the task of achieving wisdom so that he might learn to liberate men from the sufferings that befell them. Finally, after many years, he became enlightened, learned what he had sought to learn, and—his inner radiance being recognized—taught men the path of liberation.

10

Not all of us could, like Buddha, renounce love, power, wealth, ease, and the warmth of family ties to seek so intangible a thing as meaning. Yet all of us can, and ultimately must, become concerned about the selfsame problem: Why do men suffer? And what can they do to free themselves from pain?

Our Utopian novelists have envisioned an era to come in which two of the afflictions that so shocked Buddha will have been outlawed: old age and disease. But they have not yet seen the possibility—even with the most brilliant applications of modern physics—of outlawing what man thinks of as his ultimate enemy: death. And in the meanwhile, before a saner organization of the world and its resources can, if it will, bring security and health and peace and beauty and youth to all men, we are faced with a thousand insecurities, a thousand dangers, and ten thousand threats to happiness and inner peace. Fire and flood, epidemic and earthquake, disease and disaster, war and the menace of annihilation—these are some of the outer threats. And within the inner, psychic world of man, there are a throng of weaknesses and imperfections—selfishness, stupidity, envy, malevolence, and greed—that are the source of pain both to himself and to those with whom he lives.

In our moments of exaltation, swept by the sublimity of music or of a sunrise, we feel that there must be joy at the heart of the universe, and deep intention; yet turning again to the hash realities of life, with its cruelties and its crushing frustrations, we cannot but ask, if we have any perception, any compassion, any philosophic wonder at all, the ultimate questions: What, in the name of sanity, is the meaning and purpose of life, over and beyond the obvious, material one of sheer survival? Who am I? Why am I here? Where am I going? Why do I suffer? What is my true relationship to other men and theirs to me? What is our common relationship to the vast interplay of forces, and perhaps to a supreme force, beyond us and about us?

These are the most basic and the most ancient of human questions. Without an answer to these, all temporary expedients for the alleviation of pain, whether these be physical or psychological in nature, are finally without meaning. Unless the very possibility of pain has been explained, nothing has been explained. Until the suffering of the most insignificant, most remote of creatures has been accounted for, nothing has been accounted for, and our philosophic grasp on life is incomplete.

Since earliest times, even the most primitive of men have

asked these ultimate questions. They have looked up into the grandeur of the skies and felt that man's struggles and sorrows were not so ignoble or futile as they seemed; they assumed meaning by virtue of a great cosmic relationship between man and the stars. Or they have sensed presences in the forest and have said that all living things had a spirit, including man himself, and that this spirit of man lived and suffered only a brief while on earth and after death went to a happier and more peaceful place. Or they have noted the sense of right and wrong within themselves, and felt that there must therefore be a greater right and wrong in the conscience of the universe, and a great place of punishment or reward in some other, distant realm.

There have been a thousand such beliefs and explanations, some cruder than others, some more refined and reasonable. And all over the world today, men live out their lives and valiantly brave their hardships on the assumption that some such explanation is the true one. There are those who, on the authority of Mohammed, believe one thing; there are those who, on the authority of Buddha or Guru Nanak or Moses or Jesus or Krishna, believe another. And there are many thousands who believe that, beyond the need to survive, there is *no* explanation for human life; others have ceased even to wonder about it, preferring to enjoy the ease or the pleasure of the moment.

We who have been raised in the Christian tradition have our own explanation for human life and suffering, and it is this: man has a soul and this soul is immortal; suffering is a test given us by God, and heaven or hell is the reward or punishment that awaits us, depending on how we meet the challenge of our present life. Those of us who believe this explanation believe it—not because we have any proof of it, but because it has been taught to us on the authority of our parents and our prelates; and they in turn had it on the authority of their parents and their prelates; and so on back, until we come to the authority of a book called the Bible, and a man called Jesus.

This is, most people will agree, a remarkable book; and Jesus—whether he be man or Son of God—was an extraordinary person. Since the Renaissance, however, Western man has become increasingly skeptical of beliefs handed down on the strength of authority, whether it be a book or a person—a growing skepticism with regard to all beliefs that cannot be proved in the relentless laboratory of science.

Ptolemy said—and the Church accepted and taught his pronouncement—that the sun revolved around the earth; yet the instruments which Copernicus invented and used showed it was the earth, instead, that revolved around the sun. Aristotle—whose psychology and science the Church fully embraced—wrote that if two objects of differing weights were dropped, the heavier of the two would reach the ground first, yet by a simple experiment from the top of the Tower of Pisa, Galileo demonstrated that two objects of similar volume but of differing weights, when dropped, reach the ground at the same time. Numerous phrases in the Bible—together with the most obvious of common-sense observations—indicated that the earth was flat; yet Columbus and Magellan and other explorers of the fifteenth century quietly overthrew this conviction by the unanswerable accomplishment of sailing West and arriving East.

By these and a hundred other demonstrations, men came gradually to see that the ancient authorities could be wrong. Thus was the attitude of science born, and thus came about the skepticism of the modern mind. Discovery after discovery disarranged the neat world-picture in which man had believed. Spirit? Nobody has ever seen a spirit. Soul? No one has been able to detect a soul, either lurking in protoplasm or sitting on the pineal gland, where Descartes had said it ought to be. Immortality? Who has ever come back to tell us about it? Heaven? Our telescopes show no evidence thereof. God? A colossal assumption; a projection of a mind that needed a father-substitute. The universe is a great machine. Man is a little machine, made possible by an accidental arrangement of atoms and a naturalistic evolutionary process. Suffering is man's inescapable lot in his struggle for survival. It has no "meaning" other than that; no purpose. Death is a dissolution of chemical elements; nothing else remains.

For the authority of the Great Man, then, or the Great Book, or the Great Teacher, the authority of our own five senses has been substituted. Science has enlarged the range of our senses, to be sure, with microscopes and telescopes and X-rays and radar; and science has systematized our five-sense observations with reasoning, mathematics, and repeatable techniques of experiment. But basically the testimony of science and of reason is the testimony of our five senses. The edifice on which science is built rests on the eye, the ear, the nose, the tongue, and the touch of man.

In the past few decades, however, we have grown still more sophisticated and still more skeptical of what we know or what we think we know. The instruments which we have created with our brave, proud senses have ironically turned and showed us that this sense equipment itself is imperfect and inadequate to acquaint us with the world as it really is. Radio waves, radio-activity, and atomic energy, to name but a few phenomena of our times, demonstrate beyond the shadow of doubt that we are surrounded by invisible waves and pulsations of energy, and that the minutest particles of matter contain forces of a magnitude so great that our imagination cannot embrace them.

Somewhat humbled, we know now that we are looking out at the world through our eyes and ears as through tiny peepholes in the narrow cell of our body. Our vibratory sensitivity to light enables us to receive only a small fraction of the total number of light vibrations that exist. Our vibratory sensitivity to sound brings us only a narrow octave, so to speak, of the whole keyboard of sound in the universe. A dog whistle, bought at the store for fifty cents, will summon our dog, yet it will be inaudible to us because its vibratory frequency is above our uppermost limit of sensitivity. There are many other animals, and many birds and insects, whose range of hearing or seeing or smelling is different from our own; consequently their universe contains much that we do not and cannot perceive.

A thinking man begins to wonder at this curious spectacle of proud man—exceeded by animals and insects and birds and his own ingenious inventions in the perception of reality; and he begins to speculate on the possibility of seeing for himself some of these great invisibilities. . . . Suppose, for example, that we could somehow train or improve our sensory equipment in such a way that our vibratory sensitivity to light and to sound were only slightly enlarged: Would we not then become aware of many objects that were previously unavailable to us? Or suppose that a few persons among us were born with a slightly enlarged sensitivity range: Would it not be natural for them to see and hear things which the rest of us do not see or hear? Might they not hear at a distance, as if with an interior radio receiving set, or see at a distance, as if with an interior television screen?

The vast, incredible, invisible world of object and energy which our twentieth-century instruments has uncovered compels us to think about such possibilities, and—casting back into the long, strange history of man—we find that there are many cases in recorded history where such an enlarged perception seems actually to have existed. We learn that Swedenborg, the great eighteenth-century mathematician and scientist, is said by his biographers to have developed in later years a supernormal perceptive gift. One instance of his television-like perceptive power is particularly well known, since it is attested to by many distinguished persons, including the philosopher Immanuel Kant.

At six o'clock one evening Swedenborg, while dining with friends in the town of Gothenburg, suddenly became excited and declared that a dangerous fire had broken out in his native city of Stockholm, some three hundred miles away. He asserted a little later that the fire had already burned the home of one of his neighbors and was threatening to consume his own. At eight o'clock of that same evening, he exclaimed with some relief that the fire had been checked three doors from his home. Two days later, Swedenborg's every statement was confirmed by actual reports of the fire, which had begun to blaze at the precise hour that he first received the impression.

Swedenborg's case is only one among hundreds of similar instances recorded in history and biography of the great, the near-great, and the obscure. At some time in their lives Mark Twain, Abraham Lincoln, Saint-Saëns, to name but a few, had, according to their biographers and in some cases their own accounts, strange sudden visions of events taking place at a distance, or events that took place, down to the last minute detail, months or years later in their own lives. In the case of Swedenborg the ability to see at a distance developed later into a powerful and sustained faculty; in most other cases, the heightened perceptivity seemed to arise only in a moment of crisis.

We in the Western world have tended to look askance and with some slight suspicion upon such occurrences. However well substantiated they are, however well attested to by honorable and intelligent persons, however frequently they occur, we have tended to dismiss them with a raised eyebrow, a shrug, the word "coincidence," or the adjective "interesting" —and let it go at that.

The time has come, however, when we can no longer so lightly dismiss them. To a mind alert to the possibilities of high discovery within an unexplained event, to a mind aware of the great scientific currents and necessities of our times, the whole subject of the strange potential faculties of man is of tremendous import and interest.

Among the far-seeing scientists who have considered extra-sensory phenomena worthy of systematic laboratory investigation, and who have actually undertaken such investigation, is Dr. J. B. Rhine of Duke University. Since 1930 Dr. Rhine, with his associates, has been making extensive studies of the telepathic and clairvoyant faculties of man. Using closely controlled, repeatable experiments and adhering rigid-

15

ly to scientific method, Rhine has discovered that many individuals can demonstrate extrasensory powers of perception under laboratory conditions. Careful statistical techniques have been used to evaluate Dr. Rhine's experiments, and, mathematically speaking, it has been found that the results obtained could not possibly be attributed to chance. (For details of Dr. Rhine's methods and results, see his book, *The Reach of the Mind,* published in 1947.) Other scientific investigators, such as Warcollier in France, Kotik in Russia, and Tichner in Germany, also using laboratory methods, have come independently to the same conclusions as Rhine, and the growing body of scientific evidence is slowly undermining the prevailing doubts in the Western world that there exist in man's mental makeup powers of a telepathic and clairvoyant nature.

From three points of view, then, there would seem to be reason to believe that the narrow slits of man's sense perceptions can be enlarged. Inferentially, it is reasonable to believe such an enlargement possible; historically, a great accumulation of authentic anecdote demonstrates that in many instances it has occurred; scientifically, there is a growing body of laboratory data that testifies, by repeatable experiments, that man can experience awareness beyond the normal range of the senses.

To date, however, laboratories have established clairvoyance only as a possible mode of perception. Its potentialities for practical usefulness have not even been touched upon, even though these potentialities are enormous. Clearly, if man possesses a means of cognition that does not depend on his eyes or his ears; if man can, under certain conditions, "see" as if with an interior television set that which is happening elsewhere in space without the use of his physical eyes —then man possesses a new and important tool for the obtaining of knowledge about himself and about the universe in which he finds himself.

Man has achieved great things throughout the centuries. His strength and his cunning have enabled him to conquer space and subdue matter to his will. But for all his strength and ingenuity he still remains fragile and vulnerable; for all his great outer conquests he still finds himself impotent and bewildered; for all his triumphs of art and culture and civilization he still wonders as to the meaning and purpose of the sufferings which follow him and the ones dear to him from birth until death.

Of late, he has penetrated to the inner recesses of the atom. Perhaps he is now, with his newly discovered faculties of extra-sensory perception and his newly opening recognition of the strange relationship between conscious and unconscious mind, on the brink of penetrating to the inner recesses of himself. Perhaps he can finally find, after so many groping centuries, scientific and satisfying answers to the great basic riddles of his existence: the wherefore of his birth and the why of his pain.

Chapter II

The Medical Clairvoyance of Edgar Cayce

It is exciting to speculate on the possibilities of the clairvoyant faculty. It is even more exciting to find a man who, possessing the gift, was able to put it both to practical and to intellectually meaningful uses. Such a man was Edgar Cayce.

Cayce (pronounced Kay-see) was, in the last years of his life, referred to as "The Miracle Man of Virginia Beach." The title is a misleading one; though hundreds of people experienced remarkable cures as a result of his assistance, he was by no means a miracle worker in the usual sense of the term. There was no laying on of hands, no magical presence, no throwing away of crutches on the mere kissing of a garment. Edgar Cayce's so-called miracles were accomplished purely through the agency of his amazingly accurate clairvoyant diagnoses, which were frequently given at a distance of thousands of miles from the patient. Moreover, his clairvoyance was induced entirely under hypnosis—a fact which should be of special interest to those psychotherapists who are making increasing use of hypnosis as a therapeutic device or as a tool for the investigation of the unconscious mind.

One of the most dramatic examples of the manner in which Cayce's hypnotic clairvoyance demonstrated itself is to be seen in the case of a young girl in Selma, Alabama, who unaccountably lost her reason and was committed to a mental institution. Her brother, deeply concerned, requested Cayce's help. Cayce lay down on his couch, took a few deep breaths, and put himself to sleep. He then accepted a brief hypnotic suggestion that he see and diagnose the body of the girl in question. After a pause of a few moments he began to speak, as all hypnotic subjects will when so instructed. Unlike most hypnotic subjects, however, he began to outline, as if possessed of X-ray vision, the physical condition of the demented girl. He stated that one of her wisdom teeth was impacted, and was thus impinging on a nerve in the brain. Removal of the tooth, he said, would relieve the pressure and restore the girl to normalcy. Examination was made of the area of the mouth which he described; the unsuspected impaction was found. Appropriate dental surgery resulted in a complete return to sanity.

Another striking example is that of a young Kentucky woman, who gave birth to a premature baby. When four months old the child, who had been sickly since birth, experienced so severe an attack of convulsions that the three attending physicians, including the child's father, doubted that it could last the day. In desperation the mother asked Cayce to diagnose the case. Under hypnosis Cayce prescribed a dosage of the poison, belladonna, to be followed shortly by an antidote if necessary. Defying the scandalized objections of the physicians, the mother insisted on administering the poisonous dose herself. Almost immediately the convulsions ceased; after the antidote was given, the infant stretched out, relaxed, and went quietly to sleep. Its life was saved.

These instances, and hundreds like them, do not properly belong in the category of psychological "faith cures." In very few cases was the cure so nearly instantaneous as in the two just cited; and in every case a very tangible and sometimes a very long method of treatment was prescribed—whether by drugs, surgery, diet, vitamin therapy, hydrotherapy, osteopathy, electrical treatments, massage, or autosuggestion. Moreover they cannot be regarded as the exaggerations or fabrications of credulous people; careful records have been kept in the files at Virginia Beach of every one of the more than thirty thousand cases which came within Cayce's sphere of influence. These records can be examined by any qualified person who wishes to do so. They include dated letters of inquiry, appeal, and gratitude from suffering people in all parts of the world; letters, records, and affidavits of physicians; and the stenographic transcription of every word spoken by Cayce while under hypnosis. Together, they comprise impressive documentary evidence for the validity of the phenomenon in question.

Edgar Cayce was born in 1877 near Hopkinsville, Kentucky, of uneducated farming parents. He attended country school as far as the ninth grade, and though he nourished a youthful ambition to become a preacher, circumstances never permitted further study. Life on the farm did not appeal to young Cayce, so he migrated to town where he worked first as clerk in a bookstore and then as an insurance salesman.

When he was twenty-one there occurred a queer turn of fate which altered his destiny: he became afflicted with laryngitis and lost his voice. All medication proved ineffective; none of the doctors he consulted was able to help him. Unable to continue his work as a salesman, the young Cayce lived at the home of his parents for almost a year, inactive and despondent over his seemingly incurable condition.

Finally he decided to take up the trade of photography, an occupation that would make few demands on his voice. While he was working as a photographer's apprentice, a traveling entertainer and hypnotist by the name of Hart came to town and put on a nightly performance at the Hopkinsville Opera House. Hart was told about Cayce's condition and offered to attempt a cure through hypnotic means. Cayce gladly agreed to the experiment. It proved successful only to the extent that while under hypnosis he responded to Hart's suggestion and talked in a normal voice; after reawakening, however, the abnormal condition of the voice reasserted itself. The suggestion was then given him, while in hypnotic trance, that *after* awakening he could speak normally. Although this procedure, known as post-hypnotic suggestion, is frequently effective, and has helped numerous people to overcome excessive smoking and other habits, it did not succeed in Cayce's case.

Hart had theatrical engagements in other cities and was therefore unable to continue the experiments, but a local man by the name of Layne had followed the case with some interest; he himself was studying suggestive therapeutics and osteopathy and had some talent as a hypnotist. Layne asked if he might try his skill upon the still abnormal throat; Cayce was agreeable to anything that might help him regain his voice.

Layne's idea was to suggest to Cayce that he himself describe the nature of his ailment while under hypnosis. Strangely enough, Cayce did exactly that in response to the suggestion given him. Speaking in a normal voice (also in response to Layne's suggestion), he began to describe the condition of his own vocal cords. "Yes," he began, "we can see the body [He was using, here and always thereafter, a kind of editorial *we*]. . . . In the normal state, this body is unable to speak, because of a partial paralysis of the inferior muscles of the vocal cords, produced by nerve strain. This is a psychological condition producing a physical effect. It may be removed by

20

increasing the circulation to the affected parts by suggestion while in the unconscious condition."

Layne promptly suggested to Cayce that his circulation would increase to the affected parts and the condition would be allevitated. Gradually Cayce's upper chest and then his throat began to turn pink—then rose—then a violent red. After about twenty minutes the sleeping man cleared his throat and said: "It's all right now. The condition is removed. Make the suggestion that the circulation return to normal and that after that, the body awaken." Layne gave the suggestion as directed; Cayce awoke, and began to speak normally for the first time in more than a year. In the following months he experienced occasional relapses. Each time Layne made the same suggestion with regard to circulation, and each time the condition was removed.

The matter would have ended there, so far as Cayce was concerned, but Layne was alert to its implications. He was familiar with the history of hypnosis and knew of comparable cases in the early experience of De Puysegur, a successor of Mesmer, in France. It occurred to him that if, in the hypnotic state, Cayce could see and diagnose the condition of his own body, he might also be able to see and diagnose that of others. They tried the experiment on Layne himself, who had been suffering from a stomach ailment for some time. The experiment proved successful. Cayce, under hypnosis, described the inner condition of Layne's body and suggested certain modes of treatment. Layne was delighted; the description exactly fitted his symptoms as he himself knew them, and as several doctors had already diagnosed them, though the proposed methods of cure included drugs, diet, and exercises that had not been recommened before. He tried the suggested treatment, and after three weeks felt that his condition had improved noticeably.

Cayce was dubious of the entire affair, but Layne was excited and eager to see if they could help other persons suffering from ill health. As a boy of ten, when he first began to read the Bible from cover to cover once each year, Cayce had longed to be, like a disciple of Christ, a helper and healer of other people. Later he had thought he should be a preacher —but this ambition had been thwarted by circumstance. Now he was being offered, strangely enough, the opportunity to heal people—but he feared to accept it. Suppose he should say something while asleep that might prove harmful—even fatal? Layne assured him there was no danger; he himself knew enough about therapeutics to veto any recommendation that might be unsafe. Cayce searched the Scriptures for guid-

21

ance. Finally he agreed to help people who desired to be helped in so unorthodox a manner, but he insisted that it be regarded as an experiment and refused to take any money for what he did.

Layne began to take down in shorthand what Cayce said under hypnosis and to call these written transcriptions "readings." It was not a particularly accurate term, but none more appropriate seemed to suggest itself.

One of the most surprising elements of the diagnoses that Cayce now began to give for ailing townspeople in the time he could spare from his photographic studio was that they were accurately phrased in the technical terms of anatomy and physiology, though Cayce in his waking state knew nothing of medicine and had never even read a book on the subject. But most surprising of all, to Cayce, was the fact that people were actually being helped by what he told them to do. Layne's case had seemed questionable to him; perhaps it was only Layne's imagination that led him to believe he was feeling better. His own regained voice was certainly not imaginary, but perhaps that was due only to a lucky accident; perhaps the gift was reliable only with regard to himself. All these doubts, with which he wrestled continuously in the early years of the readings, were gradually dissolved by the undeniable fact that cures were being accomplished even in cases called incurable.

Word of his remarkable gift gradually spread. One day Cayce received a long-distance call from the former superintendent of the Hopkinsville public schools, whose five-year-old daughter had been ill for three years. At the age of two she had had an attack of grippe, and afterward her mind had not developed normally. The parents consulted one specialist after another, but none had been able to do anything for the child. Lately she was suffering from convulsions of increasing frequency, and the last specialist they consulted said that the girl had a rare brain affliction which invariably proved fatal. With sorrow in their hearts, the parents had brought her home to die, when they heard through a friend of the strange gift of Edgar Cayce.

Cayce was touched by the story and agreed to make a special trip out of town for the purpose of giving a reading. Since he was financially at low ebb, he found it necessary to accept the railroad fare which the father offered him; this was the first time he accepted anything tangible for the giving of his services.

He undertook the trip with misgivings in his heart, however. After he saw the little abnormal child he felt still more

22

keenly the magnitude of his own presumption. He, an uneducated farmer's son who knew nothing of medicine, attempting to help a child whom the finest specialists in the country had been unable to help. It was with a sense of trepidation that he lay down on the family's parlor sofa and put himself to sleep. Under hypnosis, however, all self-doubt disappeared. Layne was present and gave the suggestion; then he transcribed as usual what Cayce had to say. With the same calm, fluent certainty of all previous readings, the sleeping photographer began to describe the child's condition. He stated that the girl had had a fall from a carriage just previous to the attack of grippe, and that the grippe germs had settled in the afflicted area, thus causing the convulsive attacks. Proper osteopathic adjustments would relieve the pressures and would result in normalcy.

The mother confirmed the fact that the child had fallen from a carriage; it had never occurred to her, however—there being no apparent injury—that this could have had any relationship to the girl's abnormal condition.

The adjustments were given by Layne as directed by the readings; within three weeks the child was free from all convulsive attacks and her mind showed definite signs of clearing. She called the name of a doll that had been her favorite plaything before the onset of her illness; then she called her father and mother by name for the first time in years. After three months the grateful parents reported that the girl was normal in all respects, and was rapidly regaining the ground lost in the three beclouded years.

Instances like these gave Cayce reassurance that he was not wrong in using a faculty so strange and unaccountable. They also caused his fame to spread. Newspapers suddenly discovered him and publicized him; he began to receive long-distance calls and telegrams from desperate people who wanted his help. It was then that he learned it was possible to conduct readings at a distance, provided he was given in the suggestion the exact name of the person, and his location at the time the reading was made—street address, town, and state. Often he would begin these distant readings with some comment in an undertone on the surroundings of the person for whom he was giving the reading. "Pretty rough wind here this morning." "Winterhur, Switzerland. Isn't it pretty! Nice, beautiful stream." "The body is just leaving—going down in the elevator now." "Not bad-looking pajamas." "Yes. We find the mother praying." These descriptions invariably proved accurate, and provide one more piece of evidence for the validity of his clairvoyance.

The procedure, however, was always the same, whether he was giving readings for people at a distance or in the same room. He needed only to remove his shoes, loosen his collar and tie, lie down on a couch or bed, and relax completely. It was preferable, he found, to lie in a south-north direction, with his head to the south and his feet to the north. Other than the couch and a pillow for his head, no equipment was necessary; even these could be dispensed with, except for reasons of comfort. Readings could be taken at night or in broad daylight; darkness or light had no effect on the procedure. A few minutes after lying down he would have put himself to sleep. Then Layne, or Cayce's wife, or in later years his son Hugh Lynn, or any other responsible person whom he entrusted with the task, would give him an appropriate suggestion. The usual formula ran:

You will now have before you (*individual's name*) who is located at (*street address, town, state*). You will go over this body carefully, examine it thoroughly, and tell me the conditions you find at the present time, giving the cause of existing conditions; also suggestions for help and relief of this body. You will answer questions as I ask them.

After a few minutes Cayce would begin to speak, and Layne, or later on Miss Gladys Davis, recorded in shorthand what he said. Later these written records were transcribed on the typewriter; one copy would in most cases be given to the subject of the reading, or to his parent, guardian, or physician; the yellow-sheet carbon copy remained in the permanent files which he had begun to keep.

The newspaper publicity, together with his growing word-of-mouth fame, soon began to attract the attention of eager fortune hunters. A cotton merchant offered Cayce a hundred dollars a day for two weeks for daily readings on the cotton market. He needed money badly at the time, but he refused. Others wanted to know where to hunt for buried treasure; how to play the horses. Several times he allowed himself to be persuaded to try readings of this type as an experiment. A few times he was successful in predicting the outcome of a horse race; a few times unsuccessful; but each time, when he awoke, he felt depleted in energy and dissatisfied with himself. Once he was induced to embark on a venture in Texas, using his clairvoyant faculty for the discovery of the position of oil wells. Results were unsatisfactory. He came finally to the conviction that his gift could be depended on only with

24

respect to helping the sick; that it should be used for this purpose alone, and never merely to help anyone, including himself, to make money.

Offers of publicity left him as unmoved as offers of great shared fame. In 1922 the editor of the Denver *Post* heard of Cayce and summoned him to Denver. After witnessing a convincing demonstration of his work, the editor suggested an arrangement whereby he would pay Cayce a thousand dollars a day and make complete arrangements for his triumphal appearances on these terms: that Cayce should wear a turban and assume an Oriental name, and that he should give the readings hidden from the listeners by a translucent curtain. Cayce flatly refused.

David Kahn, president of the Brunswick Radio and Television Corporation and lifelong friend of Cayce's, did much to make the latter's work known among his wide circle of friends and business associates in private conversation; yet when he proposed more spectacular means of publicizing him, Cayce was adamant in his refusal. With the exception of one lecture announcement in a Birmingham, Alabama paper, he never in his entire career permitted any kind of advertising, either for his readings or for his public lectures. In conversations with people who knew him slightly, he never spoke about his unusual gift unless asked about it. Most people in his town knew little about him, beyond the fact that he taught in one of the local Sunday School classes; he was a member of no social, fraternal, or civic organization. Unswervingly he lived by the conviction that he was only an instrument through which healing and help could be given to suffering people; that attention should never be called to himself; and that those whom he could help would hear of him through personal recommendation rather than by the blazoning of headlines.

During the early years Cayce continued his trade of photographer, scrupulously refusing to accept money for the readings. It was only later, when the demand for his services became so pressing that he was unable to work at his trade, that he felt justified in making a charge for what he did in order to support his family. Even then he gave a great number of readings free to people who could not afford to pay for them. His attitude remained throughout fundamentally unbusinesslike. Carbon copies of his letters on file at Virginia Beach (where he moved in 1927, at the readings' recommendation) are eloquent testimony of this fact. Ungrammatical, badly punctuated, and badly spelled, they breathe none the less a spirit of eagerness to help and to teach his fellow-men.

Throughout these years he was besieged by doubts as to what he was doing. Sometimes, when a reading was asked for, the sleeping Cayce simply remained silent. Apparently his own health and state of mind affected his ability. Though he was on the whole a mild-dispositioned man, he was not free from bursts of temper; worry about finances frequently enveloped him. Emotional states like these evidently inhibited his gift. In most instances the unsuccessful readings were obtained at a later time, when the suggestion was repeated to him and when his physical or emotional tone was improved.

What troubled him most, however, was when people sometimes reported indignantly that the reading did not accurately describe their condition or that, after trying its recommendations, they had not been helped. Humbly and apologetically Cayce would write them long letters, explaining that he did not pretend to be infallible; that many conditions he did not fully understand seemed to affect the readings; that sometime, like a radio receiving set, he did not get clear reception. He would conclude: "Our only purpose is to help you; if you have not been helped, I want you to have your money back." And he would enclose a check in full amount of their payment.

Sometimes he would hear from these people again, many months later, telling him that a later medical diagnosis had confirmed what he had originally said and what they had disbelieved. Sometimes, too, he would discover that persons who had complained about the failure of the treatment had been careless in omitting an essential part of the diet, medication, adjustments, or mental discipline that had been prescribed.

In any case, he knew that the readings were not infallible. But as time went on their clarity and accuracy improved as he understood more and more how to use his gift. The occasional failures and apparent inaccuracies were counter-balanced, moreover, by the almost spectacular cures accomplished as years went by. A Catholic priest in Canada was healed of epilepsy; a young high-school graduate of Dayton, Ohio, was relieved of a severe case of arthritis; a New York dentist was released in two weeks of a migraine headache that had been tormenting him for two years; a young woman musician of Kentucky, given up as a hopeless case by a famous Tennessee clinic, was cured in a year of the strange malady called scleroderma; a boy in Philadelphia, born with infant glaucoma (commonly regarded as incurable), gained normal eyesight under treatment from a doctor who followed the instructions given by Cayce. It was cases such as these that cumulatively and finally convinced the ever-modest, ever-doubting, ever-scrupulous Cayce that, barring minor distortions and difficulties, his gift could be trusted; that it was in reality a gift of God rather than a tool of the devil.

At several points in his career Cayce was confronted by investigators who were as suspicious and skeptical of him as he was of himself. Hugo Munsterberg, a psychologist from Harvard University, was one of these. Munsterberg came expecting to find a cabinet, a darkened room, and the other usual paraphernalia of mediumistic charlatans. He was surprised to discover that Cayce needed none of these things, that he simply lay down on a couch in full daylight, and that, after receiving a simple hypnotic suggestion, he began to talk coherently in his sleep.

Munsterberg observed Cayce closely as he gave a reading; he interviewed persons who had experienced cures as a result of Cayce's clairvoyance; he scrutinized the records of previous readings. He went away convinced—like all others before and after him who came to expose what they thought to be a clever deception—that whatever Cayce was, he was not a charlatan. Munsterberg had been persuaded both by the testimony of the cases themselves, and by the simple unpretentious honesty of the man himself.

On the other hand, men of vision and good will appeared at various times in Cayce's life who, recognizing the humanitarian and scientific importance of what he was doing, gave him both moral and financial assistance in the vicissitudes of his strange career. Several of these persons conceived the idea of a hospital in which readings could be given and the somewhat unusual prescriptions of the readings carried out by a sympathetic staff. A wealthy man by the name of Morton Blumenthal, who had himself benefited from the readings, made this dream an actuality; in 1929 the Cayce Hospital was established at Virginia Beach, Virginia. The hospital was in existence for two years, but had to close because of the financial losses of its sponsor in the stock-market crash.

The publication of Cayce's biography in 1942 (*There Is a River*, by Thomas Sugrue), followed by the appearance of a magazine article entitled "Miracle Man of Virginia Beach" in the September 1943, issue of *Coronet* magazine, gave the phenomenon of Cayce's gift nationwide publicity. As a result he was deluged by mail from all parts of the country.

The tragic urgency of some of these cases was heartrending. Cayce could not bear to turn anyone away, and appointments were scheduled as far as a year and a half in advance. Instead of giving only two or three readings a day, he found himself giving as many as eight—four in the morning and

27

four in the afternoon. To work in one's sleep might seem to be an easy way of life, but it was a tremendous drain on his nervous energy. The strain of this constant service told on him, and on January 3, 1945, he died, at the age of sixty-seven.

So ended the life history of the man Edgar Cayce; but his significance was not buried with him. If a man's immortality can be said to rise from the transforming good he has accomplished in the lives of his fellow-beings, then Cayce's title to immortality is secure. But more important even than this is Cayce's contribution to the ever-growing body of evidence that attests to the reality of the clairvoyant faculty in man. For the clairvoyance of Cayce passed a rigorous pragmatic test. Not only did he see what other people could not see, but his seeing was afterwards verifiable. Not only was it verifiable; it was workable. Not only was it workable; but it worked.

Chapter III

An Answer to the Riddles of Life

_____

For twenty years of humanitarian activity, Edgar Cayce's clairvoyance showed itself to be reliable in literally thousands of instances. One feels the need of reminding oneself of this fact when coming to the next development in his strange career.

At first his powers of preception had been directed inward, to the hidden places of the human body. Not until many years passed did it occur to anyone that these powers might also be directed outward, to the universe itself, to the relationship of man and the universe, and to the problems of human destiny. It happened in the following way.

Arthur Lammers, a well-to-do printer of Dayton, Ohio, had heard about Cayce through a business associate, and his interest was sufficiently roused for him to take a special trip down to Selma, Alabama, where Cayce was living at the time, to watch him work. Lammers had no health problem of his own, but he was convinced, after several days' observation of readings, that Cayce's clairvoyance was authentic. A well-informed, intellectually alert man, he began to think that a mind able to perceive realities unavailable to normal sight should be able to shed light on problems of more universal significance than the functioning of a sick man's liver or the intricacies of his digestive tract. Which philosophic system, for example, came closest to the truth? What was the purpose, if any, of man's existence? Was there any truth in the doctrine of immortality? If so, what happened to man after death? Could Cayce's clairvoyance give answers to questions like these?

Cayce didn't know. Abstract questions concerning ultimate

matters had never crossed his mind. The religion he had been taught in church he accepted without question; speculation as to its truth in comparison with philosophy, science, or the teachings of other religions was foreign to his thinking. It was only because of his generous desire to help suffering people that he had continued to go into a sleep so unorthodox. Lammers was the first person who saw other possibilities in the faculty besides the curing of disease, and Cayce's imagination was stirred. The readings had seldom failed to answer any question put to them; there seemed no reason why they should not answer Lammers' questions.

Since Lammers was unable because of business affairs to remain in Selma, he invited Cayce to be his guest for a week or two in Dayton. Cayce, feeling that perhaps God wished to open new paths of service to him, agreed to go.

Lammers had recently become curious about astrology. If astrology were true, he thought, it might well be a system of analysis that related man intelligibly to the rest of the universe. This, then, seemed to him a good starting point for clairvoyant investigation. And so, when Cayce lay down one October afternoon in 1923 at the old Phillips Hotel in Dayton, it was suggested, not that he would see the interior of Lammers' body, but that he would give Lammers' horoscope instead.

Compliant as always to the suggestion given him, the sleeping Cayce obliged with a horoscope in brief, telegraphic sentences. Then, almost at the end of the reading, and still in staccato, noncommittal style, came the curious sentence: "He was once a monk."

There were only five one-syllable words in that sentence. But to Lammers, who through wide reading had become familiar with the major theories of human destiny, it was an electrifying group of words. Could it mean that Cayce's beyond-normal vision saw as a fact the ancient theory of reincarnation?

Far from gratifying Lammers' curiosity, this reading served only to fan its flame. When Cayce woke from his sleep he found Lammers excitedly discussing the implications of what had just been said with his stenographer and with his secretary, Linden Shroyer. If it could be proved that reincarnation was a fact, Lammers exclaimed, the demonstration would modify present ideas about philosophy, religion, and psychology. If Cayce would give more readings on the subject, they might discover specifically how the laws of reincarnation operated. How, for example, was reincarnation related to astrology. How did both of them together explain human life, personality, and destiny?

Avidly, Lammers requested more readings on the subject. Perplexed and somewhat reluctant, Cayce agreed to give them. In answer to Lammers' eager questions, the readings now became more specific and detailed, both with respect to his own past life experiences and to the abstract problems he had started out to investigate. Astrology, according to the readings, contained a certain amount of truth. The solar system provided a cycle of experiences for the evolving soul; man alternated experiences on earth with experiences in other dimensions of consciousness. To these dimensions tradition had anciently given the names of the planets which served as their focal points. Astrology as now practiced was only an approximation of the truth, however; it fell short of complete accuracy because, first, it did not take reincarnation into account, and secondly, it did not fully understand how the so-called "astrological" influences affected man through his glandular system and through his previous experiences in the other dimensions. Lammers had been familiar with both the concept of astrology and that of reincarnation; but such an inter-relationship as this had never entered his mind.

The whole thing seemed fantastic to Cayce, but curiosity impelled him to agree to continue giving the readings Lammers requested. It occurred to them that they might get better information on past lives if they stopped asking for a "horoscope" and gave Cayce a more appropriate hypnotic suggestion; so they asked him, while asleep, for such a formula. He gave the following command:

> You will have before you (*the person's name*), born (*his date of birth*) in (*his place of birth*). You will give the relation of this entity and the universe, and the universal forces, giving the conditions which are as personalities, latent and exhibited, in the present life; also the former appearances on the earth plane, giving time, place, and the name; and that in each life which built or retarded the entity's development.

After this the readings became more pointed and explicit with respect to past life incarnations, and soon the term "life readings" suggested itself, as distinguished from the readings for physical health, which now became known as "physical readings." The procedure for both types was the same, except for one detail. Cayce began to notice a strong feeling of dizziness whenever he gave a number of life readings in succession. He took a physical reading on himself to discover the cause of the dizziness, and was told to reverse his position from south-north to north-south (that is, his head to the north and his feet to the south) for the life readings. No explanation for this change was given beyond "a matter of polarity."

Life readings on Cayce himself revealed that he had been a high priest in Egypt, many centuries ago, who was possessed of great occult powers; but self-will and sensuality proved his undoing. In a later incarnation in Persia he had been a physician. Once he had been wounded in desert warfare and left to die on the sands; alone, without food, water, or shelter, he spent three days and nights in such physical agony that he made a supreme effort to release his consciousness from his body. (An interesting parallel to this effort at release is found in fiction in the experience of Jack London's strait-jacketed prisoner in *The Star Rover*.) He was successful in his attempt. This was in part the basis for his faculty in the present for releasing his mind from the limitations of his body. All his virtues and defects of the present were frankly appraised and attributed to one or another of his many previous experiences. The present lifetime was a kind of test for his soul; he had been given the opportunity to serve mankind selflessly, and thus redeem the pride, materialism, and sensuality of his past.

Lammers felt that this new turn the readings had taken was so important as to warrant much further research. He insisted that Cayce summon his family from Selma, to Dayton, assuring him that he would sponsor them during their stay. Mrs. Cayce, the two sons, and the secretary Gladys Davis, now almost a member of the family, agreed to come; when they arrived and learned about what had happened, their reaction was similar to that of Cayce himself: amazed incredulity, followed gradually by curiosity and eager interest. Life readings were taken on all of them. In each case the account gave a frank evaluation of the individual's character, and indicated that the origin of his qualities lay in past life experiences. "Four of your lives were spent as a research scientist," one of the sons was told, in substance, "and you have become materialistic and self-absorbed." "You have a very bad temper," the other boy was told. "You came to grief because of it, both in Egypt and England, so you had better learn to control it now."

The striking accuracy and the uncompromising honesty of these character delineations, not only of people Cayce knew closely but also of relative strangers such as Lammers, Linden Shroyer, and other friends of Lammers, caused Lammers to become increasingly enthusiastic, but inspired Cayce, as he became more aware of the implications, with a growing uneasiness. Another period of torturous self-doubt and self-examination now began for him. He had finally become persuaded that his clairvoyance could be relied upon, with its diagnoses and prescriptions, to do the work of God rather than that of the devil; but now that it had come up with this pagan, this sacrilegious notion, how could he be sure of anything any longer?

Cayce's inner turmoil is not difficult to understand. He had been brought up in an atmosphere of strict, orthodox Christianity, with no instruction in the teachings of the great world religions other than his own. At that time, therefore, he was unaware for the most part of the many profound points of similarity between his faith and other faiths, and had had no opportunity to appreciate the ethical and spiritual light which burns in lamps other than that of his own form of Christianity. He was particularly uninformed with regard to that cardinal teaching of Hinduism and Buddhism—reincarnation.

He was repelled, in fact, by the very word, confusing reincarnation, as some people do, with the doctrine of transmigration of souls—namely that man returns to earth, after death, in an animal form. He seemed to recall having read somewhere about Hindus who refuse to kill cows because they may be their reincarnated grandfather; he seemed to have heard somewhere of people who do not kill beetles—or was it eat beans?—because they may contain the spirit of a departed ancestor.

The readings themselves soon disabused Cayce of this confusion. Reincarnation, the readings explained, does not mean the return of human beings to animal form; it is not merely a superstition of ignorant people. It is a thoroughly respectable doctrine, both from the religious and the philosophic point of view. Millions of educated people in India and Buddhist countries believe it intelligently, and guide their lives by its ethical principals. There are, to be sure, many sects in India and the East that teach the transmigration of the human soul to animal forms; but this is only a misinterpretation of the true reincarnation principle. Even Christianity has garbled and mistaken forms; one must not permit a narrow acquaintance with the distorted versions to close one's mind to the possibility of truth in the original.

Lammers was able to add to the clarification given by the readings themselves. Reincarnation means *evolution*, he explained: the evolution of the spirit of man through many successive lifetimes on earth—sometimes as a man, sometimes as a woman, now as a pauper, now as a prince, here belonging to one race, there to another—until finally the spirit has reached the perfection enjoined on us by Christ. The soul is like an actor who takes different roles and wears different costumes on different nights; or like a hand, that puts on the glove of a material body for a little while, and when the glove is threadbare, slips out and later dons another glove. Any number of men of intellect in our hemisphere have accepted this idea, and written about it. Schopenhauer thoroughly believed in it. So did Emerson, Walt Whitman, Goethe, Giordano Bruno, Plotinus, Pythagoras, Plato.

That is all very well, was Cayce's rejoinder; but how about Christianity? If I accept reincarnation, am I not thereby denying Christ and his teachings?

Not at all, returned Lammers. After all, what was the essence of the teachings of Christ? A lawyer among the Pharisees had once asked Christ this question, and his answer was: "Thou shalt love the Lord thy God with all thy heart, and with all thy soul, and with all thy mind . . . And thou shalt love thy neighbor as thyself. On these two commandments hang all the law and the prophets." (Matthew 22:35-40)

How did this simple and profound teaching conflict with the framework of life's evolution as proposed by reincarnation? How, indeed, did this law of love conflict with the teachings of any of the world's great religions? "Hurt not others in ways that you yourself would find hurtful," Buddha had said. "This is the sum of duty: do naught unto others which would cause pain if done to you," taught the Hindu scriptures. And both Hinduism and Buddhism had found no discrepancy between the law of love and the law of spiritual evolution called reincarnation. They had emphasized the latter rather than the former, to be sure; but they had seen no conflict between them.

Cayce was still unconvinced. When he was ten years old he had been given a copy of the Bible—and the book had fascinated him. He conceived the ambition then of reading it through completely once every year of his life and so—after he had caught up with the years he had missed—he proceeded systematically from Genesis through Revelation once each year. In all those years of reading his beloved book he had never once come across the word reincarnation. Why was it that the Bible, and, more important, Christ himself, never spoke of reincarnation?

Well, said Lammers, perhaps Christ had. One must remember first of all that he taught many things to his disciples that he did not teach to the multitudes. Besides—even had he taught reincarnation more generally, one must remember that the original records of his teachings have undergone many changes through the centuries because of the interpretations placed upon what he said, and because of translations through several languages. Consequently many of the authentic teachings of Christ may be lost to us. One passage at least seems to have remained—the one in which Christ told his disciples that John the Baptist was a reincarnation of Elias (Matthew 17:12-13). He did not use the word *reincarnation,* but he indicated definitely that "Elias is come already. . . . Then the disciples understood that he spake unto them of John the Baptist."

The very fact, too, that his disciples asked Christ of the blind man: "Master, who did sin, this man, or his parents, that he was born blind?" was significant. Other passages hinted at or even clearly pointed to reincarnation. Revelation, Chapter 13, Verse 10, said: "He that leadeth into captivity shall go into captivity: he that killeth with the sword must be killed with the sword. Here is the patience and the faith of the saints." This passage hints that a law of moral retribution operates from life to life.

Gradually Christian orthodoxy had crystallized, to be sure, about those portions of what Christ taught that did not seem to refer to reincarnation; yet how can we be sure that orthodoxy was right in its interpretations, its selections, and its rejections? Besides—Lammers went on—if one studied the history of the early Christian Fathers one learned that many of them had written explicitly of their acceptance of reincarnation, and had openly taught it as well. Origen, for example, in the early years of his life; Justin Martyr; St. Jerome; Clemens Alexandrinus; Plotinus; and many others. Could it be possible that they—being so close in point of time to the fountainhead of Christ's actual presence—had somehow learned and perpetuated teachings that he had given his twelve disciples in secret, and that had come down through the esoteric tradition since the most ancient times?

It was worth noting, too, said Lammers, that the Catholic prelate Cardinal Mercier did not himself admit to a belief in reincarnation, but he stated that the doctrine did not conflict with the essential teachings of the Catholic Church. And Dean Inge of St. Paul's said that he found no conflict between reincarnation and modern Episcopalianism. So neither Protestants nor Catholics need feel themselves to be treading on unholy ground when they consider reincarnation as a religious and scientific possibility.

True—there were certain ideas in Christian theology that might appear to be in conflict with the reincarnation idea. The teaching of the resurrection of the dead, for example, and the last judgment day would be regarded by most orthodox Christians as a direct contradiction of reincarnation. But is it not possible that the phrases "resurrection of the dead" and "last judgment day" were meant to be understood symbolically rather than literally? And that the parables and poetical metaphors, like "hell fire" for example, with which Christ and the New Testament writers had dramatized their perception of spiritual truth, had been crystallized into a rigid, literal dogma?

Cayce found these answers thought-provoking, and they served to still the almost frightened bewilderment which had been his when he began to feel that his peculiar power was being used contrary to the religion he had known as a child. But other objections soon rose in his mind—scientific ones, now. How about the vast increase in the world's population, for example? Can this increase be reconciled with the notion that all souls have been on earth before? Where did the surplus come from?

The whole Cayce family, together with Gladys Davis, Lammers, and Linden Shroyer became a forum for the lively threshing out of all these questions. When they reached a stalemate in the argument they consulted the readings themselves; when the readings seemed too preposterous to believe they referred to books from the public library.

They found an answer for the population question without too much difficulty. After all, someone argued, how can we be sure there has been an absolute increase? Many of the readings so far have referred to vanished civilizations in Egypt and Atlantis. Archeological ruins in Cambodia, Mexico, Egypt, and the Orient confirm the fact that great civilizations once existed where now there is only wasteland; great waves of population could conceivably mount and subside in numbers at any given point in history, without altering the total number of souls in the universe. The unseen world may well be host to millions of souls at times when conditions are unfavorable to their being on earth.

This seemed a reasonable enough explanation, even to the stubbornly skeptical Cayce. But Atlantis was another stumbling-block. How do we know there really was such a place? Wasn't it just another myth? The readings themselves answered this question, in considerable detail and at considerable length.

Plato was the first writer of the Western world, they said,

to refer quite casually to the ancient existence of Atlantis, beneath the waters of the Atlantic Ocean. And though the general public today gives the matter no serious thought, geologists have turned their scientific attention to it for some time. There is a division of opinion among them—some denying, and some affirming most emphatically that Atlantis actually did exist. At any rate, a number of scholarly books on the subject presented the accumulation of mutually corroborative historical, cultural, and geological evidences. Cayce found one such book: Ignatius Donnelly's *Atlantis, the Antediluvian World*. He was astounded to discover that his readings had given an accurate account of the major lines of evidence.

These discussions, probings, and exploratory excursions into books on history, science, comparative religion, ancient esoteric teachings, Atlantis, and the psychology of hypnosis —all of which topics were touched on in the substance of the readings—soon gave Cayce an historical and cultural perspective which he had never before had. Gradually he came to feel less fearful of the things he said in hypnotic sleep and more receptive to the possibility of their holding some truth. With eager but critical curiosity he began to scrutinize the readings for inner and outer checks of their validity.

He found for one thing that they were always consistent with themselves. One reading never contradicted another, even when a long period of time had elapsed between them. For example, a second life reading might be taken on an individual several months or several years after the first. Yet the information of the second reading coincided exactly with that of the first, and proceeded somewhat in the manner of a person who opens a book to a page marked by a ribbon and reads on from where he left off. Most readings contained some background information about past eras of history, such as ancient Egypt and Atlantis. When a group of these readings was compared it was found that all fragmentary details agreed with each other; each reading either repeated part of what had been said elsewhere, or else added some new detail to the mosaic.

Not only did the readings agree with each other, but they also agreed in many respects with the facts of recorded history, no matter how obscure. For example, one of the early readings referred to a man's previous incarnation as a stool-dipper. Cayce had no idea what a stool-dipper was, but on consulting an encyclopedia found that the term referred to the early American custom of strapping supposed witches on stools and dipping them into a pool of cold water.

Another and perhaps more striking example of the historical accuracy of the readings, independent of Cayce's conscious-mind ignorance, was a reference to Jean Poquelin, or Molière, whose mother died when the boy was very young. The name of Molière, the great French dramatist, was unknown to Cayce, and all the more so was the fact that Molière was a pseudonym, his real name having been Poquelin. Reference works disclosed that the sleeping Cayce had been accurate both in the fact of Molière's real name, and in the fact of his mother's early death. Still another example was found in the case of a young man who was told that in a previous life he had lived in France where he had befriended Robert Fulton and had been of assistance to him in some of his inventions. Cayce knew who Robert Fulton was, but doubted that he had ever lived outside the United States. Upon consulting a biographical dictionary, he found that, true enough, Fulton had spent several years in France, and had met many stimulating people there who had influenced his career.

The readings customarily gave the exact name borne in previous lives; but in several instances they also told the individual where he might find records of this former personality —either in a book, an old registry, or on a tombstone. Perhaps the best example of this was the case of a man who was told that his name had been Barnett Seay in his former life, and that he had been a southern soldier in the Civil War. He was told further that he had lived in Henrico County, Virginia, and that he could still find the records of this former personality if he looked for them. At the first opportunity the man eagerly made a trip to Henrico County. The records he sought were not there, but the Clerk of the Court informed him that many of the old registries had recently been transferred to the Department of Old Records of the Virginia State Historical Library. Finally, in the archives of this library, he actually did find the records of Barnett A. Seay, who had enlisted in Lee's army as colorbearer in 1862, at the age of twenty-one.

In addition to these curious historical confirmations of the past-life data, there were innumerable confirmations of the present-life material. Cayce soon learned that the readings' psychological analyses were accurate, not only of himself and members of his family, but also of total strangers. The accuracy of the readings with respect to his family could perhaps be explained away on the grounds that in the waking state Cayce knew himself and his family very well indeed; it could be argued that he was drawing on this personal knowledge while in the hypnotic state. But he soon discovered, as in the case of the physical readings, that it was immaterial whether he was acquainted with the persons for whom he gave the reading. They could be complete strangers to him and be at any spot anywhere on earth; yet if he had their full name and the date and the place of their birth, he was able to describe their circumstances and their most intimate character accurately, listing their abilities and weaknesses, and plausibly ascribing them to previous incarnations when they had, presumably, begun to develop.

Had accurate characterizations of a distant stranger occurred only once, one might dismiss it as being due to coincidence. But in view of the infinite number of human abilities and the infinite diversity of human circumstances, the coincidence would be an extraordinary one. Multiply such correct delineations, and it becomes difficult to regard the matter as a series of coincidences.

Still another aspect of the life readings' accuracy, Cayce found over a period of years, was the correctness with which they characterized young children both as to temperament and vocational aptitude. A life reading for a Norfolk child, taken on the day of birth, stated that she was a headstrong, self-willed, and obstinate entity—one that would be hard to control. As she grew older, these traits began to manifest themselves unmistakably—and, we can perhaps safely assume, at no deliberate prompting on the part of the parents.

An even more impressive case was that of a boy whose life reading, taken three weeks after birth, stated that he could become an outstanding physician. All the defects of character attributed to him by the reading began to appear at an early age, as well as a pronounced interest in medicine. At the age of eight he began to cut up dead animals to find out how they were made; before he reached his teens he was avidly devouring medical encyclopedias; at the age of twelve, he announced to his father his intention of going to Johns Hopkins and becoming a doctor. The boy's father was a New York businessman; his mother, an actress; both parents at first looked with disfavor on his idea of entering the medical profession and tried to discourage him. But his determination overrode all obstacles, and the boy is now taking the pre-medical course in a large eastern university. Here again the parents were in no way abetting the prediction of the reading, and once again it would seem as if there must have been a bona fide clairvoyant perception at birth of the child's potentialities, on the basis of his past-life development.

Instances like these would seem to indicate the high predictive value of the readings—using the word "predictive" not in the sense of fortune-telling, but in the same sense that psychologists use the term when they speak of the predictive value of psychological tests. For example, the widely known Rorschach ink-blot test was administered to aviation cadets as they began their course of training. The test interpretations showed that six in a group of about two hundred students were emotionally unfitted for the life of a pilot. All cadets were permitted to continue the course, but at the end of the year all six designated as unfit had dropped out of school for psychological reasons. The Rorschach test is, therefore, on the basis of many such examples, regarded as having high "predictive" value.

Cayce's life readings had high predictive value in this same sense; and it was observable, not only in the case of infants, but also in the case of adults. A young woman telegraph operator in New York City became curious about the strange telegrams that she was asked on several occasions to send to Virginia Beach. She made inquiries about Cayce's identity; her curiosity heightened, she decided to have a life reading. She was told in the reading that she was wasting her time as a telegraph operator, and that she should study commercial art, as she had been a competent artist for several past lifetimes and could be one again. The notion of entering commercial or any other kind of art had never entered her head; but on the strength of a daring sense that she might as well try anything once, she put herself through art school. To her surprise she found that she had genuine talent; she soon became a highly successful commercial artist, and incidentally transformed her personality in the process.

As the years went by, then, and Cayce observed the outworking of this information in people's lives, he became gradually convinced that it was true and it was good because of the good it was accomplishing. There was much about the readings that could not be proved; yet the parts that could be proved gave him confidence in the parts that could not. Many people were being guided into suitable vocations; others were being led to an understanding of their marriage difficulties; still others were given self-knowledge to help make better social and psychological adjustments.

At the very outset Cayce had wondered if he might be giving this information only because Lammers believed in reincarnation and had somehow implanted the suggestion in his mind. But the facts seemed to belie this suspicion. First of all, Lammers had not used the word reincarnation in his suggestion for the first reading—he had asked for a horoscope, no more, no less; Cayce's unconscious or superconscious mind had volunteered the information about a previous life.

Moreover, almost all the evidential information which later was given on distant strangers was completely beyond the range of either Lammers' or Cayce's knowledge. Had Cayce's unconscious mind merely been elaborating, fancifully, on a suggestion given him by Lammers, the information could hardly have tallied so often with unknown, but verifiable, facts.

All these considerations, put together, gradually convinced Cayce of the validity of the life reading material and of the explanation of human destiny which they advanced. Above all else, however, he was convinced by the thoroughly Christ-like spirit that pervaded the readings, both in the brotherly helpfulness with which they were being given, and in their easy integration of Christian ideals with the reincarnation framework. Barely a reading was given which did not use some Biblical phrase or some admonition of Christ. Perhaps most frequently quoted of all were Christ's words: "As ye sow, so shall ye reap"; and "Do unto others as you would have others do unto you." Sometimes they were direct quotations, sometimes they were paraphrases or elaborations on direct quotations, as: "Be not, be *not* deceived; do not misunderstand; God is not mocked! For what man sows, man reaps. Man constantly meets himself. Do good, then, as He said, to those who have despitefully used you; and you overcome then in yourself what you have done to your fellowman."

Such statements were made in comment on an affliction presumably brought over from a past-life iniquity. They were so earnestly spoken, and invariably so appropriate and meaningful, that they carried conviction. This concurrence of the reincarnation idea with a thoroughgoing Christian outlook would, of course, have no scientific force and would mean nothing whatever to an agnostic. To Cayce, however, it was the decisive weight in a balance which was wavering.

After the first excitement had subsided somewhat, the group began asking questions about the character of the information itself. For one thing, they were curious about the frequency with which certain eras of history recurred in the life readings that they took. Many people were given a similar historical background; in fact, the outline of people's past lives seemed almost to fall into a pattern. One common sequence was: Atlantis, Egypt, Rome, the Crusades period, and the early Colonial period. Another was: Atlantis, Egypt,

Rome, France in the time of Louis XIV, XV, or XVI, and the American Civil War. There were variations, of course—including China, India, Cambodia, Peru, Norseland, Africa, Central America, Sicily, Spain, Japan, and other places; but the majority of readings followed the same historic lines.

The reason for this, according to Cayce, was that souls of a given era in general incarnate in a later era together. In the intervening centuries, other groups of souls are on earth—taking their turn, so to speak. This proceeds with orderly and rhythmic alternation, almost like the shifts of laborers in a factory. Consequently most of the souls on earth today were also together in previous ages of history. Also, souls related to each other closely by family ties, friendship ties, or the ties of mutual interests were likely to have been related before in similar ties in previous eras—and most of the people securing readings from Cayce were, in some such way, releated.

Another question asked was: Where is this information coming from? The answer was that there were two sources of knowledge which the mind of Cayce could, while in hypnotic trance, succeed in tapping.

One source was the unconscious mind of each individual whose life history he was asked to give. The unconscious mind, the readings explained, retains the memory of every experience through which the individual has passed—not only from the time of birth, but also before birth in all its previous experiences. These pre-birth memories exist below what might be called a trap door, and at deeper levels of the unconscious mind than those commonly tapped by modern psychotherapists; but they are there nonetheless. The unconscious mind, moreover, is more easily accessible to other unconscious minds than is the conscious mind—as it is generally easier to travel between two points in New York City by subway than by surface travel. Under hypnosis, then, Cayce's mind was put in immediate touch with the unconscious levels of other minds.

This explanation was not too difficult to accept; it coincided, at least in part, with the discoveries of psychoanalysis about the existence and content of the unconscious mind. The explanation of the other of the two possible sources of information, however, seemed fantastic. It had to do with what the readings called "Akashic Records." As always, with unfamiliar words, the sleeping Cayce spelled out the term—*Akasha*, the noun, *Akashic*, the adjective. In brief, Cayce's explanation was this:

Akasha is a Sanskrit word that refers to the fundamental etheric substance of the universe, electro-spiritual in composition. Upon this Akasha there remains impressed an indelible record of every sound, light, movement, or thought since the beginning of the manifest universe. The existence of this record accounts for the ability of clairvoyants and seers literally to *see* the past, no matter how remote it may be and no matter how inaccessible to ordinary human knowledge. Akasha registers impressions like a sensitive plate, and can almost be regarded as a huge candid-camera of the cosmos. The ability to read these vibratory records lies inherent within each of us, dependent upon the sensitivity of our organization, and consists in attuning to the proper degree of consciousness— much like tuning a radio to the proper wave length. In his normal waking state, Edgar Cayce was unable to subjugate his physical consciousness sufficiently to make this attunement; under hypnosis, however, he was able to do so.

Of all the strange statements that had come from his sleeping lips, this, to Cayce, seemed the most utterly strange. Yet by repeated incredulous questioning the same explanation always came through, sometimes in the same words, sometimes with elaborations. Frequently the readings indicated that the "Akashic Records" could also be called "The Universal Memory of Nature" or "The Book of Life." They also advanced the point taught about the reality of Akasha many centuries ago. In view of the fact that several other Hindu notions—namely the illusory, non-solid nature of "matter"; the interchangeability of matter and force; and the reality of thought transference through telepathic means—had only recently been confirmed by Western science, why not be open-minded at least as to the possibility of this other Hindu idea, Akasha, as well?

Cayce suspended judgment on the point for a long time. The unconscious-mind explanation might conceivably cover past-life individual histories, but how account for the ready, copious, and detailed material that flowed from him in "research readings" on past eras of history, such as Atlantis, Egypt, or the times of Jesus? Could it be that this information was being drawn from the unconscious mind of somebody who had lived in those eras, even though the individual was not ostensibly the subject of the reading? Or was he really reading some vast tapestry of history, preserved in an unknown and tenuous dimension of the universe?

In the end Cayce came to accept even Akasha—not because there was absolute proof of it, but because the readings had said it was so, and the readings in all other provable respects had proved themselves honest. Perhaps investigators into extrasensory perception will demonstrate that on this point the Cayce information went off the beam; perhaps some other explanation will account for the facts of his clairvoyance into the past. Perhaps, on the other hand, some scientific mind of our era will be able to show that Akasha really does exist—no more fantastic a thing than radio waves, radium, atomic energy, or the memory engrams of the human nervous system.

In any event, the life readings that Cayce gave, and their astonishing demonstrable validity, remain a fact, regardless of what their ultimate source may have been. In the twenty-two years that elapsed between 1923, when he first stumbled on them, and 1945, when he died, Cayce gave some 2,500 of these life readings. Like the physical readings, they have been carefully preserved and annotated. Letters and other documents bear witness to the accuracy of many of them, at least insofar as their accuracy could be ascertained; the investigator who wishes to do so can still interview many of the subjects.

If then we can, with Cayce, finally come to believe in the validity of these strange documents, and the explanation for human destiny which they propose, we find ourselves in possession of an extraordinary mass of information. In the first place, we have here a large body of circumstantial evidence in favor of a revolutionary principle, reincarnation. If we cannot accept the evidence as absolutely conclusive, it seems worthwhile, in the interests of scientific alertness, at least to direct our attention to the area of speculation which it points to. Many great discoveries have been made by probing unlikely sources. When Einstein was asked how he discovered relativity, he answered: "By challenging an axiom." Secondly, we have here a large body of information of a psychological, medical, and philosophical nature which, when sorted and analyzed, yields a transformed picture of the nature and destiny of man.

In those twenty-two years, a procession of suffering and bewildered humanity passed in review before the profound insight of Cayce's hypnotic clairvoyance. Physical and psychological ills of every description preoccupied these people; like the psalmist, who cried in uncomprehending anguish, they wanted to know *Why has this thing come upon me?*

Not all cases were of desperate or tragic proportions—many of the past-life histories of these people were of no greater dramatic interest than the commonplace, ordinary lives they were leading in the present. But invariably, whether their problem was mild or severe, it was demonstrated that their situation of the present was a link in a chain of sequence that had begun centuries ago. In case after case, people were shown the cosmic relevance of their disease or their frustration. This knowledge had a transforming effect upon their lives; insight into the long-range pertinence of their situation enabled them to achieve dynamic equilibrium at higher levels of integration.

If the validity of these readings can be accepted, then their staggering implications must be considered. Their importance certainly does not lie in the fact that they present a new theory to the world—the theory itself is an ancient one, found among many widely separated peoples in every continent of the world. The importance of the Cayce readings lies rather in two things. One is that here, for the first time in the Western world, specific, well-defined, coherent, and psychologically credible accounts have been given of the presumable past lives of many individuals. The second is that here, for the first time in the known history of the world, these accounts were kept in record form such as to be available to the general public.

Moreover, Cayce readings integrate the philosophy of the Orient with a Christian dynamics of living; new life is thereby imparted to both. Thus there is accomplished a much-needed synthesis between the two outlooks, introvert and extravert, which have respectively characterized the East and the West for so long.

But above all, the Cayce readings achieve a synthesis between science and religion. They do so by showing that the moral world is subject to laws of cause and effect as precise as those that govern the physical world. Human suffering, they make clear, is due not merely to materialistic mischance, but rather to errors of conduct and thinking; the inequalities of human birth and human capacity do not arise from the capriciousness of the Creator or the blind mechanism of heredity, they arise from merits and demerits of past life behavior. All pain and all limitation have an educative purpose; deformities and afflictions are of moral origin; and all man's agonies are lessons in a long-term school for wisdom and perfection.

Chapter IV

Some Types of Physical Karma

_____

THE lame, the deaf, the deformed, the blind, the incurable—these are perhaps the most conspicuous examples of human suffering. When we see such an affliction in another, we are moved to pity of the deepest kind. When we experience such an affliction ourselves, and know its sad frustrations, we begin bitterly to question the ways of God to man. *Why* has this thing happened to me? we ask plaintively. Why has it happened to *me?*

Job was known to be one of the most righteous and patient of men. He suffered the loss of all his worldly goods and even of all his children with anguish in his heart but not a word of complaint. But when, as a final test, the devil inflicted his body with loathsome boils, then did Job for the first time curse God and for the first time cry out in desperation for the why of his affliction. "Teach me, and I will hold my tongue," he exclaimed *"and cause me to understand wherein I have erred!"*

This belief that suffering must be due to wrongdoing of some kind has been discarded by the modern mind as a superstition of outworn religions; few people nowadays are inclined to think of suffering in terms of "sin." Yet in the view of the Cayce readings, sin and suffering *have* an exact cause-and-effect relationship, even though the point of origin of the sin may be hidden from view.

In order to understand this idea, which is basic to the Cayce readings, it is essential to know the meaning of the word *karma* because this word is the only one that expresses the sin-suffering causal relationship. Karma is a Sanskrit word literally meaning action; in philosophic thought, however, it has come to mean the law of cause and effect, or action and reaction, to which all human conduct is subject. Emerson, who was steeped in the Brahmic philosophy of India, referred to this concept as the law of compensation. Christ formulated it very concisely when he said, "Whatsoever a man soweth, that shall he also reap." Newton's third law of motion, namely that every action has its reaction which is equal and opposite, applies as much to the moral law as to the law of physics.

The Cayce life readings are fascinating by virtue of the fact that they trace human afflictions and limitations of the present to specific conduct in the past and thus bring the abstract notion of karma into sharper and more immediate focus. A thorough examination of these cases indicates that there are various types of karma. One type might well be called Boomerang Karma because, like the Australian boomerang, which when thrown returns to the thrower, a harmful action directed toward another person seems to rebound to the perpetrator of the action.

There are many instances of this type of karma in the Cayce files. One example, a college professor who had been born totally blind, heard about Cayce on a radio program called "Miracles of the Mind." He applied for a physical reading and experienced conspicuous improvement in health and vision by following its instructions, which included osteopathic adjustments, electrical treatments, and a change of diet. Within three months he had achieved 10 per cent vision in his left eye, which had been considered hopeless by eye specialists. The professor's life reading outlined four previous incarnations: one in America during the Civil War period, one in France during the Crusades, one in Persia about 1000 B.C., and one in Atlantis, just before its final submergence.

It was in Persia that he had set in motion the spiritual law which resulted in his blindness in the present. He had been a member of a barbaric tribe whose custom was to blind its enemies with red-hot irons, and it had been his office to do the blinding.

The question inevitably arises here: How can an individual be held morally responsible for a duty imposed on him by the customs of the society in which he lives? This is a thoroughly valid question; it shall be discussed at some length in Chapter XXIII.

The second example worthy of note is that of a girl who earned her living as a manicurist and who had been afflicted with infantile paralysis at the age of one year. She was left with both legs crippled and both feet stunted in size, to such a degree that she had to use crutches and braces.

The karmic cause of her condition was attributed to an Atlantean incarnation in which through some means—whether through drugs or hypnosis or telepathy the reading does not specify—she made people "weak in limb and unable to do other than follow. . . . Thus we find the entity meeting itself in that very thing which it brought to others." ("The entity" is the term used by the readings to refer to the immortal individual who, for the sake of gaining experience on its path to perfection, incarnates again and again.)

A third interesting example of Boomerang Karma is found in the case of a woman of forty who since childhood had suffered from symptoms which had been most recently diagnosed as allergies. When she ate certain foods—principally bread and all cereal grains—she began to sneeze, as if the victim of hay fever. When she came in contact with certain materials—mainly shoe leather and plastic rims of glasses—she experienced excruciating neuritic pains in her left side. She had consulted innumerable doctors over the years, but the only relief she had ever had, she stated, resulted from hypnotic treatments when she was twenty-five. The relief lasted for six years; then the symptoms gradually returned.

This woman's primary concern in obtaining a Cayce reading was to achieve a cure; but the Cayce clairvoyance included the karmic origin of her condition. "In another experience," the reading relates, "we find that this entity was a chemist, and used many of these things for the producing of itching in others. She therefore finds it in herself in the present. . . . The entity also used certain substances that caused the breath itself to be poisonous to others. Similarly, the entity now finds itself immediately poisoned in the presence of certain metals, plastics, odors, and leathers. If these leathers are tanned with oak, they do not harm the body. If they are tanned with the very same things that the entity once used to hinder someone else, they hinder the entity."

A second type of karma in the physical realm might be called Organismic Karma. It involves the misuse of the organism in one life, and results in an appropriate retribution arising from the organism in a succeeding life. A good example of this type of karma is to be seen in the case of a man of thirty-five who since infancy has suffered from digestive weakness. He needs constantly to limit himself to certain foods in certain combinations; yet even after taking these precautions, he requires several hours to digest a meal. Because of this sensitivity, he frequently experiences inconveniences and social embarrassment.

The origin of his disability was attributed by the Cayce reading to an incarnation in the court of Louis XIII of France, when he had been a kind of escort and protector of the king, and an adviser on the king's wardrobe. His duties he had performed faithfully and well; however, he had one serious weakness—the weakness of gluttony. Even in a preceding life as a court physician in Persia he had been given to the pleasures of the table. Thus for two lifetimes he had committed the psychological sin of excess; the imbalance needed somehow to be equalized, and thus we find him forced, through predisposed bodily weakness, to become temperate in the present.

A third type of physical karma which is frequently found in the Cayce readings might be given the name Symbolic Karma. This is perhaps the most surprising and most interesting type of karmic consequence among the physical cases.

One of the early life readings was given for a young man who had suffered since early childhood from anemia. His father was a physician, and the boy had been given every known treatment for his condition, but to no avail. A malfunction which so stubbornly resists cure is highly suggestive of a deep-seated karmic cause. And, in fact, the life reading traced the condition to an incarnation in Peru, five lifetimes back, where the entity had ruthlessly seized control of the country, thereby becoming its ruler. "Much blood was shed," says the reading; *"hence anemia in the present."*

The significance of this phrase becomes fully apparent only when we compare the case with other examples of physical karma. It is clearly not a case of Organismic Karma, since the man's sin had not been that of misusing his own body through intemperances of any kind. It is not strictly speaking an example of Boomerang Karma either; for had it been this type, the young man would have been the victim, in battle, of a ruthless conqueror's slaughter—perhaps a young Pole, whose blood was shed by Hitler's troops.

Instead, we see that his own body became the field of slaughter; it became, as it were, the sacrificial altar on which his crime was expiated. This lifelong bodily deficiency constitutes a far more protracted form of educative justice than bloody death on a battlefield could possibly have accomplished. The entity once shed the blood of a people for whom he felt a conqueror's contempt; now he himself is a weakling, by virtue of his own bloodstream deficiency, and thus one part of his body has taken over his karma symbolically.

This might seem a fantastic notion if we were not prepared for it by the clinical findings of psychosomatic medicine. There was a time, not long ago, when it was believed that all diseases were physically caused. The advance of psychiatry demonstrated that at least some physical conditions were due to mental and emotional disturbances; and from this discovery branched what is known as psychosomatic medicine (from two Greek words: *psyche*—soul, and *soma*—body), a new but fully accredited development in the field of medicine.

Clinical practice in psychosomatic medicine has demonstrated that tensions of emotional origin, when they cannot be expressed in word or action, often express themselves symbolically in the body through a kind of "organ language." "For example," say Weiss and English, authors of the standard text in the field, *Psychosomatic Medicine,* "if a patient cannot swallow satisfactorily and no organic cause can be found, it may mean that there is something in the life situation of the patient that he 'cannot swallow.' Nausea, in the absence of organic disease, sometimes means that the patient 'cannot stomach' this or that environmental factor. . . . The patient who has lost his appetite and as a consequence has become severely undernourished is very often emotionally starved just as he is physically starved. . . . The organ which 'speaks' is most likely to be the organ whose function was in the ascendancy when environmental conditions were bad and produced pain (anxiety) in the mind. But constitutional predisposition, identification with a parent, or other factors, may also determine the 'choice of organ.' "

There would seem to be a close correspondence between the "organ language" of psychosomatic medicine and what we have here termed Symbolic Karma. In the latter case it is as if there were so deep a feeling of guilt in the consciousness of the entity with regard to its sin, that the guilt feeling was projected, or acted out, in the body itself—the choice of the organ being dependent on certain symbolic appropriateness.

Here are a few typical examples of the many instances of such symbolic retribution in the Cayce files. In a severe case of asthma, the sufferer was told: "You cannot press the life out of others without seeming at times to have it pressed out of oneself." A person who was deaf was admonished: "Then do not close your ears again to those who plead for aid." (This entity had been a nobleman at the time of the French Revolution.) A sufferer with tuberculosis of the spine was informed: "The entity thwarted others and is meeting it now in himself." A victim of progressive muscular atrophy learned that: "This is not merely the atrophy of the nerves and muscles of the lower limbs; it is the result of what you built in your life and the life of others in other experiences."

Perhaps the most striking case of Symbolic Karma in the files is that of a young boy of eleven who had been a chronic bed-wetter since the age of two. The case is worth discussing at some length because of the rather unusual nature of the boy's cure.

As a baby, he was a very quiet child; he gave his parents no difficulty until the time of the birth of a second child, when he began to wet his bed during the night. This became a regular nightly occurrence. Both parents were aware of the fact that a first child may feel insecure at the time of the birth of another, and frequently revert to infantile habits for the sake of regaining attention and supremacy. Every effort was made to show the boy that he had not been replaced in their affections by the baby sister, but the bed-wetting continued.

Finally, when the boy was three, the parents decided to consult a psychiatrist. For over a year he was under psychiatric care; when the parents saw that the condition would not yield even to psychiatry, the treatment was discontinued. For five years thereafter the boy continued to wet the bed every night. The parents consulted every known specialist, tried every known treatment—all to no avail. At the age of eight the childish habit still persisted. Once again the parents decided to seek the help of a psychiatrist. There followed two more years of treatment which proved helpful to his general personality growth, but the condition continued. In his tenth year, after two years of fruitless trial, psychiatric treatment was abandoned.

When the boy was eleven, the parents heard of the work of Edgar Cayce, and the father determined to obtain a reading on the peculiar case of his son. According to the boy's life reading, in the life previous to the present he had been a minister of the gospel in early Puritan days, at the time of the witchcraft trials; he had been active in punishing supposed witches by ducking them, on a stool, into a pond.

This karmic explanation given, the reading held out definite hope for cure. The parents were told to use suggestion on the boy before he went to sleep at night; the implication was that the suggestion should be of a spiritual rather than a physical nature.

Soon after obtaining the reading, the mother sat by the boy's bedside one night, and waited until he was about to drop off to sleep. She then began to repeat these words, in a slow, monotonous voice: "You are good and kind. You are going to make many people happy. You are going to help everyone with whom you come in contact. . . . You are good and kind . . ." The same idea was expressed in various forms for perhaps five or ten minutes to the now sleeping boy.

That night, for the first time in almost nine years, the boy did not wet the bed. For several months the mother continued the suggestions, always in the same vein; not once, in that period, did the condition recur. Gradually she found it possible to give the suggestion only once a week; and finally not even that was necessary. The boy was completely cured.

There are several interesting features in this case. That on the very first night of the trial the suggestion broke a habit of nine years' standing is in itself a fact of singular interest, yet had the mother not been a woman of trained intelligence and unquestioned integrity one might almost imagine the circumstance to have been exaggerated. She is a lawyer and a trusted member of a District Attorney's staff; she is not gullible or superstitious or dishonest.

The second singular feature of the case is that the suggestion which proved so efficacious mentioned nothing about not wetting the bed. It was not directed to the boy's physical consciousness at all, but rather to what might be called his spiritual consciousness. That is to say, it was directed to the consciousness of guilt which he carried over from his Salem incarnation, and which had been symbolically expressed, through an appropriate kidney mechanism, in his own body. He once ducked others, or was responsible for their ducking; now he felt obscurely the need for retribution upon himself.

Though in this life the child had not harmed anyone, a certain stratum of his mind still doubted his own kindness, his own social acceptability, because of the persistent memory of the cruel punishment he had once inflicted upon others. The suggestion reached that particular stratum, reassured him that his guilt had been, or could be, expiated through social service and kindness, and consequently erased the necessity for further symbolic retribution.

The boy has since become well adjusted; he is well liked, popular, a good student, and a leader. The initial introversion of his nature has been so well modified that on a Johnson O'Connor Human Engineering Laboratory test he was rated as a perfectly well-adjusted extravert. For this change in personality the mother feels that credit should be given in part to the psychiatric treatment, in part to the Cayce reading.

Now, at the age of sixteen, one of the boy's marked characteristics, according to the observation of both parents, is a great tolerance of other people. For any defect of character in other people he finds some psychological explanation, some justification. It would seem, therefore, that the intolerance of which his physical disability was the symbolic self-chastisement had been transmuted into an active tolerance. The equilibrium has been so thoroughly re-established that the physical karma could justly be withdrawn.

As we review these cases of karmic action we find that certain generalizations can be made about them. Karma has often been defined as action-reaction; this definition is substantiated in the Cayce readings. But the retributive reaction which characterizes all karma is usually neither exact nor literal. The blind professor, for example, who once blinded his enemies with irons was not born this time into a barbaric tribe; he did not, as a young man, become the victim of an alien tribesman's cruelty in having his eyes branded out. Instead he was born, already blind, in modern twentieth-century society, and in no respect were the events of his present life exact duplicates of the earlier life.

This and other comparable examples leads us to generalize that: *Karma is a psychological law and acts primarily in the psychological realm, the physical circumstances being merely the means whereby the psychological purpose is fulfilled. Therefore the reversal or reaction on the objective physical plane is not exact, but only approximate; on the psychological plane, the reversal is more nearly exact.*

Another generalization appears warranted with regard to the agency of the reaction. In no case in the Cayce files was the present-life affliction found to have been instigated by a former victim of the person in question. That is to say, the professor was born blind; no indication was given that his parents had been former victims of his. The manicurist who was the victim of polio did not, so far as can be determined, receive the contagion from one of her former victims in Atlantis. The person cursed with digestive weakness suffered it with respect to a different stomach from the one which he first abused. In short, the reaction or retribution would seem to arise, not from the identical individual or the identical organism whereon the act was first committed, but rather from the same field wherein the action was directed. A few diagrams may make this generalization clear.

When we address a letter to John Doe, 614 Birch Street, Madison, Wisconsin, we are specifying four successively larger environments which encircle the person called John Doe. Like John Doe, the spiritual ego finds itself, when it assumes material form on the physical plane, in several concentric environments. These environments not only surround the ego; they offer it spheres or fields of operation.

The analysis of what constitutes the ego's spheres of operation can be made in a variety of ways and more or less minutely. But there would seem to be three major fields on which the ego imposes its will: first, its own body (variously subdivided into its numerous organs and capacities, and also, perhaps, into its subtler and more etheric aspects); second, its natural environment (in the sense of all external physical surroundings); and third, its social environment (meaning all the persons with whom it has relationships).

Diagram 1 illustrates these concentric fields.

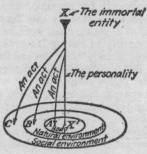

DIAGRAM 1

The letter X represents the immortal entity who, at the point X′, finds itself in embodied form. The entity XX′ is surrounded by the three major fields of action: A, his own body, B, the natural world, C, other human beings. The arrows radiating from XX′ to circles A, B, and C signify willed actions affecting these fields.

Diagram 2 illustrates the reactions arising from these fields and affecting XX′ as a consequence of his original acts. Thus if XX′ misuses his body (A) through overeating, a bodily reaction will arise from that same area in the present or in a future life. The fact that he may have a different body is of no importance; the field of operation is the same, and the displacement of equilibrium can be corrected in one place as well as another.

This concept may seem less strange if we regard it in the light of a simple analogy from a tennis game. Suppose that two people are engaged in an amateur tennis match and have

54

reached the crucial score of 5-5 in games when they are interrupted because of the expiration of their court permit. The excitement of the contest impels them to go to another park nearby and engage another court, whereupon, half an hour later, they resume their match. The scene of operation is different, but the score remains unaffected; their friendly rivalry demands that they begin from the same tie score where they found themselves at the time of the interruption. It must be noted that this score, which is their principal concern, is an intangible in the sense that it cannot be seen; but it is fully

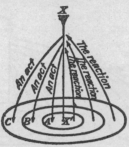

DIAGRAM 2

as real as the visible court upon which the players are engaged. Similarly with the score of the spirit in its contests with materiality, and the court of the body upon which the contest takes place.

To continue with our explanation of Diagram 2: if XX′ wantonly destroys forests or constructively uses minerals (Field B), the reaction will arise from the same field later to bring him future misfortune or fortune with respect to forests or minerals. There are many examples of this type of reaction in the Cayce files.

If at the same time XX′ treats his fellow beings (Field C) with cruelty or inconsideration, cruelty or inconsideration will return to him—not necessarily from the same specific person, but from the same general field. The reaction may, however, be a delayed reaction, affecting not the immediate personality but a later one.

Diagram 3 illustrates the lines of force affecting a personality, XX″, known to his associates as Olaf Olsen, from his own past conduct as XX′, or Michel Guion. At the same time that Olaf Olsen is being bombarded with the energy reactions of his past actions, he is setting in motion still newer causes which in turn may react upon a later self.

The Cayce readings, then, lead to many stimulating avenues of thought with regard to the problem of human bodily afflictions. They would seem to indicate that, with our normal five-sense perception, we see only a limited piece of a vast and intricate piece of tapestry; beneath the smooth surface visible to us are innumerable underside threads and innumerable invisible entanglements. The tapestry, moreover, extends far in one direction and far in another; no thread can be said to begin at the illusive margin which we call "birth," nor to end at the equally illusive margin which we call "death."

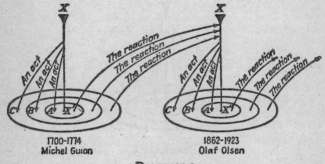

1700-1774
Michel Guion

1862-1923
Olaf Olsen

DIAGRAM 3

Chapter V

The Karma of Mockery

ONE of the seven cardinal sins of Christian theology is pride. Like many another theological tenet, this one is intellectually interesting but seems remote from the practical, medical problems of human affliction. Yet if we are to accept the testimony of the Cayce readings, the sin of pride can result karmically in very tangible physical suffering—and particularly so when this pride has expressed itself in mockery or scorn. Cruel laughter and disparaging words seem to be the equivalent of a physical act of aggression, and thus set in motion Boomerang Karma which results in the same physical affliction as that suffered by the person mocked at.

There are seven cases of severe physical disability in the Cayce files in which the affliction is attributed to a cause of this kind. Curiously enough, six of them are traced to the era of the Christian persecutions in Rome; here again we see how groups of souls of one era of history apparently return to earth as contemporaries in another era of history.

Three instances are cases of polio. The first one is that of a woman of forty-five, wife of a professional man and mother of three children, who at the age of thirty-six was stricken with infantile paralysis and has not walked since. Her life is lived in a wheelchair; she is completely dependent on others for transportation to any point outside the home. The karmic cause is attributed by the reading to the entity's behavior in ancient Rome. She had been among the royalty of the time, and was closely associated with Nero in his persecution of the Christians. "And the entity laughed at those who were crippled in the arena—" says the reading—"and lo! that selfsame thing returns to you!" The second case—and perhaps no

57

more pathetic case is to be found in all the Cayce files than this one—is that of a woman of thirty-four who was stricken with infantile paralysis at the age of six months, which resulted in spinal curvature and a limping walk. Her father, a farmer, regarded her condition with indifference, and callously appropriated for purposes of his own money she had painstakingly earned through raising chickens. Destiny ill-served her twice again in two unfortunate love affairs. Her first lover was killed in World War I. Afterward she became engaged to another. He fell dangerously sick; when he recovered, he married the trained nurse who had attended him. Add to all these physical and emotional disasters the picture of quarreling parents, a lonely farm life, and a fall from cement steps which confined the girl to bed with an additional spinal injury and you have a picture of misery hard to surpass.

Here again the karmic cause—for the physical condition at least—is seen to have been two lifetimes back in Rome. The reading says: "The entity was then a member of Palatius' household, and often sat in the boxes viewing the struggles of man with man and man with beast. In the present, much of the physical struggle arises from the entity's scornful laughter then at the weakness of those who fought for a cause."

The third case is that of a motion-picture producer who was stricken with polio at the age of seventeen and still limps slightly, though he can ride horseback and engage in some active sports. Rome in the early Christian era is again the scene of the transgression. "The entity was among the soldiery, and jeered at those that became afraid, or those that submitted without outward show of resistance. The entity lost through this experience—not from doing his duty, but from jeering at those who held to an ideal. The breaking of the body this time was an experience necessary for the awakening of the inner self, and the development of spiritual forces."

There are four interesting cases of afflictions other than polio whose karmic cause is shown to have been mockery. One is that of a girl lamed by tuberculosis of the hip joint. A life as an early American settler preceded the present one; the karmic cause, however, arose in the second life back, in Rome. Here the entity had been one of the aristocrats in Nero's court and had found it amusing to watch the persecution of Christians in the arena. She had laughed in particular at the girl whose side was ripped open by the claws of a lion.

Another is the case of an eighteen-year old girl who would have been attractive had it not been for her very overweight body. Doctors diagnosd the condition as overactivity of the pituitary gland. The Cayce physical reading concurred in calling it a glandular condition, but elsewhere in the readings the information is given that the glands themselves are focal points for the expression of the heredity of the psyche, or its karma. We would expect, then, that this girl's glandular condition and her consequent excess weight were karmic in origin; and the life reading bears out this supposition.

Two lifetimes ago she had been an athlete in Rome; she excelled both in beauty and in athletic prowess, but frequently ridiculed those who were less nimble than herself because of their heaviness of body.

The third case in this group is that of a young man of twenty-one, a Catholic, whose parents wished him to become a priest. He did not feel the call, however, and did not accede to their wishes. The central problem of his life was a marked homosexual urge. The life reading taken on this young man at his request shows him to have been in a previous life a satirist and gossipmonger in the French court who took particular delight in exposing the homosexual scandals of the court with his cartoonist skill. "Condemn not, then," concludes the reading, "that you be not condemned. For indeed, with what measure you mete it shall be measured to you again. *And what you condemn in another, that you become in yourself.*"

The fourth case is that of a boy who at the age of sixteen was in an automobile accident in which his spinal cord was severed. Specialists doubted he would live, but he pulled through. Below the fifth vertebra he was completely paralyzed, and his life has been confined to a wheelchair ever since. Seven and a half years after the accident when he was twenty-three, his mother obtained a reading for him from Cayce. The life reading gave the boy two past incarnations, one at the time of the American Revolution, when he was a military officer of much determination and courage. From that experience he brought over to the present "the characteristics of orderliness, cheerfulness, the ability to make the best of a bad situation and to use what is in hand."

The incarnation before this was the crucial one, so far as his affliction was concerned. He had been a Roman soldier in the early Christian era, "and one given to self-indulgence. He gloried in seeing the suffering of those who held to the principles of the Nazarene. He fought in the arena and later watched many whom he had met in combat fight again with beasts. The entity saw much suffering and made light of it. Hence the entity sees suffering in himself in the present, and must again make light of it—but for a different purpose.

That some purposefulness that he mocked at then must arise within himself in order to meet what he has created."

It is interesting to note that in these seven afflictions—which included three cases of polio, and one each of tuberculosis of the hip joint; overweight; homosexuality; and spinomuscular paralysis from a fracture—none of the persons was born with the affliction. In every case the condition arose some time after birth, ranging from the age of six months to that of thirty-six years, and in one case it was "caused" by an automobile accident. Behind the veil of ostensible causation, however, there would appear to be another and deeper cause. The strange fatality of accidents wherein one person is killed and another is not, one goes without a scratch and another is cruelly disfigured, seems to man to be a matter of chance. Cases such as those just cited, however, would seem to indicate that some inner imperceptible line of force is operative even in the sudden chaos of accident such that karmic dues are accurately apportioned. Even susceptibility to the polio germ would appear to be similarly induced.

Though at first glance the penalties may appear disproportionate to so trifling a matter as laughter, on deeper consideration the justice becomes more apparent. He who laughs at the affliction of another is condemning a set of circumstances for which he does not understand the inner necessity; he is despising the right of every man to evolve through even the meanest form of folly; he is deprecating the dignity and worth and divinity which inhere in every soul, no matter how low or ridiculous the estate to which it may have fallen. He is, moreover, asserting his selfhood as being superior to the selfhood of those he laughed at. The act of mockery is an act of self-assertion in the most ignoble sense of the term.

These considerations remind us forcibly of certain phrases of an ancient book of wisdom. We begin to see that blessed indeed is he who does not sit in the seat of the scorner, and right indeed was the instinct of the psalmist when he resolved: "I shall keep my lips with a bridle, that I sin not with my tongue." *Judge not that ye be not judged!* suddenly stands out like an apocalyptic commandment, written in tongues of flame; *for with what judgment ye judge, ye shall be judged*. And those other words of Jesus: "He who says 'thou fool!' shall be in danger of hell fire!" suddenly acquire, in the light of these cases of mockery tragically expiated, a new depth of psychological meaning.

Chapter VI

An Interlude of Comment

─────────────────────────────

A THOROUGH study of the Cayce files provides a vast panorama of human woe not to be equalled in variety and scope by the combined case-history files of doctor, psychiatrist, psychologist, and social worker. This may sound like an exaggeration, but it is not; the human pain represented here not only touches all these realms of therapeutic approach, but also embraces the evil and error and folly and pain of hundreds of past forgotten centuries.

The negative aspects of karma are conspicuous in the Cayce files because it was primarily the sick and afflicted who turned to him for help. The healthy person has no reason to consult a doctor and the well-adjusted person rarely finds it important to question the ultimate meaning of life. And so the vast majority of the Cayce readings were given for people who had very definite and sometimes very appalling personal problems that had not been solved by medical, psychological, or religious practitioners.

A study of the readings might be overwhelmingly depressing if it were not for the fact that in these cases—unlike the usual medical or psychiatric case history—the ethical and spiritual significance of the suffering is made clear. For this reason, a passage through the readings gives one the same sense of grandeur in time and space as in reading Dante's account of hell and purgatory—without the intellectual reservations occasioned by Dante's medieval theological limitations. The Cayce readings give a continuous evaluation of suffering in an ethical, universal, and thoroughly intelligible frame of reference—and it is this that makes the study of them bearable. More than bearable, they are engrossing, encouraging, inspiring, and deeply reassuring, even though the springboard is more often than not some kind of disease or deformity.

Not all the karmic examples in the Cayce files are instances of frustrations and abnormalities, however. We shall see later, when we come to cases on vocational guidance, how human ability, talent, genius, distinction of any sort are the karmic rewards of lives well spent along these same directions in the past.

A favorable environment and a healthy body are also positive karmic consequences, but explanation is not often given by the readings for their karmic basis—possibly because the source of information, like a good news reporter, recognized that it is not the good, but the calamitous, that has news value. People who obtained readings shared the general human tendency of feeling that there is no need of an explanation for good fortune; man usually feels instinctively that it is his inherent right. It is only when he suffers ill fortune that he begins to question why it has happened.

Personal beauty is likewise a positive karmic consequence. The readings have occasionally indicated, in general terms, that a beautiful body in the present is the result of care devoted to the body, the temple of the spirit, in the past. There is one interesting instance in which the reading gave another karmic reason for beauty. This is the case of a striking New York model whose unusually beautiful hands bring her much in demand with nail polish, hand lotion, and jewelry merchants who feature hands in their advertisements. The karmic cause for her gift of beauty was found in the incarnation immediately preceding the present, when she was a recluse in an English convent. Her life had been spent in performing menial and distasteful tasks with her hands; she did them with such a dedicated spirit of selflessness and service, however, that her consecration of spirit was transmuted into the unusual beauty of her person and of her hands.

Here, indeed, is a heartening example to those who long for beauty. It should serve also to remind us that all karma is not disciplinary and constrictive in effect. Examples of the punitive aspects of karma are perhaps more impressive than illustrations of its beneficent aspects—more impressive and more necessary to the generally confused and morally bankrupt outlook of our time. Intelligent human beings must have an intelligent moral basis for life; the orthodox dogmas of the church are no longer acceptable to many critically trained scientific minds. Thus the traditional sanctions and ideals have crumbled, but no new, scientifically acceptable notions have risen to take their place.

For almost twenty centuries the moral sense of the Western world has been blunted by a theology which teaches the vicarious atonement of sin through Christ, the Son of God. Even skeptics, in the face of the strange events and the tremendous influence that emanated from this man, may concede that Christ was in a sense a Son of God and that—noble and compassionate—he lived and died so that men might be free. But more and more, in the light of the advances of modern physics, people are coming to feel that all life in the universe, down to the minutest power-charged atom, is in essence related to each other life in the universe by virtue of a common sustaining source in one central energy, or God. By this view it seems necessary to conclude that all living things, and all men and women, are the sons of God—like rays from some vast central sun. It can be felt then that perhaps the personality called Jesus was different from us only in that he was closer to the central light than we are.

Moreover, Christ's giving of his life that men might be free is no unique event in history; the study of comparative religions reveals other saviours, among other peoples, who suffered martyrdom and death. In our own Western culture, many idealists have given their lives willingly for humanity's sake. Mazzini, Bolivar, Lincoln, St. Francis, Toussaint L'Ouverture, Semmelweiss, St. Teresa—a hundred names and more can be cited of men and women who lived and died that other human beings might be free. But no one feels that their effort redeems us from effort, or that their sacrifice absolves us of our own personal guilt.

To build these two statements, therefore—that Christ was the Son of God and that he died for man's salvation—into a dogma, and then to make salvation depend upon believing that dogma, has been the great psychological crime not of Christianity but of some of its theologians. It is a psychological crime because it places responsibility for redemption on something external to the self; it makes salvation dependent on belief in the divinity of another person rather than on self-transformation through belief in one's own intrinsic divinity. It violates the sense of justice and psychological verisimilitude because it declares that belief in vicarious atonement is necessary, the penalty for non-belief being everlasting damnation. Twentieth-century minds, trained rigorously in physical and psychological sciences, find it difficult to take such a doctrine seriously.

Despite the handicap of its rigid theology, the church has been unquestionably a great force for good in the world. The more enlightened Christian churches today, moreover, no longer teach this dogma narrowly and literally, and profession of belief is not universally considered a condition for entrance into heaven. But the vestiges of this attitude are apparent even where it does not prevail in its original theologically uncompromising form; the Christian world is still permeated by a conviction that lifts responsibility from the realm of conduct and places it to a large degree in the realm of uncritical belief.

The cardinal importance of conduct in personal salvation becomes strikingly apparent as one studies the laws of karma and reincarnation; for this reason ancient wisdom provides a tonic corrective to the anemic lassitude into which many Christian sects have fallen. Our grim recital here of the disciplinary aspects of karmic law according to Cayce should not be unduly depressing to those who come to accept the validity of reincarnation; on the contrary, it should lead to hope, optimism, and a renewed religious faith founded on confidence with regard to the cosmic justice that underlies all human affairs.

Examples such as these should serve as deterrents to persons who feel that all reason for morality disappeared when "science" undermined "religion," and that conduct consequently can be free and untrammeled by the scruples of the church. That cruelty can result karmically in blindness or anemia or asthma or paralysis; that sexual excesses can result in epilepsy; that the selfish thwarting of others can result in the paralysis of one's own limbs—facts such as these, which illustrate a sensitive, scientific, impartial, and appropriate operation of *law*, have the power to startle people into good behavior, if nothing else.

Further, cases such as the ones we have seen should suggest an explanation for the tragic condition of the millions of afflicted people who populate the earth. We do not ordinarily see the lame, the halt, the blind—the lunatic, the epileptic, the bedridden, the leprous—the mutilated victims of war and accident; they are hidden from ordinary view in the privacy of saddened homes or in the concentrated colonies of institutions. We see the defective only occasionally upon our busy streets, and we are made aware of their numerical extent only indirectly, as we read an occasional magazine article on the subject.

But their number is legion and their plight is sad. We need to be reminded of their existence in order to realize how tragic indeed can be the lot of man when deprived of the normalcies which most of us tend to take for granted. The usual Christian explanation for such tragedies is indicated by the phrase, "the will of God." But it is difficult to reconcile an all-loving Father with a will that visits such pitiful afflictions on innocent persons. And so the will of God is regarded as "inscrutable"; but the adjective does not dispose of the essential contradiction.

The reincarnation principle resolves such dilemmas by indicating that the "will of God" may indeed be a fact in the universe; but it is not a matter of whim or inscrutable purpose. It is rather a law of spiritual intention, whereby only those who deserve to be afflicted are afflicted: no person is given a cross to bear in life any better or any worse than he has earned in lifetimes past.

It is difficult for people of Western heritage to accept the concept of reincarnation on first hearing. It seems incredible—a thing far outside the bounds of observed or observable experience. And yet how many other incredible things there are in life, to which we do not give a second thought! An egg hatches out a tadpole which becomes first a fish and then a frog. A caterpillar spins itself a silken shroud and emerges not long afterward an exquisite butterfly. Here are truly amazing instances of the way in which the same life can, without losing its identity, successively inhabit different physical forms—yet we take them for granted. Thoughtfully considered, they are perhaps no more unnatural than that a human spirit should inhabit successively different forms without losing its essential selfhood.

The processes of birth are themselves a miracle in which we probably would not believe if our microscopes did not show us they were so. That two minute cells should join and multiply in cellular composition by mathematical laws, and finally, after a recapitulation of the race experience, produce a human creature with eyes, lips, hands, feet, and a brain to guide them, would stagger sextillions of infidels, in Whitman's picturesque phrase, if only they stopped to think about it. A succession of lives, therefore should really be no more startling, no more preposterous than one life: as Voltaire said, "After all, it is no more surprising to be born twice than it is to be born once."

The Cayce life readings, with their psychological and ethical plausibility, serve to take something of the edge off our incredulity. Perhaps these documents, so strangely originated and so strangely given, can be regarded as vehicles for raising us from one dimension of perception to another. Perhaps, for all their strangeness, they can teach us—like fish at the bot-

65

tom of a sea—that there is such a thing as air; that there is a vaster framework of existence than the little world in which our lives are embedded, and a vaster meaning to life than we have yet been able to surmise.

Chapter VII

Karma in Suspension

_____

A CURIOUS fact, observable in the cases of physical karma already discussed, is that the karmic consequence of an action sometimes shows itself only after an interval of one or more lifetimes. The question arises as to why this karmic suspension is necessary. Why should not the reaction begin immediately, with the promptness of a ball rebounding from a wall?

There would seem to be several answers to this question. One is that the ego must wait for a time and place appropriate to the karma which it has created. It may take centuries before such a suitable opportunity presents itself, and the intervening centuries are to be used for the working out of other character problems. A good example of this type of karmic suspension is seen in the Cayce data on entities who once lived on the lost continent of Atlantis.

The existence of this vast ancient continent beneath the Atlantic Ocean has never been fully proved or disproved by science, though a fairly good case for it has been made on the basis of historical, geological, and cultural evidences. The principal historical secondary source is Plato, who refers to Atlantis quite seriously in the Critias and Timaeus dialogues. One of the geological evidences often cited is the discovery made when a trans-Atlantic cable snapped and sank to a depth of ten thousand feet; when dragged to the surface the cable brought with it pieces of lava which under microscopic examination were shown to have been hardened on land areas *above* water. Among the cultural evidences perhaps the most striking are, first, the universality of the flood story (it is found not only in the Bible but also in the legends and religions of almost all primitive peoples in the world); and second, the close similarity of language and architecture between Egypt and Central America at an age when no communication between the two continents is known to have existed. All considered, the total evidence is persuasive, though by no means conclusive.

At any rate, if the Cayce readings are to be accepted, Atlantis did very definitely exist. According to Cayce, certain unopened chambers in the Great Pyramid may some day disclose full records of its history and civilization. These records were brought there, he said, when some of the inhabitants of the doomed continent fled to Egypt at the time of the third and last cataclysm, about 9500 B.C. Cayce also referred to the island of Bimini, off Miami, Florida, as an Atlantean mountain peak; he stated that on the sea-bottom here could be found a fine example of an Atlantean temple with its dome constructed for the capture of the sun's energy by means of specially designed crystals. According to the readings, the Atlanteans had reached a much higher peak of scientific efficiency than we have. Electricity, radio, television, air travel, submarines, and the harnessing of solar and atomic power were highly advanced among them; they had much more efficient techniques of heating, lighting, and transportation than we now possess.

All this is of absorbing interest, whether one takes it seriously or not; but the significant thing to note here, if one *does* take it seriously, is this: the life readings repeatedly stated that the Atlanteans became evil in their misuse of the titanic forces that they had learned to develop. They committed some of their greatest depravities in connection with electrical and psychic powers, and especially with a form of hypnosis which was used to enslave others for forced labor or sexual gratification.

If this can be accepted as a true account, then it is understandable that this ancient corruption of character could not very well be completely redeemed in eras when neither electricity nor occult and psychological knowledge was available. The final test of a man's having surmounted gluttony is to surround him once again with his favorite food, and see if he remains temperate. A man cannot be said to have conquered his sexual desires if, when placed in the midst of desirable women, he does not resist temptation with the stubborn tenacity of St. Anthony. Similarly, the entities who misused the tremendous power available to them by Atlantean science at its height cannot be said to have transmuted their selfishness and lust for power unless, when offered the same opportunities, they can use them constructively.

The cyclic progress of history has made the twentieth century just such a period; consequently we find, according to the Cayce readings, that Atlanteans are incarnating at present in great numbers. The amazing technology of the present age can therefore be understood under two aspects: first, as the consequence of the bold, inventive genius of egos who brought with them a remembrance of Atlantean achievements; and second, as the testing ground for these same egos, to determine whether in the intervening centuries they have acquired qualities that will withstand the renewed temptation to selfishness and civilized barbarity.

The need to wait for an appropriate culture epoch, then, seems to be a major factor in determining karmic suspension. It would seem to be related to some cyclic progression of history and some rhythmic alternation of groups of souls in their periods of embodiment and non-embodiment on this planet. It seems reasonable that great waves of races and peoples could follow such cosmic and rhythmic regularity of return. Various passages in the Cayce readings indicate, however, that the incarnation of smaller groups within the waves, and even of individuals within the groups, may not be merely a matter of mechanically rhythmic predetermination. Souls and groups of souls do not return with the automatic regularity of a revolving door; here, as everywhere in creation, there is freedom of will and an individual or a group may *choose* to manifest at certain times if it wishes to.

This leads then to the further complexity that if an individual entity needs to develop some quality with respect to another individual soul, or group of souls, he may need to delay his own incarnation to conform with the period chosen for embodiment by the others. And if such a delay is extensive he may find it expedient to return meanwhile to work on some other aspect of his development—thus giving rise to the phenomenon we have noted as suspended karma.

These generalizations cannot be made with scientific certitude, of course, but are proposed only on the basis of scattered but repeated indications that this is so in the Cayce readings.

The above-mentioned factors represent purely external determinants of karmic suspension; but there would seem to be inner determinants as well. Of equal if not greater importance is the psychological fact that strength is needed to meet karma; some opportunity must be given the entity to acquire the necessary combative qualities, otherwise the karmic obligation will be so overwhelming as to result in annihilation rather than growth.

Several afflicted people who learned in their Cayce reading that the origin of their affliction was to be found several lifetimes previous were curious about the reason for the karmic lag. All who inquired about this point in a later reading received substantially the same answer as the lame girl mentioned in Chapter 5 who asked: "Why did the entity wait until this incarnation to make good the karma from the Roman period?" The answer: "Because it was unable to do it before." The context it clear that this inability was a matter of inner capacity rather than outer restriction; in this and other cases of affliction, close analysis of the intervening lives shows that they were necessary experiences for the acquisition of certain positive qualities.

If we refer back to the case of the sixteen-year-old boy injured in an automobile accident, for example, we will observe that the karmic seed in this case was sown in ancient Rome. An experience in the American Revolutionary period, however, gave him the opportunity to develop certain qualities of courage and cheerfulness and the ability to put to good account whatever came his way. These were necessary qualities for the bearing of the karmic affliction that came to fruition in the present.

An instructive parallel is found in the commonsense practice of men with regard to monetary debts. The man who borrows five thousand dollars from a bank is in no position to repay the debt the following day, week, or month, and probably not even the following year. For this reason time is allowed the borrower, that he may gather together sufficient resources; there would be no point in demanding repayment the following week when it is obvious that he has nothing with which to pay. Possibly cancellation of debts incurred in the moral realm is handled in a similar way.

If the reincarnation principle should some day win popular acceptance, and the concept of karma be at least roughly understood by the masses of the West as it already is by the masses of the East, the notion of suspended karma may become a source of concern to many people. The thought that some past act of cruelty may demand future payment in the form of blindness in this or in a forthcoming life is, admittedly, an unwelcome one; to an impressionable imagination an unknown karmic debt may appear to hang like the sword of Damocles over one's head, or lie in wait like a beast of prey beyond the bend of the road. Suspended karma might well become the bugaboo of the first decades of the Reincarnationist Age as the devil and hell-fire were the bugaboos of a former one.

To counteract this tendency toward fear, the leaders of New Thought schools may, in fact, go so far as to make wholesale denials of suspended karma, much as the Christian Scientists make denials of sin, disease, death, error, and matter. There is no doubt that such denials would have great suggestive power and, as in the case of Christian Science and New Thought generally, might even accomplish healthful results in the direction of spiritual strength. However, to "deny" matter and sin and karma verbally does not actually annihilate them. Our task in life is not to hide from the reality of matter, with the cheerful but deluded evasion of the ostrich; our task is to govern it, order it, and even create it from the higher levels of spirit. In reality, matter is only a condensation of an energy which may be called spirit; or matter is merely spirit at a lower degree of vibration.

Similarly with respect to sin and karma. According to reincarnationists, to "deny" karma, either presently operative or in suspension, is equivalent to denying the existence of debts to be paid and lessons to be learned and is an essentially dishonest attitude. A man who is deceitful and fraudulent in regard to his obligations, whether they be of a material or spiritual nature, commands no respect. Just because the attempted fraud consists of mental acrobatics of denial does not alter the fact that it partakes essentially of the effort to dodge accountability.

This is not to say, however, that suggestion should not be used. On the contrary, it may be very helpful in dissolving mental fixations, mechanisms of guilt, or crystallizations of attitude. We have seen one remarkable case—that of the boy cured of bed-wetting—in which suggestion was directed to the subconscious sense of guilt. It was his feeling of worthlessness that was inflicting symbolic punishment upon himself. By dissolving this guilt feeling and thereby freeing him to express helpfulness to his fellowman, both his bodily condition and personality were transformed.

In the case of allergy, also, deep suggestion and hypnosis were recommended by the reading. But in neither case was the suggested treatment one of denial—on the contrary, it was to consist of "affirmation of virtue" and "consciousness of spiritual attunement." If mental healers wish to "treat" for karmic conditions or for the oppressive sense of impending karma, the treatment, it seems, should make honest acknowledgment of past obligation, then express honest willingness to meet that obligation, and finally affirm that particular strength the absence of which led to the karma to begin with.

If the reincarnationist view is to be accepted then, it is

71

necessary to face the fact that the human race is spiritually immature and consequently its members must expect unpleasant karma in future lives. But this fact should not be a source of fear or anxiety, and this for two reasons: first, *Sufficient unto the day is the evil thereof* is a maxim that applies not only to the living of each day with unconcerned tranquillity; it applies also to the living of each life in the calm assurance that whatever may be its hardships the individual portion is a just one, tempered to individual strength. At no time do we become involved in karma too great for us to bear. Second, the uncertainty of the future is always with us, whether or not we believe in karma; and if future calamities that may befall us are karmic rather than haphazard our fears should be alleviated rather than intensified, if only for the simple reason that karma represents the operation of a law which is so ordered as to guarantee justice always.

It is understandable in man to fear future hardships, but it is not becoming in him to fear future hardships that come to him justly, for the sake of his education and the expansion of his consciousness. An honest man who has incurred a debt is anxious to pay it; he conscientiously takes care of the financial affairs of each day so that on the first of the month, when his bills come due, he will be in a position to pay them. He does not live all month in fear of the day when he will inevitably receive the bills; he devotes his energies instead to making himself able to fulfill his obligations.

We are not aware, in our limited conscious minds, of the exact nature of the moral debt that we may have contracted in our ignorant past, but we should have that integrity of mind and that acquiescence of spirit that mark honest men everywhere, such that we go forward to meet our debt with simple willingness to pay.

But perhaps the word *debt* is misleading—perhaps the more appropriate word would be *deficit*, or *deficiency*. A deficiency disease must be fought by supplying the vitamins and minerals in which the body is deficient; until the deficiency is repaired the body is not healed of the disease. Similarly, karma is made possible, in one important and fundamental sense, only by the *absence* of spiritual qualities; only by the *lack* of awareness of one's spiritual identity. The proper correction of karmic conditions, then, consists in supplying the spiritual qualities the deficiency of which induced the condition to begin with, and in evoking the awareness of spiritual identity.

But whether karma is regarded as a debt or a deficit or a sort of spiritual deficiency, the fact remains that its redemption must be approached in a spirit of willingness rather than

72

of rebellion. To "deny" its existence partakes more of the nature of rebellion than of acquiescence; for such a "denial" is expressive of the self-will and desire for convenience of the present personality, rather than of the long-term wisdom of the eternal identity.

The Cayce readings frequently give counsel for the proper attitude to take with regard to karma. The following passage gives a particularly pointed suggestion:

> If the experience is used for self-indulgence, self-aggrandizement, or self-exaltation, the entity does so to its own undoing, and creates for itself that which has been called karma and which must be met. And in meeting every error, every trial, every temptation, whether they be mental or physical experiences, the approach to it should always be in the attitude of: "Not my will, but Thine, O God, be done in and through me."

"Thy will" can be understood, of course, in two senses: either as the "will" of God, which expresses itself through the impersonal laws of the universe, or as the will of the eternal identity, the Oversoul, who, in the esoteric tradition, is the Father to whom we address our prayers. Whichever interpretation is placed upon the phrase, acquiescence and trust should mark our attitude toward whatever karma may come our way.

In the universe of order and justice and beneficence which the reincarnation principle reveals, there is no need for fear.

Chapter VIII

Karma and Problems of Health

UNFORTUNATELY, karma has become associated in the minds of many with passivity, lethargy, and fatalism. This is largely because the people of India, where belief in karma is almost universal, appear for the most part to be passive, lethargic, and fatalistic.

It is true that social conditions in India are deplorable; it is also true that the passivity of the Hindus in the acceptance of their karma is partly to blame. However, the teachings of India's religious sages filter down through so much time-encrusted superstition that the character of the teachings changes radically in the process; by the time they are absorbed by the uneducated masses their psychological effect cannot be considered an optimum example of the results of belief in reincarnation. Moreover the enervating effects of India's climate are an important element in the psychology of its people and would affect their mental outlook and character no matter what their religious belief.

In reality there is no psychologically necessary association between apathy and belief in karma—any more than there is a psychologically necessary association between hypocrisy and Christianity. Christianity has developed multitudes of hypocrites, both in the present and in the past eras of its history, but this hypocrisy cannot be charged to the teachings of Christ.

If an individual comes to accept the concept of karma, acquiescence and trust must characterize his inner attitude toward it, as it must characterize his inner attitude toward any law of the universe. But he cannot help but wonder to what degree he should acquiesce, to what degree he must accept the constrictions that are placed upon him. This problem becomes particularly apparent in situations involving physical karmic affliction.

Here, as elsewhere, the Cayce readings are interesting because speculative questions on ethical and practical implications of the reincarnation theory are given specific and tangible answers. We turn to them, then, with the questions: What treatment, if any, was prescribed for people suffering from a physical karmic penalty? What hope, if any, was held out for their cure?

Every reading in the Cayce files belies the view that passive acceptance must accompany the belief in karma. The consistent point of view throughout is: "This is your karma. Now here is what you can do about it."

One of the most striking elements of the original documents is the way in which the statements of karma invariably flow into suggestions for treatment. In many cases of physical karma the reading holds out definite hope for cure. In other cases, where the karmic debt is more serious, it frankly states that a complete cure cannot be expected, but improvement can be achieved through effort; it then proceeds to outline the type of treatment.

An interesting case is that of a thirty-four-year-old electrician afflicted with a disease finally diagnosed by the doctors as a hopeless case of multiple sclerosis. For three years he had been unable to work; he had become too blind to read or write, and often fell when he attempted to walk. He was accepted as a charity patient by several hospitals in succession; meanwhile his wife clerked in a department store to support herself and their five-year-old son. Though no life reading was taken, the man was told in the physical reading that his condition was a karmic one. However, he was urged not to lose hope.

"Yes, we have the body here," the reading began, using the same simple but extraordinary phrase with which the clairvoyant description of all physical readings began. "As we find, conditions here are very serious, but do not lose hope, For help is nigh, if you will but accept it."

Then follow three pages of singular beauty and force. First there is given a pathological description of the condition in medical terms, then an essay on the recuperative energies within the body, then a reference to the fact that the man's situation is karmic, followed by an exhortation to change his mental outlook and eliminate all hate and malice from his consciousness. The reading concludes with a careful prescription of treatment.

About a year later the man wrote again for another reading, reporting that he had religiously followed the prescription and had immediately noted an improvement. This improvement continued steadily for a period of four months, after which a relapse and decline of strength appeared. Apparently he had applied the material side of the prescription without paying much attention to the spiritual, for the reading calls him to task in no uncertain terms.

Yes, we have the body here; this we have had before.

As we find, there have been physical improvements in the body, yet there is much, much to be desired.

As already indicated, this is a karmic condition and there must be measures taken by the entity to change its attitude toward things, conditions, and its fellow man.

So long as mechanical things were applied for physical correction, improvements were seen.

But when the entity becomes so self-satisfied, so self-centered, as to refuse spiritual things, and does not change its attitude; so long as there is hate, malice, injustice, jealousy; so long as there is anything within at variance with patience, long suffering, brotherly love, kindness, gentleness, there cannot be a healing of the condition of this body.

What does the entity want to be healed *for?* That it may gratify its own physical appetites? That it may add to its own selfishness? Then, if so, it had better remain as it is.

If there is a change in mind and purpose, and if the entity expresses the change in speech and action, and if there is the application of those material things suggested, we will see improvement.

But first there must be the change of heart, of mind, of purpose, of intent. . . . All of the mechanical appliances that you can muster will not bring about complete recovery *unless* your purpose and your soul have been baptized with the Holy Spirit. . . . Will you accept, will you reject? It is up to you.

We are through—unless you make amends.

We are through with this reading.

It will be noted in the above passages that hope is held out for cure on condition that the man changes the contents of his consciousness and his spiritual purposes in life. What do you want to be healed *for?* the source of information asks, frankly and searchingly. So that you can gratify your physical appetites? So that you can add to your selfishness? In that case you might as well remain as you are.

This outspoken reading typifies the antiseptic moral outlook of a great physician, whose vision included far more than the mere temporary expedience of a personality. Not once, in more than 25,000 physical readings, did Cayce refuse to give suggestions for cure to an afflicted person, no matter how depraved or how infamous that person's sin had been. But many times, as in the present instance, infinitely compassionate though he was, he could not refrain from pointing out that disease has a morally corrective purpose, and that the moral fault that was its source must be corrected. The person who suffers from disease should make every effort to correct it with all the means as his command, but concurrently he should take the cue that life presents him to amend the inner weakness of his soul. The storehouse of nature and the miracle drugs of modern science may produce temporary relief, but in the path of the moral force of karma they must finally remain impotent. Ultimately, healing must come spiritually from within, or it cannot long endure.

The following case of blindness is another among the hundreds in the files that illustrate this consistent point of view.

Yes. Conditions here are mostly karmic. The better application of spiritual ideals in relationship to others will bring a great difference in the life experience of this entity.

While there will not be at first a great deal of change in the vision, we find that the body will be materially improved as adjustments are made in the inner self.

The conditions in the spinal system, as well as in the mouth and gums, have had much to do with the eye condition.

Then, as we find, there should be first the effort to manifest the fruits of the spirit and to apply the Christ-consciousness in the daily experiences. Practice, then, brotherly love, kindness, patience, long suffering, gentleness.

Also have osteopathic adjustments especially in the 4th, 3rd, 2nd, and 1st dorsals, the 3rd cervical, and 1st, 2nd, and 4th cervical. The adjustments here should be made in the orders indicated, and then those nerve centers that supply the teeth—especially in the area just under the ear connecting with the mastoid areas of the head—should have particular attention. . . .

It will be seen in both of the above cases that the reading lays primary stress upon a change of consciousness and character as the *sine qua non* of a change of physical karmic condition. When it is remembered that the purpose of karma is moral education, it will be seen how natural and inevitable this approach to karmic therapeutics is. The "sin," of course, that karma corrects is not sin in the superstitious primitive sense of offended gods and spirits, nor sin in the sense of fundamentalist theologians, nor even sin in the sense of Victorian or Puritan morals. It is sin, rather, in a psychological sense; sin that is universally definable and universally subject to a cosmic law.

Sin in this sense consists basically in selfishness or separativeness, and the self-exaltation may take many forms. It can consist of violence against the will or body of another; it can consist of violence against one's own body, through intemperance or neglect; it can consist of pride or exclusiveness of the spirit. These varieties of error are possible because of one cardinal error, one cardinal misunderstanding, one cardinal forgetfulness. For man is a spirit, not a body; sin arises from his forgetfulness of this fact as he identifies himself with his body. It is against this illusion of identity with his body that he must fight. And the surest way of combating that illusion is not through the negative process of denial, but through the positive process of identification with spirit.

In the attainment of this sense of identity with spirit one achieves what the Cayce readings and other mystic sources call the Christ-consciousness. It will be found in the above-cited cases, and in almost every other case of physical karma in the Cayce files, that the primary recommendation for cure is that the sufferer shall attain, in some measure at least, this Christ-consciousness.

The Christ-consciousness is not, however, an exclusively Christian attribute. Christ, it must be remembered, is not the name of the man Jesus, but a term whose literal meaning is "the anointed one," and whose mystic or rather psychological meaning is that of the liberated or spiritual consciousness. Krishna and Buddha were, we may believe, equally the possessors of Christ-consciousness; and men are striving, dimly and confusedly, in all parts of the world, toward the possession of this consciousness no matter who their teacher and no matter by what name that degree of unfoldment is called.

It happens that the language in which the Cayce readings are couched uses the phraseology of the Christian tradition; this in all probability is because Cayce himself was brought up in the Christian faith; his conscious mind was steeped in

Christian imagery and point of view, and thus every statement of his superconscious mind while in the hypnotic state was filtered through this screen. Conceivably, had Cayce been born in a Buddhist country, he might have adapted his wisdom to the culture setting in which he found himself, and used a predominant Buddhist terminology. But this particularized style of expression does not limit the applicability of what he said.

Here, for example, is the enjoinder given to a man suffering from tuberculosis of the spine:

> Remember, the source of this condition is the meeting of yourself; it is karmic. This can be met best in Him who, taking away the law of cause and effect by fulfilling the law, established the law of grace. Thus the need for the entity to lean on the arm of Him who is the law, and the truth, and the light.

"The law of grace" referred to here is likewise not the exclusive attribute of Christendom or of those who "believe in Jesus Christ"; grace can be achieved by a Buddhist or a Hindu or a Mohammedan as much as by a Christian. "The law, the truth, and the light" is a phrase usually applied by Christians to Jesus—but law and truth are equally applicable to other great religious teachers and their teachings, and light as a symbol of truth and of God and of his purest manifestations is a universal symbol.

Similarly the phrase, "until your soul has been baptized with the Holy Spirit," used in the case of the multiple sclerosis victim is typically Christian. But the idea behind it—the flow of new life consequent upon the realization of one's divine identity—has been phrased in dozens of different images in all the esoteric religions of the world. When the Cayce readings speak, then, of Christ-consciousness, they are using the term most acceptable to people brought up in the Christian tradition. The term, however, refers to a psychological state or stage which could be called by a dozen other names.

The attainment of the Christ-consciousness of spiritual consciousness is the "law of grace" that dissolves the exact retribution of karmic effect. Spiritual consciousness "fulfills the law," to use Jesus' phrase, in the sense that it annuls the error that was the source of the karmic action to begin with. "I come not to destroy the law," is what Jesus might have said "but to teach you how to fulfill it through spiritual consciousness."

But the full attainment of this consciousness is not an easy achievement. "Remember," says a reading, "there is no short cut to a consciousness of the God-force. It is a part of your own consciousness but it cannot be realized by a simple desire to do so. Too often there is a tendency to want it and expect it without applying spiritual truth through the medium of mental processes. This is the only way to reach the gate. There are no short cuts in metaphysics, no matter what is said by those who see visions, interpret numbers, or read the stars. They may find urges, but these do not rule the will. Life is learned within the self. You don't profess it; you learn it."

The use of affirmations, meditation, and prayer, the study of the Scriptures, the practice of the virtues, and the rendering of service to one's fellowmen are methods often recommended by the readings for the attainment of a changed consciousness. But genuine growth cannot be mechanically induced. Unless and until the heart is sufficiently tenderized, these practices will be, in Paul's apt phrase, as tinkling brass; without true charity they are essentially worthless. As disciplines they will be valuable; as suggestive forces they will have an effect; as educative experiences they will start the soul on the proper path. But for those multitudes of souls who are at the kindergarten stage, spiritually speaking, they cannot lead immediately to college. Not all people are sufficiently evolved spiritually to be capable of achieving in one lifetime that all-consuming, all-embracing love which is the essence of the true Christ-consciousness, and thus achieve liberation from the debt of karma.

In the case of a young man suffering from arthritis, the source of information was apparently aware of this impossibility for the youth in question. Therefore, with the probity of a physician who knows the utmost possibilities of an organism and does not wish to mislead the patient with false hopes, he says, "There may be relief here, but not complete cure."

Yet he does not let the matter drop therewith. In this and in all similar cases, he proceeds to suggest curative measures of a physical nature, so that the entity, regardless of the possibility or impossibility of achieving direct liberation, is guided to make active efforts to overcome his affliction. Patience, persistence, fortitude, and whatever other qualities of humility or goodness learned in the process will contribute indirectly at least to the moral fulfillment of the karmic debt. It is obvious, then, that far from promotiong a passive attitude toward a karmic condition, the readings encourage a vital and dynamic attitude of activity.

Another important aspect of the matter of therapy is this:

the readings were always aware of the necessity of counseling people at their own stage of development. They did not propose exclusively mental methods of healing to people who were incapable of understanding such methods, or were averse to them. According to the testimony of scientist Alexis Carrel in his books *Man, the Unknown* and *The Voyage to Lourdes,* many persons of deep religious faith have been instantly cured at the shrine of Lourdes of cancers and other seemingly incurable afflictions. Assuming that such cures happened, it is certainly not to be expected that similar cures could be effected in persons who lacked the same degree of faith, the same outlook of mind, the same readiness to abjure the physical.

A comparative study of many of the Cayce physical readings indicates clearly that the source of information always tacitly acknowledged the limits of belief of the individual in question. In many cases of specific illness, for example, the readings were apparently confident that some individuals could achieve a cure through sheer mental suggestion—such is the remarkable power of suggestion and the obedience of the unconscious mind. In other cases of the same illness, the patients were apparently incapable of being cured in this way, because of ignorance, or skepticism, or too great absorption in a material point of view. For them it was simpler and wiser, the readings recognized, to recommend specific physical treatments.

One is reminded of the classic story told by Hindu teachers about the eager young student of a great yogi. The student had been given basic instruction on accomplishing miraculous feats with his mind. An apt pupil, he withdrew into solitude and returned ten years later to his teacher. "What have you been doing all these years?" asked the yogi, with affectionate interest. "I have learned how to govern my mind so that I can walk on the water," said the pupil, with some pride. "My dear boy," said the teacher, sadly, "you have been wasting your time. Don't you know that you can get the ferryman to take you across for only two pennies?"

This story, told by a people who for centuries have devoted themselves to the cultivation of the powers of the mind, has a commonsense force that should be thoughtfully considered by those who resist all physical means in the treatment of disease. To be sure, the effort to achieve a purely mental cure is a praiseworthy one and productive of strength. Christian Science, Religious Science, Unity, and similar metaphysical movements are making a tremendous contribution to the public awareness that the mind is the source of much disease and therefore can be the source of its cure as well. It is important, however, that it be recognized in metaphysics, as it has been recognized in psychosomatic medicine, that there are times when a condition is not of mental origin, and there are times when a condition, no matter what its origin, can best be reached through physical rather than mental means.

One other significant aspect of the Cayce therapeutic outlook was this: the readings did not regard one healing method to be more "spiritual," in an ultimate sense, than another. All healing methods have the same divine source.

A woman who suffered excruciating pain in her back wondered if she should have physical adjustments or whether Unity treatments should be relied on. The reading answered her question as follows:

Much of this can be overcome mentally. But meet conditions as they arise. If there is excessive pain, then have a treatment or adjustments to meet the physical need. There is *no* difference, for the good in each form of treatment comes from the same source. They are not contradictory, as some people believe.

Did the Master heal all people alike? Didn't he use mechanical applications with some? Didn't He tell others to pass the word along? Didn't He simply use the spoken word in others? Remember this basis, this first principle: "The Lord thy God is *one*."

In every realm, then, of mind, body, and soul, there is an attunement to that Oneness. Each phrase has its attributes and its limitations. Only in Him is the full oneness.

A Pittsburgh newspaperman who had suffered with arthritic ill health for ten years, and who had leanings toward metaphysical rather than physical cure, was instructed to try hydrotherapy treatments to stimulate circulation and elimination, and ultraviolet ray treatments. He was told:

All the healing that can be accomplished is within yourself. All healing comes from the Divine. Who heals your diseases? The source of universal supply.

All these various sources come from One Source, and the applications are merely to stimulate the atoms of the body. Each cell is like a universe within itself.

Whether the influences that act upon a body come from medicine, mechanical appliances, hydrotherapy, or what-not, they must of necessity come from the One Source—Life itself.

One other matter must be mentioned in connection with the Cayce philosophy of healing, and that is this: though all causation is, in an ultimate and absolute sense, in the mind —either of God or of man—we are living in a realm of such submergence in matter and such involvement with many groups of souls and many levels of activity that we can call into play, and be affected by, many different levels of causation.

For example: we may go into a restaurant, eat tainted chocolate cream pie, and suffer ptomaine poisoning as a result. Some analysts and metaphysicians would diagnose this as having been caused by an inner state of mind—perhaps a psychological rejection of some life situation. Following this logic to its reasonable conclusion, would we then not have to assert that the other 250 people who ate the same batch of chocolate cream pie in the same restaurant were experiencing the same kind of psychological rejection and hence were led (presumably by their unconscious mind) to the same restaurant which would supply them with the tangible excuse to vomit?

If we insist on the mental causation of everything that happens to us, down to the minutest detail in our lives, we are inevitably led to such a conclusion. And, to be sure, the explanation, however far-fetched it may seem, may even be a correct one. In a world where, by the testimony of the Cayce readings, most causation springs from invisible lines of force and attraction, we cannot presume to deny such a possibility. However it would seem more probable that the 250 persons had been victimized by the carelessness or venality of a baker who used spoiled ingredients; that purely on a physical level, the chemical content of their stomachs was acted on by the poisonous chemical content of the tainted cream. It would seem a more realistic and comprehensive view to recognize that at our present level of evolution and involvement in matter we are inevitably affected by many chemical, biological, mechanical, social, racial, and economic forces for which we have no inner, immediate responsibility except insofar as we must ultimately acquire the strength to be invulnerable to them. Hence Cayce frequently recommended a purely physical remedy for a purely physical condition: a simple antidote for poison; a simple application of heat for congestion; a simple change of locale in order to experience a better climate.

A fall on the street resulting in a broken arm may—as psychiatrists and psychosomatic specialists have amply demonstrated—be due to an "accident-prone" temperament, to a state or trait of personality. But it may also be due to nothing more complex than a broken sidewalk or the protruding wheel of a careless child's bicycle—in which case there is no need for soul-searching to discover the deep inner cause. Mental means of suggestion, affirmation, visualization, prayer, or faith may in any case, whatever the true cause, favor or hasten the knitting of the bone, for psychosomatic reasons we yet know little about. But we will do well to recall a thought the sleeping Cayce often expressed: "Accidents happen often, even in creation." And this one rather cryptic sentence should give us pause before we attribute everything that happens to some watertight theory of causation.

Apart from considerations of causation the physical therapeutics of the Cayce readings are interesting in themselves. These methods of cure, recommended alike in cases called karmic and those in which no mention of karma was made, would constitute a separate study in themselves. As a physician, the source of information was thoroughly eclectic in its choice of healing methods; a list of all the curative measures recommended in the readings would include diet, exercise, drugs, vitamin therapy, operation, herbs and herbal compounds, massage, osteopathy, hydrotherapy, electrotherapy, and the use of two appliances called the Radio-active and the Wet-cell appliances.

These latter two devices are, in a way, inventions of the readings themselves; that is to say, directions for their construction came unasked for through a reading, and their use was subsequently recommended in hundreds of cases. Both the preventive and therapeutic values of osteopathy were continuously stressed, and some thoroughly remarkable results were reported in cases varying from the cure of infant glaucoma to making childbirth possible, as well as easing the birth process.

These and many other original methods of treatment emerge from the Cayce readings. The task of examining and presenting the evidence of their efficacy in cases that medical science had given up as hopeless, and of extracting the principal features of the treatments in various diseases, awaits the efforts of a qualified investigator with medical training.

But the material surveyed so far suggests the rough outlines of a great new philosophy of healing, a great new unitary science of man. For man would seem to be a unit, composed of three basic aspects: body, mind, and soul. This triplicity of man is derived from the triune nature of Divinity, and is in turn reflected in three great bodies of knowledge that man has evolved through the centuries: medicine, psychology, and religion. These branches have pursued separate and often conflicting courses; but perhaps the separation and the conflict have been due to man's ignorance of the truth about himself. Perhaps, in reality, the doctor, psychologist, and priest are three workers at the same laboratory table, three molders of the same ductile clay, three tenders of the same divine fire.

Chapter IX

A New Dimension in Psychology

THE solving of riddles is an instructive pastime. Underlying the solution of many a child's trick is a significant principle of logic or of thought. Perhaps, then, when we come to that most important of all riddles—the riddle of man's identity, his origin, and his ultimate end—we can apply to it the wisdom learned from a simple match trick.

In this trick a person is given six matches and asked to form with them the outline of four equilateral triangles. He begins confidently to make triangular arrangements, but his confidence soon wanes. Indeed, he finally despairs of finding the solution. The problem cannot be solved until it occurs to him to manipulate the matches in three dimensions rather than two, and to make an upright pyramid rather than a fruitless combination of flat triangles.

The enigma of man is, in a sense, comparable to the problem of the matches. Only through an added dimension—in this case, the dimension of time—does it seem likely that man will be able to understand himself.

The birth and death of man's body are commonly considered to be the beginning and ending of man. But if it could be demonstrated scientifically that man is not merely a body, but also a soul inhabiting a body; and that, further, this soul existed before birth and will continue to exist after death, the discovery would transform psychological science. It would be as if a shaft had been dropped from surface levels of soil to deep-lying strata of the earth; modern "depth" psychology would appear as superficial as a two-inch hole for the planting of an onion by comparison with a two-mile shaft for the extraction of oil.

First of all, such an added dimension of time would enlarge man's understanding of personality traits. Psychologists have for some time been making close statistical and clinical studies of the qualities that compose personality. These studies are monuments to the ingenuity of man's mind; they have had many practical applications in personnel work, vocational guidance, and clinical psychology—and yet they represent what would seem to be only the narrow foreground of man.

Acceptance of the reincarnation principle throws a floodlight of illumination on the unnoticed background. The landscape so illumined has a strange and beautiful fascination of its own, but its principal importance is that within it can be discerned the slow, winding paths by which traits and capacities and attitudes of the present were achieved. Or, to change the analogy, it is as if reincarnation revealed the submerged eight-ninths of an iceberg, of which psychologists had been painstakingly examining the visible ninth.

The Cayce files provide numerous examples of this added dimension—time—and of the manner in which it explains the present personality. In one reading Cayce told of a soldier of Gaul who was taken prisoner by Hannibal and forced to row in the galleys of the trade ships. He was cruelly treated by his colored overseers, one of whom finally beat him to death. This took place three lifetimes ago, but a hatred against the colored race engendered by that intensely painful experience persisted, deep in the unconscious, over almost twenty-two centuries of time. In his most recent incarnation, the entity was an Alabama farmer. Throughout his long life he hatred Negroes with a fierce and unrelenting venom; at one time, indeed, he founded a Society for the Supremacy of the White Race.

This is a typical example of an attitudinal carryover from one life to the next. There are dozens of similar ones in the life-reading files. A certain newspaper columnist has for many years nourished an intense anti-Semitic attitude. This is seen by her life reading to stem from an experience in Palestine when she was one of the Samaritans who came into frequent and violent conflict with their Jewish neighbors.

A thirty-eight-year-old unmarried woman had had several romances in her lifetime, but she was never able to commit herself to marriage because of a deep-seated distrust of men. This wariness sprang from an earlier experience when her husband deserted her to go on the Crusades.

A woman whose tolerance of religious beliefs was outstanding was told that she had gained that quality while a Crusader among the Mohammedans. Meeting these people of an alien faith she realized for the first time that idealism, courage, kindness, and mercy exist even among non-Christians; and the impression was so strong as to leave her with a lasting sense of religious tolerance.

On the other hand, an advertising writer of notable skepticism in religious matters had also been a Crusader, and had been so profoundly disgusted by the disparity between religious profession and practice among the people with whom he associated as to acquire a deep-seated distrust of all external professions of faith.

Here, then, we see three types of attitudes—toward race, toward the opposite sex, and toward religion—the basis for which was presumably laid in a previous incarnation. Naturally there had to be in each case certain contemporary environmental circumstances to evoke such a response. The man who hated Negroes was born in the South in 1853, and the customs and traditions of his environment provided a favorable culture for the germ of race-dominance sentiment. Similar possibilities of contemporary influence can be argued in the other cases cited, or in any of the numerous similar instances in the Cayce files, but the intensity of many such attitudes, and the fact that other persons exposed to the same environmental influences do not react in the same manner, would seem to favor a more deeply founded cause than that observable in present-life circumstances.

Psychiatrists concur in the view that the major life attitudes of the psyche arise from the unconscious. The reincarnation principle merely expands the scope of the unconscious to include the dynamics of past-life experience. As in the case of physical disease, there is added a longer range of time within which the point of origin may be found.

Like attitudes, the likes, dislikes, and interests of people are an important component of human personality. The basic instincts of self-preservation, reproduction, and mastery are intimately involved in all the more superficial interests of our life. However, over and beyond the basic needs common to all humanity, there is wide diversity in the way these primary urges express themselves as interests and enthusiasms in different people.

In the same family of five children, for example, one child may take an eager interest in butterflies, another in music, a third in mechanics, a fourth in painting, and a fifth in mischief. For this diversity of talent and outlook the usual psychological explanation is that each individual's makeup is primarily determined by the hereditary endowment of his genes, and secondarily by psychoanalytic factors of position and experience in the family constellation. This explanation is thoroughly reasonable as far as it goes; but to one whose horizon of inquiry includes even the possibility of reincarnation it is inadequate. The Cayce readings place talent and interest firmly in the heredity of the soul itself rather than in the heredity of one's grandparents. In our hypothetical family of five, there must have been, by the Cayce view, circumstances in previous lives which laid the basis for the present bent.

The Cayce files contain the following instances of past-life origin or interests. A certain New York dentist was born and brought up in the metropolis where he now successfully practices his profession. His family for many generations were city-bred people. Though happy in his profession and an enthusiast of city life, he periodically feels an urge to go out into the fields and streams with his gun and fishing rod and camp in the wilderness alone. This intense interest in nature and outdoor life, while not unusual, is an inconsistent element in his thoroughly urban character, but by the reincarnation principle it becomes understandable. According to his Cayce reading he was, in his former life, a Dane who came to this country at the time of the early Dutch settlements. He lived in New Jersey, in a region of many marshes, lakes, and streams, and became a trapper and dealer in furs. The hunger for woods and streams remains with him, though it must now be subordinated to the principal life task of the present incarnation.

Many persons feel an intense attraction for a specific geographic locality. Such an attraction is frequently attributed by the readings to a happy previous sojourn there. A certain East Coast businesswoman, for example, longed for many years to go to the southwestern part of the United States. She finally was able to make the change, and now lives in New Mexico, where she works as a hotel executive. According to her reading she had had two previous experiences in this portion of the country, and her love for the region had persisted through the intervening centuries.

Four persons who had, respectively, a pronounced love of the South Sea Islands, New Orleans, India, and China, were told that they had had experiences in these places before and for this reason felt a strong affinity for them.

Interest in certain types of artistic or professional activity is similarly traced by the readings to past experience. One woman's absorbing interest in the Greek dance and drama arose from an experience in Greece when these art forms were at their height. A boy's marked interest in telepathy had its basis in an incarnation in Atlantis as a teacher of psychology and thought-transmission; a beautiful girl's almost fanatic interest in aviation also stemmed from an Atlantean experience as a pilot and director of communications. A woman's interest in helping crippled children had its origin in a Palestine experience, when, under the influence of the teachings of Jesus, she began to succor the crippled and sick. A research engineer, for many years active in the Technocracy movement, was once an Atlantean active in the scientific administration of the country.

This interest carryover from the past would seem to display itself with particular distinctness in the life history of notable people. We are speaking here not on the basis of a Cayce reading taken on such people, but on the basis of known biographical facts interpreted in the light of the Cayce data.

Consider, for example, the case of Heinrich Schliemann, the German archeologist who discovered the remains of the buried city of Troy and thus established the historical basis for the great Homeric epic. He was the son of a poor pastor of a North German village, yet since early childhood had been fascinated by the story of the Iliad, and conceived the ambition of learning Greek and finding the original site of the Trojan story.

During the first thirty-five years of his life Schliemann amassed the fortune which enabled him later to achieve his archeological purpose. He became an extraordinary linguist, but was especially an enthusiast about Greek and all things Hellenic. In later years he used Homeric forms of address in conversation, and his biographer relates that he held a copy of Homer over the head of his son and recited Homeric verses to him before he handed him over to the Greek priest to be baptized. This is only one of his hundreds of similar enthusiastic extravagances. So inordinate an ardor becomes understandable if one sees it as a form of homesickness of the soul which remembers an era when it was happy and attempts to reestablish itself in the same milieu.

Numberless other examples of the same sort suggest themselves from the annals of biography. Another striking instance is the case of the writer, Lafcadio Hearn. Born on an Ionian island, son of an Irish father and a Greek mother, Hearn wandered from Greece to England to America to the French West Indies and finally found his "true spiritual home" in Japan, where he married a Japanese woman, assumed a Japanese name, and became a teacher in a Japanese school. His amazing intuitive grasp of the Japanese point of view, his extraordinary ability to interpret the Japanese to the Occidentals and the Occidentals to the Japanese appear less extraordinary if one sees them as the outgrowth of a possible former Japanese incarnation, that he was impelled irresistibly to recreate.

T. E. Lawrence is another example of a man who "had it in his blood," as one biographer puts it, to deal with masterly skill with the Arabs and, indeed, to become one of them. He was never "at home" in his English fatherland or with his English family. School bored him except for the Crusades and the study of medieval castles and fortifications. His phenomenal success as a military leader of the Arabs can perhaps be understood as the completion of some previous adventure in the Middle Ages, when he himself was an Arab and a military strategist, and died before fulfilling what he conceived unconsciously to be his incarnation purpose.

Exotic interests like these are found not only among the great and near-great; they are found also among the people who form one's circle of acquaintance.

Traits, like interests and attitudes, are important elements in the analysis of personality, and the Cayce files yield some fascinating examples of their past-life origin. The wife of a certain Middle West millionaire was extremely dictatorial and domineering. Her life reading attributed this tendency to the fact that she had been a schoolteacher in early Ohio, and had held a position of authority in Palestine and India incarnations.

A young boy showed, from early childhood, an extremely argumentative turn of mind and displayed acute reasoning powers. These traits took rise from an incarnation as a man of law at the time of the establishing of trial by jury by Alfred the Great, and from another incarnation as a judge in Persia.

A woman of mystic, quietistic tendencies had been in the life previous to the present the head of a religious retreat in the early nineteenth century. A wealthy young man, whose escapist drinking was the despair and disgrace of his distinguished family, had laid the basis for the weakness in a dissolute experience during the Gold Rush.

Hundreds of instances similar to these are to be found in the life-reading files. Anyone familiar with the Psychology of Individual Differences and the problems with which it deals, cannot but recognize that this material, if true, gives a whole new depth and comprehensiveness to Differential Psychology.

The crux of the matter is this: Modern psychology assumes that differences between human beings are determined primarily by the genes of the parents and secondarily by environmental influences. By the reincarnationist view, however, heredity and environment are themselves the result of past-life karmic determinants, and every quality of the soul is self-earned rather than parentally transmitted.

There is a certain fallacy in the theory of heredity that is not generally recognized. By the hereditary view, it is presumed that phenomena of a mental order can be created by phenomena of a biological order. Remembering Einstein's engaging and ingenuous audacity ("How did you discover relativity?" *"By challenging an axiom!"*), it is perhaps worthwhile to challenge the fundamental assumption on which the hereditary theory is based. Man's knowledge of the mind-body relationship is still in its infancy, to be sure; yet it seems more credible, and psychologically more sound, to believe that phenomena of a mental order must in large part be caused by previous phenomena of a mental order also. "All that you are," said Buddha, "is the result of what you have thought." In that excellent and psychologically rigorous religion, Buddhism, reincarnation is, of course, a cardinal teaching; Buddha taught that a man's qualities are the result of his modes of thinking and acting in past lifetimes. Merely from a mechanistic point of view it seems reasonable to argue that only repeated personal effort can account for personal capacity. If this is so, then it is inferentially necessary that the differences between human endowment in the present are due to differences of human effort in the past.

Ralph Waldo Emerson—an avid student of Eastern thought and a devoted reader of the *Bhagavad-Gita,* the Hindu bible—understood this concept thoroughly. It appears by implication in much of what he wrote, but becomes particularly explicit in his essay on experience. The essay begins:

> Where do we find ourselves? In a series of which we do not know the extremes, and believe that it has none.
> We awake and find ourselves on a stair; there are stairs below us which we seem to have ascended; there are stairs above us, many a one, which go upward and out of sight. But the Genius which according to the old beliefs stands at the door by which we enter, and gives us the Lethe to drink, that we may tell no tales, mixed the cup too strongly, and we cannot shake off the lethargy now at noonday.

Emerson's use of the word "series" suggests the evolutionary nature of all life; his image of the stairs is a particularly graphic representation of how human capacities seem to advance upward as lifetimes progress. The growth of traits and talents does seem to exhibit, in the Cayce data, a kind of continuity that is stairlike in nature. This fact suggests the name Continuity Principle, which can be illustrated in the following manner:

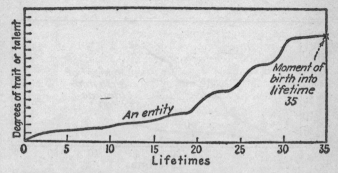

The preceding table portrays how an entity gradually advances in the acquisition of any trait (such as honesty, courage, unselfishness) or talent (music ability, artistic faculty, mathematical insight, etc.) If we were to trace the progress of the entity here represented with respect to musical ability, for example, we might see that in Lifetime 1 he began to use a rudimentary musical instrument, perhaps a reed. In Lifetimes 2, 3, and 4 he used other musical instruments of later culture epochs, increasing gradually the faculties of pitch, rhythm, melodic memory, and so forth, which are the components of what we call musical talent. Finally, in Lifetime 35, he was "born with" extraordinary talent or even what is known as genius.

The new depth given by this concept to the Psychology of Individual Differences is shown still more completely by the following table in which John and Peter are compared in musical talent from the moment of birth into Lifetime 40.

The chart reveals that the entity called Peter has devoted himself to music for many lifetimes past. The entity called John has given some attention to music, but not much. On our arbitrary scale of degrees of musical talent, say that 60 is the equivalent of "genius." At the moment of birth, Peter, then, is a musical genius; John, merely the possessor of a simple degree of talent. Similar diagrams could be drawn with respect to any human capacity, and thus the basis for a science of Individual Differences is revealed; the reason for differing human endowments at birth becomes clear.

Unfortunately, many persons who accept the karmic idea tend to think of karma only in terms of punishment and suffering. But it must be remembered that karma literally means *action*, which is a neutral word. Everything in the

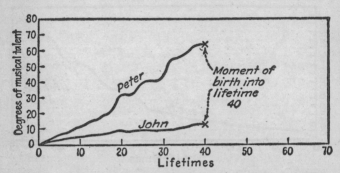

manifest universe has its polarity, or its positive and negative aspects; karma is no exception. Obviously, action can be evil or good, selfish or selfless. If conduct is good, there is nothing to prevent it from the continuing; this proceeds by natural growth, and can, as suggested, be called the Continuity Principle of karma. If, however, conduct is flagrantly evil or impure, it must be corrected; this proceeds by the law of action and reaction, and might be called the Retributive Principle of karma.

By the Retributive Principle we are brought back through the painful equilibrating force of karma to the narrow path of self-perfection. But by the Continuity Principle we make tranquil, uninterrupted progress along that selfsame path. Like the chambered nautilus, we build ourselves, as the lifetimes pass, more stately mansions for the soul. And at length we are free.

Chapter X

Human Types

WHEN Robert Benchley said: "There are two kinds of people in the world: those who divide the world into two kinds of people, and those who do not," he was formulating, with his wonderfully zany genius, a typology fully as valid as many another.

He was also putting his finger on a basic distinction between psychologists in recent years, with respect to their views on human personality. There are the psychologists who have divided the world into certain types of people, and there are those who have not. The former adhere to what is called the "type theory" of human personality; the latter, to the "trait theory." Both theories are attempts to analyze the differences between human beings.

In our daily experience with others, all of us come to recognize certain different types which we classify by value systems of our own devising. There is the sociable, easy-to-talk-to-type, the reserved, difficult-to-talk-to-type, the selfish type, the egocentric type, and so on. Many psychologists have concluded also that people array themselves into fundamental groupings; and it was natural that they should attempt to establish a scientific basis for the groupings or types which they felt existed. From this point of view many typologies have emerged, notably those of Jung, Spranger, Kretschmer, and Rosanoff, all of which have merited serious scientific recognition.

Like a wise Solomon, the reincarnation principle supports both the trait and the type theory of personality; it also points up the incompleteness of both. If we take into consideration one system of types in the light of the Cayce readings, we shall see how this is so.

The scientific typology perhaps best known to the general public is that originated by Carl Jung—namely, the introversion-extraversion typology. According to Jung's original formulation of the concept, the fundamental distinction between all human personalities lies in their concern with outer or inner realities. This can be seen in the original Latin of the terms which he chose for his purpose: *vert*, meaning "turned"; *intro*, "within"; and *extra*, "without." In the opinion of reincarnationists, however, Jung and the psychologists who have come after him have not provided satisfactory ultimate explanations of why one person should be allotted by life, so to speak, the fate of introversion and another the fate of extraversion. These two basic psychic situations are attributed by June and most other authorities to biological causes; the reincarnationist view is, here as elsewhere, that biological causes are only secondary, while past-life conduct is a primary determinant.

The manner in which the experience of past incarnations predisposes toward introversion is clearly seen in many cases in the Cayce files. An examination of such cases indicates that the Continuity Principle apparently operates here in the carrying over of certain attitudinal elements, or mental "sets" in the psyche.

A case in which this is clearly shown is that of a girl of twenty-one, a college student of some musical ability. In spite of personal attractiveness, she was abnormally shy and fearful, had great difficulty in making friends, and was concerned over not having been admitted to a college sorority. The early life circumstances of this girl are not known—very probably there were factors in her family conditioning which would account for her being an introvert or as Overstreet called it, a contractive type.

According to her life reading, however, this temperamental outlook was of past-life origin. She had been a French lady of much talent, beauty, and affability, but her husband, like the haughty Duke in Browning's "My Last Duchess," could not bear to see her graciousness extended to all and sundry. Consequently he suppressed her every natural impulse with cold and merciless tyranny, sometimes even beating her with a whip. This caused her to withdraw fearfully into herself; the dread of being misunderstood and chastised had persisted in her unconscious even to the present.

A similar sort of suppression pattern appears in the following case, though the personal and historical circumstances are widely different. The young man was twenty-eight at the time of his reading; he was of a studious and introverted nature. In his past life, according to Cayce, he suffered persecution in Salem in the course of the witchcraft trials. This experience had a twofold effect on his present temperament. First, it left him with a hatred of all forms of oppression. Second, it gave him a strong urge to study, and an equally pronounced urge to keep his knowledge to himself.

It should be noted here that the readings placed a slightly different interpretation on the Salem witchcraft trials than that ordinarily given by historians. That is to say, the readings indicate that there was then a genuine epidemic of spiritistic phenomena, and that a number of people were undergoing authentic experiences of a psychic or mediumistic nature, which of course offended the orthodox views of the time. In the case of this young man, the reading does not indicate precisely what his experience was, but—judging from other Salem period cases in the files—it may have been that in an impulse to tell some strange psychic experience of his own or one that he had witnessed, or through an impulse to defend someone whom popular frenzy had condemned, he was seized and brutally persecuted. Even a dog or cat who has been mistreated will learn to distrust mankind. And so it is not difficult to understand why, deep in the unconscious recesses of this man's mind, there was the instinct to be wary of men, to be hesitant of seeking their company or of telling all he knew.

The Cayce files record many cases dealing with experiences in Salem similar to the one above and which have resulted in a similar contractive tendency. Still other cases reveal different causes for psychic withdrawal. A doctor of marked uncommunicative nature had acquired the tendency in the practice of silence as a Quaker in a previous life. The temperament of a New York sales manager showed great lack of sociability; in a previous life he had been an explorer who had led a lonely and self-sufficient life in South Africa. A high-school girl felt a deep sense of inferiority; an experience as an American Indian girl who felt hopelessly inferior to the white settlers laid the basis for her diffidence. An Ohio doctor, though competent in his profession, was of an extremely retiring disposition and experienced self-doubt constantly. The origin for this tendency was seen in a Colonial experience in which he had made disinterested efforts in behalf of public welfare in early Georgia. His contribution was unjustly belittled and scorned; hence he became disillusioned and bit-

97

ter, and, doubting both himself and mankind, withdrew into himself.

Introversion, then, on the testimony of the foregoing and of many other cases in the Cayce files, proceeds in a natural continuity from one life to the next, stemming from an experience which has caused the ego to withdraw.

The continuity principle operates in a similar manner in the case of extraversion. An outstanding example is that of a woman—a divorcee in her late thirties—with a completely uninhibited personality who is currently preoccupied with her third matrimonial venture. The basis for her vivacious social competence was, according to the Cayce reading, laid in two past lives: one as a dance-hall entertainer in early frontier days; another as one of the mistresses of Louis XIV in the court of France. From the latter experience came her gifts of diplomacy and fascination, and the ability, as the reading puts it, "to wind everyone around her finger, from king to scullery maid." As a dance-hall entertainer she capitalized on these gifts and developed them still further, until a reversal of fortunes and a change of heart led her to become a kind of ministering angel in her community.

A second interesting example is the case of a New York entertainer and magician of great personal charm who makes friends easily and has a marked gift for the comic. These enviable extravertive tendencies are attributed to the reading to two past experiences. The first was as an early settler in the Mohawk Valley, where he tried to unify the various settlements in the locality. "Though the entity was short-lived, the abilities gained through the sojourn and the one just previous give him his powers to attract and control people in the present."

Much of the leadership quality and the charm of the man stem, then, from his idealistic struggles in early America; much of his quickness of wit and perception of the comic from the previous life as a kind of court jester in England to Henry VIII. Apparently he was active in politics, had a serious interest in promoting the welfare of the country, and developed his art to diplomatic advantage at court.

In short, all cases of extraversion in the Cayce files seem to be the result of socially outgoing activity of one kind or another in previous lives.

It is interesting to analyze how introvertive personalities become extravertive, and vice-versa, over the span of many lives. It must be remembered that by derivation the words introversion and extraversion mean a turning inward or a turning outward of attention; the words themselves imply a direction of psychological movement. It would seem, then, that psychological motion inward or outward, like any other type of motion, tends to continue on its path until forcibly stopped.

A soul may go along for many lives with the healthy placidity of an animal which can be said to be neither introverted nor extraverted. But then, in Life 19, let us suppose that something happens which makes this soul turn inward on itself. Perhaps a lame foot or a weak physique makes it impossible for him to live with the same healthy, relaxed extraversion of his fellows.

The inward tendency thus begun is at first a healthy (though perhaps uncomfortable) thing. Even though it first appears as a compensation mechanism, it is good in that it sharpens the man's power of analysis, his sense of values, his awareness of non-material realities. But the inertia of motion leads him to persist in his inward direction until with his increasing self-preoccupation he has built himself an ivory tower where the rest of the world seems no longer necessary or worthy of concern. A sense of aloofness and cold superiority isolates him more and more from his fellows; a negativistic attitude begins to render him inactive and unsocial.

These tendencies persist with increasing intensity through Lives 20 and 21, until finally the unhealthy ingoing and the karmic causes set in motion by the accompanying sins of omission or commission toward his fellows occasion a breakdown of one kind or another. This intolerable situation, this impasse, finally frightens the ego into a determination to change the direction of his attention. To invoke a homely (and incomplete) analogy, it is as if an ingrowing toenail were permitted to continue its growth with unconcern, until finally the pain became so great that the indolent host decided to go to a chiropodist and have it removed.

The bankruptcy of his situation in Life 22, then, leads to the desperate efforts of the ego to become more social and outgoing. In Life 23 the impulse will have gathered momentum by virtue of the earth life plus the planetary sojourn; the momentum continues in force through Lives 24 and 25, until finally in Life 26 a full-fledged extravert or expansive type comes into being.

But now there is another crucial period. Can he remain extraverted and happily adjusted to society without exploiting his social gifts for self-indulgence and self-aggrandizement? Just as the extreme of introversion holds subtle dangers to the self-exalting tendencies of the solitary ego, so the extreme of extraversion holds subtle dangers to the self-gratifying ten-

99

dencies of the socially competent ego. And so in Life 26 our subject becomes arrogant and sensual, and we discover in him selfish conduct born of his complacent social competence and self-assurance.

Once selfishness acts, however, karma comes into play. So in Life 27 or 28 we find him, a richly endowed personality, but constructed by early life circumstances into introvertive and very possibly neurotic tendencies such that he is forced to think in social terms once again, and act upon more spiritual bases, if he is to survive as a personality.

Again a struggle for balance ensues. And thus we discover that Hegel's classic *thesis, antithesis,* and *synthesis* may be more than a hypothetical pattern of movement in historical events; it may also represent the pattern of movement in the growth of the soul. It would seem, then, that the general areas of temperamental outlook called introversion and ex-traversion, or expansiveness and contractiveness, actually exist as conditions of the soul; they represent a true intuition on the part of Jung and Overstreet respectively, and are two fundamental and polar-opposite attitudes of the psyche. But they exist, not as pigeonholes in a desk, into which the names of all the people in the world can be consigned, but more in the nature of tourist-camp hostels, in which at one time or another, all travelers encamp.

Introversion and extraversion would seem to be polar op-posites as female and male are polar opposites. And just as the soul sometimes incarnates in a female and sometimes in a male body, but must learn the virtues of both polarities in be-coming androgynous, similarly the soul becomes (in succes-sive lifetimes or cycles of lifetimes) both a predominantly in-trovert and predominantly extravert personality, though his ultimate purpose is to acquire the strength of both and be-come ambivert. The process seems to continue through pen-dulum swings, until finally the soul becomes so exquisitely poised in an attitude of pure receptivity and pure expression, pure inward-looking and pure outward-going, that the terms introverted or extraverted could no more be applied to it than to an oak tree.

In the Cayce files there are many cases of successful and unsuccessful social adjustment which provide substantiating evidence for the principles just outlined. One such case con-cerns a woman of a pronounced talkative, aggressive, extra-vertive nature. Her early ambition had been to be an actress, but difficult family circumstances plus a rather short, squat figure made this an unattainable goal, and she entered the business world instead. According to her life reading she had

100

been an entertainer at the time of the American Revolution. She had achieved social position and luxury, but at the expense of personal principle. Her abilities to influence others and her conversational and dramatic gifts arose from that sojourn, but because she had used them then "without spiritual insight," as the reading puts it, she is faced with frustrations in the present.

This entity apparently finds itself now in that crucial period referred to above. Her bodily structure and her family circumstances have inhibited the expression of her dramatic gifts in a professionally spectacular way; her conversational ability appears relatively uninhibited, but she is explicitly warned by the reading not to use her gifts of expressiveness without spiritual insight, the implication being: lest something worse befall you.

Cases such as this show the inextricability of spiritual and vocational problems. Frequently a vocational frustration occurs, as in this case, not for any lack of ability, but because of the existence of some spiritual defect whose correction would be impossible if the vocational ambition were fulfilled. The reading advised this woman—she was thirty-two at the time—to become a reader of stories, or a companion to the young or to shut-ins, or, in any case, to use her gifts in a constructive and unselfish way.

Another case which presents a picture of corrective psychological circumstances in the present necessitated by misuse of extravertive gifts in the past concerns a woman forty-nine years old, a private secretary in Washington, D. C. Her letters reveal that she feels herself unwelcome in any social group that she enters—probably because as a child her older sisters and brothers excluded her from their company.

She writes: "I grew up with a fear complex, which has followed me all the way. When out with a crowd, I always feel that I am not wanted, and am at a loss to know what to do or say. I want to enter into things but don't know how . . . I always have the feeling that I must do more than is expected of anyone else for fear I won't be liked. So I sacrifice my comfort and health to do something for someone else. I want to be needed." She further relates that she had three disappointing love affairs, in two of which the man, though assuring her of his love, left her and married someone else.

The life reading indicates that she had previously been an early settler in Ohio; she had been gracious in her treatment of others, but only for her own selfish purposes. "Thus the entity disappointed many, though it was satisfied with what it had attained. The entity wielded power among those very individuals who are problems in the experience today. To use others as stepping stones is to bury yourself in karma that must be met within yourself."

The universe is honest. It gives back, measure for measure, what has been put into it. Like a true reflecting mirror, the circumstances of this woman's life revealed the circumstances she had once created in the lives of others. In reality, in her previous incarnation, she had not wanted other people's company—except insofar as it might benefit herself. In her present incarnation, her childhood position in the family was such that she felt her own company to be unwanted. She was thus led to an insecurity and an introversion which persisted throughout her adult life. She was sufficiently personable and had sufficient social gifts to attract several men, but though they led her to believe they loved her, in all of them she was disappointed.

By her own admission, her sense of being unwanted and her introversion led to the effort to help other people, so that she might be liked and needed. In this way the beneficent corrective purpose of karma is being accomplished. The social competence, misused in selfishness and insincerity in the past, led to social inhibition in the present, from which she can escape only through sincere unselfishness.

The experience of being disappointed in people appears to be a fairly common one and seems almost invariably to be an example of boomerang karma on the psychological level. No terser summary of this could be found in the readings than the following paragraph, spoken, as indicated by the italics, in emphatic tones:

> The entity has often been disappointed in others. *Know that first rule, a law that is eternal: The seed sown must one day be reaped. You disappointed others. Today, from your own disappointments, you must learn patience, the most beautiful of all the virtues, and the least understood.*

It is typical of the extravert to be heedless of the feelings of others; no better corrective could be found than that he should later find himself the victim of the insensitivity of others, at their mercy through his own now introverted social ineptitude.

These and many similar cases substantiate the concept that a tendency of soul proceeds unhindered, as though by the inertia of motion, until some inner corruption sets up a corrective check. The opposite direction is then induced, so that eventually the diametrically opposite state is reached. These alternations proceed with pendulum swings until equilibrium is reached. The passage between the extravert and the introvert states offers, then, an almost exact parallel to alternations of health and fortune.

We have here scrutinized the readings with respect to only one current system of types, the Jungian; but the same conclusion can be reached in all the typological systems yet formulated. Whether they be psychological typologies, like Spranger's classification of men on the basis of their "values," or bodily typologies like that of Kretschmer, they are all concerned with the outer manifestation of deep-lying qualities of mind and spirit—qualities which change from lifetime to lifetime through an evolutionary process. Whatever the final judgment of science on the validity of typologies, it would seem that the Cayce readings establish, for those who accept them, at least one fact: that current systems of typology place no eternal and final brand upon the soul. For the sake of convenience a personality may be said to belong to one type or another; but whatever type that may be, it is only a temporary fixation of consciousness, only a provisional stage in the growth of the eternal identity.

Chapter XI

Examples of Retributive Psychological Karma

WE HAVE already seen how pride—a sin of the moral realm —can have tangible consequences in the physical realm in the form of crippling disfigurements. The Cayce files also include many cases where sins of the moral realm result in serious psychological problems. Among these are two outstanding cases of maladjustment which had their karmic origin in the sin of intolerance.

The first case is that of a nun in a French convent at the time of Louis XIV. She had been stern, cold, and intolerant of human weaknesses. Her understanding of the Scriptures was purely literal, consequently she held in contempt those who violated the letter of the law.

The karmic result of her intolerance first manifested itself in her present incarnation in a glandular disturbance that persisted throughout adolescence. This disturbance—an excessive menstrual flow—made it impossible for the girl to attend school regularly, confined her to bed for almost two weeks out of every four, made her shy and seclusive, and by putting her out of touch with people of her own age affected all areas of her personality.

The disturbance finally passed. The girl developed a beautiful figure and became a professional model in New York, and eventually married. Her choice of a mate was an unfortunate one, however. They had little in common—he was cold and unaffectionate; she was starving for affection. World War II broke out and her husband went overseas. Now began a period of intense loneliness. The strain was too great to bear and the girl went to a resort town, where she took to drinking and loose living. She had discovered that only a glass or two

104

of liquor freed her from the social inhibitions which still oppressed her.

Once started, she was incapable of stopping; her drinking sprees became longer and longer. Sometimes she drank continually day and night, for three weeks, sleeping meanwhile with any soldier, sailor, aviator, or marine who happened to strike her fancy. While drunk she had not a single civilized inhibition as to clothing. She would unconcernedly carry out the garbage to the backyard wearing only an unfastened housecoat, or would—unless restrained—walk blithely into the boardinghouse parlor completely unclothed.

Finally her health began to break under the strain of alcoholic saturation. Her hands began to shake so that she was unable to sign her name to her husband's allotment checks. In a moment of sensible sobriety she decided to leave the resort, which was the rallying point for a half-dozen neighboring army camps and naval bases, and return to the city where she was born. Her latest letters show that she holds a responsible secretarial position, but there are several indications from other sources that she still drinks to some extent. She has divorced her husband.

It seems apparent that her degradations arose primarily from her personality difficulty, and that this in turn arose from a glandular disturbance. (The glands, Cayce often pointed out, are focal points for the expression of karma.) This malfunction was the direct karmic consequence of her own condemnation of others, her own uncharity of spirit; the weaknesses she so unfeelingly condemned in others have become her own weaknesses. She was in this way made to understand the inner necessity of error, the hunger which impels the erring to their sin, the weakness and loneliness which compel them to find solace in the gratification of the senses. Like those who mock, those who condemn must meet within themselves the circumstances of their condemnation.

A second case is that of a woman whose two previous lives present an interesting picture of pride and prejudice. In the first of these two lives we find her in Palestine at the time of Christ, where she was the wife of a Jewish priest; because of her social position she was scornful and intolerant of the activities of the unconventional young man who was causing such a stir in religious circles.

Time apparently did not wither nor custom stale the pleasure she took in superiority. She returned for another incarnation in Salem, Massachusetts, with an undiminished readiness to exclude and condemn—in fact, she seemed to have grown even more unrelenting. This time, to quote the reading, "the entity was among those who were very hard, very questioning, very condemning of those who had convincing evidence of the survival of personality. . . . The entity then caused many hardships. When some were ducked, the entity was present and gave consent. When some were beaten with many stripes, the entity gave evidence and approval. Hence in the present the entity finds itself bound with those periods when consciousness is hampered. There have been in the lacteal ducts and in the first and second cervicals lesions formed by pressures in the inco-ordination between the sympathetic and cerebro-spinal systems. This brings on the periods of physical reaction."

The "physical reaction" to which the reading refers here is a nervous breakdown which the woman experienced in the present lifetime at the age of thirty-nine, followed by fourteen years of periodic mental depression. She was unmarried; her fashionable New York address plus the fact that she had no occupation would seem to show that she was a woman of independent means. Undoubtedly there were typical medical or psychiatric syndromes here; surely idleness may have been an important factor in her depression. But, as has been pointed out before, such factors are only apparently and immediately causative, not ultimately so. At the core of this woman's nature was an intolerance of human beings, a cold indifference alike to their enthusiasms and their sufferings. The harsh intolerance she expressed caused hopelessness in many people in previous lives; it is only just that she should herself experience hopelessness now.

The question might be raised as to why this woman did not experience the karmic consequences of her Palestine intolerance in the Salem experience. There are two possible answers to this question. First, her Salem incarnation may have had a purpose other than that of correcting her intolerance—hence the tendency begun in Palestine had free rein while the entity was preoccupied with another major life task. Second, the intolerant attitude of her Palestine period may not have been sufficiently overt to have expressed itself in an act of intolerance that seriously injured another human being; it was intolerance in its beginning stages, hence it did not have sufficient force to generate a karmic consequence of major proportions. Moreover, each moment of life is, as it were, a test. In Salem she was placed in a position where she could be tolerant or intolerant. She failed the test, thus fortifying rather than erasing the intolerance of Palestine, and thus actively generating the karmic consequence of the present.

In the same family of traits with intolerance is the tendency to be critical. The following case is an interesting example of the karmic results of being over-critical. It concerns a young man, a twenty-seven-year-old first lieutenant in the army, who suffers acutely from the sense of personal inadequacy. We have no way of discovering the ostensible cause of his personality difficulties in his early youth. It is possible that he had a critical and unreasonable parent; it is also possible that his physical appearance in some way made him the target of the ridicule of his schoolmates. We infer these possibilities because of the nature of his karmic sin. "As one sows," says the reading, "so must he reap. *As you have criticized, know that you yourself must be criticized.*"

The disclosure is then made in the reading that the young man had been in the past life a literary critic, whose custom it was to write pitilessly and caustically of whatever did not please him. Having engendered much self-doubt in others in the past, it is to be expected that he should himself suffer self-doubt in the present. And here we see one more facet of the infinitely various law of karma—a facet of so much importance that its moral implications deserve to be pondered.

Criticism as a profession, of course, claims a very small minority of people, but on the planet earth at present there are approximately two and a half billion critics of nonprofessional standing. Probably no other one profession claims so many amateur practitioners who pursue their avocation with such unfailing interest from the time they first learn to talk to the time death seals their lips. It is not an expensive pursuit in terms of coin of the realm. It is more universally available than eating. Unlike other forms of human amusement, it can be engaged in outdoors, indoors, and the year round without any equipment other than a pair of tongues. Let two or three be gathered together, and there will be criticism.

However, although it costs nothing in terms of money, criticism may be a very expensive amusement in terms of the psychological price that must someday be paid. The source of information, as Edgar Cayce called his power, from its vantage point of seeing cause and consequence over long spans of time, frequently gave sharp and explicit warning to people who erred conspicuously in this direction. The following is a pointed example, among hundreds of similar cases:

We find that the entity has the inclination to become, when aggravated, rather severe in its criticisms of others. *This should be tempered; for what one says of another*

107

will usually become one's own state also, in one form or other.

Here we have an explicit statement of moral cause and situational consequence which suddenly recalls certain rather cryptic declarations of the Christian Bible. Jesus said:

> But I say unto you, that every idle word that men shall speak, they shall give account thereof in the day of judgment. For by thy words thou shalt be justified, and by thy words thou shalt be condemned.

It does not seem illogical to identify the "day of judgment" referred to with the time when the karmic debt falls due. Again:

> Not that which goeth into the mouth defileth a man; but that which cometh out of the mouth, this defileth a man.

And again:

> Judge not, that ye be not judged. For with what judgment ye judge, ye shall be judged.

These quotations take on, suddenly, in the light of the karmic consequences we have seen, a virile, exact, sensible meaning the practical force of which cannot be mistaken.

It must be noted in these cases there, here as elsewhere, *motive* and *purpose* are the impelling force of the karmic action. It was not the profession of literary critic in itself which had damned the young lieutenant in his previous life, but rather the attitude he had held and the self-doubt he had engendered in others through the unwise practice of his profession. A similar situation was seen in the case of the Roman soldier (Chapter V) who jeered at the Christians. His karma proceeded not from the performance of his duty as a Roman guard, but from his jeering at those who were helpless in his power. As always, it is not the letter but the spirit that matters; not the form but the substance; not the act but the motive.

In the section on traits it has been shown how the authoritative tendency can begin in past experiences of command. Leadership is an admirable quality, but it often degenerates into tyranny; more than once in the history of man has the

108

power of office led to insolence and unscrupulous self-gratification. Several flagrant instances of authority misused and its karmic consequences come to light in the Cayce files.

There is, for example, the case of an entity who in the days of the Salem witchcraft trials was a gentleman in authority; he was largely responsible for the persecution of women suspected of being witches. It seems, however, that this righteous Puritan who was bent on purging this outbreak of deviltry for the protection of public morals and the safeguard of the Christian faith saw in his official situation other possibilities of a more personal nature: he took advantage of those imprisoned for gratification of his own sexual appetites.

The files show this Puritan scoundrel in his new incarnation as a boy of eleven, the son of a woman in straitened circumstances because of being abandoned by her husband, and the victim of a violent case of epilepsy. At the time of his reading he had lost the use of his left side and also his faculty of speech. He was unable to dress or undress himself or attend to his own bodily functions. His shoulders were bent, and after an attack of several days' duration in which he experienced convulsions every twenty to thirty minutes, he was unable to hold his head up or to sit up alone.

According to Cayce, epilepsy is frequently the karmic result of sexual excesses.* However, the misuse of authority is in this case an important element in the situation. The poverty and low social status of the mother seem an appropriate reversal of his former financial security; the epilepsy proper, the karmic consequence of the sexual excess which was one of the forms of his abuse of office.

The following case is an example of authority misused which stems back to the period of Christian persecution in Rome. Romus was a soldier; his rank was sufficiently high to place him in a position where he could earn a tidy sum over and beyond his salary as a Roman soldier. The reading does not state whether his method was one of extortion, blackmail, or an early version of protection money; but some such un-

---

* Epilepsy is also traced karmically to the misuse of psychic powers. In both cases, the exact principle of karmic action involved is obscure. Perhaps the appropriateness of the affliction inheres in the occult constitution of the human body, and will be better comprehended when we understand the seven *chakras* or wheels of Hindu psychology. The readings called the chakras the "life centers" and attributed to them great significance. They would seem to be the points of contact between the physical body and the soul and are whirling vortices of energy.

scrupulous conduct enabled him to make handsome gains in a material way and "lose and lose and lose" in a spiritual way. "And from this," says the reading, "came Saturn's influence."

This last detail is notable because it indicates that the man's corrective experience began in the inter-between planetary sojourn, near Saturn—apparently a limiting, purgatorial sort of realm. It indicates also Cayce's whole version of the interrelationship between incarnations on earth and "astrology," he himself using the latter term with extreme caution and insisting again and again that our understanding of planetary influences is as yet very imperfect.

Romus' present-life circumstances are certainly restrictive enough to suggest to anyone of astrological persuasion a pronounced Saturnine influence. Poverty, dispossession, homelessness, and hunger have dogged his steps throughout his adult life. A tailor by trade, he has been unable to earn enough money to provide adequately for his wife and five children. Only through the generosity of American relatives have he and his family been able to eke out a precarious existence in the slums of London.

Here again the abuse of authority seems to have been appropriately corrected in the realm where the abuse was committed. The man's economic hopelessness exactly duplicated the privations he once visited on others.

One other case of misused authority worthy of note is that of a woman who was, at the time of the French Revolution, one of the bourgeoisie who roused her compatriots to rebellion against the aristocrats. In this respect, and in her sincere idealism and dedication to a cause, she made great spiritual progress. But when the tables were turned, and she was placed in a position of power after the revolution was over, she herself became dictatorial and misused authority almost as badly as those whom she had struggled to dethrone. "Hence," says the reading, "we find throughout the present experience it has been necessary for the entity to take orders from others, as well as to subjugate much of that which seeks expression."

In the present this woman finds herself in very difficult circumstances. She was forty years old at the time of her reading—a widow for ten years, and the mother of a little girl. She had been struggling against great odds to support herself and her child. For some time she worked on a government W.P.A. project, but at best her situation was precarious, and her loneliness and lack of opportunities for recreation gave her a desperate sense of frustration. The situational prison in which she found herself was no mere result of chance; it was the accurate reflection of the constriction which she had formerly placed upon others through misuse of authority. On the surface of it, she was victimized by a ruthless economic system or an unfair allotment of destiny; in terms of karmic reality, she was victimized only by herself.

Such cases provide an important inferential clue in whatever analysis might be made of the difficulties of other human beings, or whatever attempt might be made to reason backward from visible effect to possible cause. When Aeschylus wrote, two thousand years ago in Greece, that "character is fate," he formulated a proposition the converse of which is also true. For it would seem from the cases considered above that the fate of today reveals the character of yesterday.

An important issue then arises—one that is bound to occur to the thoughtful student of reincarnation. If poverty and low station are the necessary educative karmic consequences of certain kinds of misuse of authority, why, then, should any effort be made to improve the social order? Would it not frustrate karmic intention if the tailor, for example, were well taken care of in a less ruthless economic system than our own?

The issue will be more fully discussed in a later chapter, but for the moment it should be stated emphatically that acceptance of the reincarnation theory is not equivalent to a laissez-faire attitude with regard to human society. Entities who need to learn the lesson of terrible privation are born into a period and place of history when social injustice permits of the destitution that they need to experience. At the same time, however, those who do not work actively for the betterment of the lot of others are committing a sin of omission; those who live in the conscious exploitation of others are committing a sin of commission; and both sins toward one's brother will someday need to be expiated.

Rightly understood, the reincarnation theory offers no haven to tyrants or those who would defraud their fellow man. The reincarnation teaching is psychological in its primary emphasis, because it is concerned with the individual soul and the laws and conditions through which the soul achieves perfection; but by extension it is also social, for love is the ultimate purpose and only solvent of the law of karma by which personal evolution is regulated.

By the reincarnationist view, it is held certain that cosmic law is never brooked by human arrangements. The Retributive Principle, like water, always finds its own proper level. No matter what the social structure of the time, it seems certain that within its framework exists, for those souls who have chosen it as their milieu, the proper means for the correction of their inner defect.

Chapter XII

Past-Life Origins of Mental Abnormalities

_____

THE name of Freud and the term "unconscious mind" are well known today. Many persons, however, are unaware of the fact that Freud's discovery of the unconscious mind was due to his investigations in hypnosis. It was because hypnotized subjects could recall incidents from their childhood that were completely forgotten in their conscious state that Freud was forced to postulate an unconscious mind to account for the preservation of the otherwise irretrievable material. Freud later abandoned hypnosis as a clinical technique because it proved unsatisfactory in many cases, and proceeded to develop other methods of exploring the unconscious depths. But hypnosis must nonetheless be regarded as the parent of psychoanalysis.

In the realm of reincarnationist psychology, hypnosis may have a similar role to play. The Cayce clairvoyance would seem to indicate that it is possible for a hypnotized subject to discover the past-life history of other individuals. But perhaps even more important than this, it would seem that it may be possible for an individual using hypnosis, or some similar technique such as the dianetic reverie, to relive his *own* past lives. Age-regression experiments in hypnosis have established the fact that there is stored in certain strata of the mind a detailed and sequential memory of every event lived through since birth. A hypnotized subject, for example, "regressed" to the age of ten and told to write his name will write it as he did at the age of ten; regressed further to the age of six will write in a still more childish scrawl; regressed to the age of three will be unable to do more than make meaningless lines with his pencil. These age-regression experiments are commonly conducted in university classes and are familiar to students in the field.

Less well known, however, is the work of the French scientist De Rochas, who in the latter half of the nineteenth century claimed that he was able, through the same age-regression techniques, to evoke memories of past-life experiences. His book *Les Vies Successives* (Successive Lives) has not been accorded scientific recognition; but perhaps he will one day be hailed as a pioneer in the realm of reincarnationist psychology. More recently, A. R. Martin of Sharon, Pennsylvania, has made similar studies and has published a remarkable book called *Researches in Reincarnation and Beyond.* Past-life memories experimentally induced in this manner would seem to be contradictory to the intention of nature at this point, or else all of us would recall our past spontaneously. Efforts such as these, however, made in the interests of science, are interesting and valuable; they may, before long, provide the final experimental laboratory evidence for the reality of reincarnation.

In turning to the instances of mental abnormality that were scrutinized by the Cayce hypnotic clairvoyance, one finds that they tend to illuminate the nature of memory and the unconscious mind and that they tend to confirm the belief that the unconscious mind is far deeper than is thought even by present-day psychoanalysts. These cases are not always evidential —that is to say, they do not always provide us with direct or indirect proof that what Cayce said about the past was true. But some of the cases are evidential at least to a degree; and those that are not can only be regarded as further fragments of the whole intricate mosaic which—once its total reasonableness is seen—automatically provides the details with credibility.

One of the most curious of the abnormalities of mental life is the phenomenon known as phobia. A phobia is generally understood by analysts to be an exaggerated fear which had its origin in a complicated series of situations or relationships conducive to antagonism, suppressed aggression, or guilt feelings of an intense nature. These submerged feelings later express themselves as an intense and seemingly irrational fear of closed places, high places, cats, thunderstorms, or some other of an almost endless variety of possible phobia objects, the object chosen having some direct or indirect relation to one of the basic precipitating experiences. The Cayce readings, however, seem to show that *in some cases at least* these strong and seemingly unreasonable fears can have a very reasonable origin in some directly related experience of a past life.

One interesting example is the case of a woman who even as a young girl was afraid of closed places. In theaters, she insisted on sitting near an exit. If the bus on which she was riding became too crowded, she would get off and wait for another. On excursions to the country, she was fearful of entering caves, grottoes, or any small, enclosed place. Neither she nor the members of her family could understand this peculiar attitude, since no one could remember any unusual childhood experience that might have induced such a fear. According to the Cayce reading, the explanation was that in her past life she had been smothered when the roof of a cave collapsed upon her. The memory of this horrible death still persisted in the unconscious mind.

Another case is that of a woman who has two phobias: one of cutting instruments and the other of all furred animals, especially domestic pets. She is gripped by nervous fear whenever she sees cutting instruments close to her, or sees anyone else using them. The life reading accounted for this phobia in stating that she met death in a Persian incarnation by being run through with a sword.

Her aversion to animals is difficult to understand on the basis of her present life, since she came from a large family, all of whom had pets. Her brother in particular was very fond of animals. Yet the very sight of a cat or dog in the house repels this woman as much as the sight of a snake repels another. Furthermore, she had never been able to wear a fur coat or even a coat trimmed with a fur collar. Psychiatrists might explore her phobia in terms of her relationships to the members of her family—possibly jealousy of the brother who was especially fond of animals, for example—and explain it as an expression of antagonism. The readings, however, traced her curious aversion to an Atlantean incarnation in which she had some sort of experience in relation to repulsive creatures.

Many other phobias were similarly explained by the reading on a past-life basis. A morbid fear of darkness was attributed to a dungeon experience in France, when the entity was a political prisoner at the time of Louis XVI. A fear of sharp knives was traced to an experience in a torture chamber in France, where the entity suffered the rack and other instruments of torture. A fear of impending wholesale destruction was explained by the fact that the entity had had a Peruvian experience at the time of one of the submergences of Atlantis: he had been left alone on a high mound to which he had retired for study, and had seen the water mounting everywhere around him. An overpowering fear of wild animals was attributed to an experience in Rome, when the entity's husband had been made to fight wild beasts in the arena. Two persons who had a morbid fear of water were told that they had been drowned in the last life; a third person who feared water was told that he had been shipwrecked in a storm, during the time of the expansion of the Roman Empire.

Examining these cases critically, from the point of view of ordinary psychology, we might wonder if in all instances there had not been a present-life situation which could adequately explain the phobia. Granted, it is conceivable that some repressed emotional disturbance might be found, but this would still not negate the possibility of anterior memory which was the true basis for the phobia. For example, the woman who had a morbid fear of closed places may have been locked in a dark closet at the age of four, and the incident forgotten. Under free association or hypnosis the incident might be unearthed, and the psychiatrist might work from that information into an understanding of emotional problems which could have caused the nervous disorder.

An important fact is often overlooked in these cases. Although it must be acknowledged that in the emotional realm algebraic equivalents are not to be expected, countless people have emotional experiences similar to those that produce phobias in others and yet do not themselves suffer from phobias. Why, then, is this particular person susceptible? If everyone who had experienced the kinds of emotional upsets to which claustrophobia is frequently attributed got claustrophobia, we would have a population of claustrophobes so great that telephone booths, dormitory rooms, one-room apartments, and some of the smarter nightclubs would need to be abolished as menaces to public health and sanity.

The answer to the problem as indicated by the Cayce data is this: that the greater nervous susceptibility of one child over another to an emotional situation *may* be due to a past-life experience. The present-life situation merely acts as the reawakening agent of the tragic buried impression.

By the reincarnationist view, then, we see that the unconscious mind, like a box with a false bottom, is far deeper than is ordinarily supposed. Certain analysts—notably Carl Jung—have already sensed the necessity for the existence of deeper levels in order to explain otherwise unexplainable facts of mental life and have spoken of the "collective unconscious," "race unconscious," or "racial memory," on the assumption that there exists a sort of reservoir of memory of racial experience which all individuals tap. Although it cannot be said with certainty that such a mass memory does not exist, it seems more difficult to accept than the theory that memory is individual and extends back in the unconscious through previous lifetimes. At least the individual memory theory cannot be said to be less plausible than a concept that holds that memories are stacked like corn in a granary and then withdrawn and used by the rest of the community. If such a phenomenon of pooled experience occurs, it would seem to be no longer a memory, in the strict sense of the term, but rather a cognition, or knowing process.

According to the point of view of the Cayce readings, an individual *does* have unconscious memories surging up from the ancient past, but they arise—not from some hypothetical pool of race memories, or from some long-dead ancestor, but rather from his own previous experience. All his unconscious fears and hates and loves and impulses are his own inheritance, bequeathed by himself to himself, as a man bequeathes his own today unto his own tomorrow. He himself once was a savage many times, hence it is natural for him to have certain unredeemed savage impulses. He himself once was threatened by the terrors of the jungle and the abominations of man's cruelties, hence it is natural for him still to feel unreasoning fears and unfounded apprehensions. He himself once had good reason to hate and love many of the people whom he is now associated with; it is only natural for him now to feel seemingly irrational loves and hates toward these same people in the present.

The abnormal emergence of subterranean elements can apparently occur in other ways besides phobias. In several instances recurrent dreams were explained by Cayce on the basis of past-life experiences. One of the most interesting examples is that of the woman who asked the question: "Why in early childhood did I dream so many times that the world was being destroyed, always seeing a black destructive cloud?" The answer indicated that this dream arose from her Altantean experience when she had been a priestess and physician. She had experienced one of the terrible cataclysmic destructions of Atlantis, and the impression remained so deeply engraved in her soul memory as to arise again repeatedly during sleep.

Another interesting case is that of a child of four who alarmed her mother because almost daily she awoke from sleep in tears and obvious distress. The child was in good physical health, and the mother wrote to Cayce for an explanation of the nervous condition. According to the reading, the child had met a violent death in France during World War II. Eager, though, to take incarnation again, she had returned to American parents only nine months later. In so short an intermission between lives the fearful memories of bombardments and fires had not been erased; and they surged upward in the child at the sleep level of consciousness.

Cases such as those just observed point unavoidably to an examination of the whole problem of memory. The first objection raised by most people against reincarnation is the fact that we do not remember our past lives. This is, indeed, a curious circumstance, and yet not so curious after all when one considers that we remember nothing of our infancy and little of our childhood. Conscious memory is so tenuous a thing, events slip by us with a fluidity so streamlike, that to say "I do not remember" is not equivalent to proof that something did not occur. If we were to ask any of our friends, "What, exactly, were you doing at 10:26 in the morning of April 5th, 1939?" we could stake our bank balance on the fact that he could not honestly, and precisely, answer the question; yet this lack of recollection of that point of time in his life by no means proves that he did not live through it.

This objection to reincarnation, therefore, is easily met—first on the score that forgetting and repression of memories is a very natural and common human phenomenon and second, on the score that the nature of memory is such that details escape us but principles remain. For example, any educated adult will be able to tell you that 7 times 7 equals 49 and 12 times 12 equals 144. He will not recall all the unhappy hours that he spent in third and fourth grade learning how to perform these operations, but the ability to perform them, and the knowledge of the facts, remain as the useful residuum in his mind of many repeated efforts of attention.

Similarly with man's caution as to fire, his wariness as to dogs, his ability to dance, or his skill in performing anything. The ability to walk argues clearly a period of time when effort was expended in learning how to walk—though not one out of a hundred thousand people would actually remember the specific and exhaustive efforts made in order to acquire that skill.

Forgetfulness of detail, then, does not invalidate memory of principle; and the answer of reincarnationists to those who raise the lack of memory objection is that man's conscience (or level of ethical insight) and his degree of intelligence and capacity represent the carry-over of sum totals from past-life experience, the details of which have escaped him.

The second and more subtle objection raised by the opponents of the reincarnation theory is that it is not ethical to hold a personality responsible for deeds done by another personality. Consciousness of wrong, they say, surely should be present if an offender's punishment is to have any real meaning. The reincarnationists' answer to this objection is based on what they believe to be the relationship of the personality to the eternal identity.

The eternal identity—like an actor offstage—can remember all its past, but as soon as it takes on a personality, as an actor takes on a role, then it is prevented by a protective provision of nature from remembering anything but the sum totals or the principles which he had learned before. In a sense, it compares with a Shakespearean actor who in his home can recall scenes from any of the dramas in which he has played; while he is acting Hamlet, however, the role of Shylock is completely excluded from his mind.

Similarly the over-soul or eternal identity contains the remembrance of all things that have happened to it in all its personality roles; but these memories are unavailable normally to the little personality (even in immediate afterdeath stages) unless somehow, through some departure from the normal, it taps the memory stream of the identity. Whether this is done through the "unconscious" or the "superconscious" is not of primary importance, though future investigation should be able to define more clearly the realms of mind which these two terms represent. The point is that such a reservoir of memory exists—no matter what it is called or where it is located—and that it can be tapped in a variety of deliberate or accidental ways. This, at least, is the view of reincarnationists.

The objection that it is not ethically sound for an individual to suffer from something he did in his past which he no longer remembers seems, in the last analysis, no more tenable than the complaint that it is unethical for an adult to suffer for unconscious conflicts established in infancy. Dynamic processes follow laws of their own. We must learn to conform our notion of ethics to nature as it is (and nature is supremely ethical) rather than expect to fit nature to the Procrustean bed of our own preconceived ideas.

The blinders of forgetfulness which conceal the past from us and cause us to see only the small segment which constitutes the present are protective and necessary blinders. At first glance this may seem an odd and improper provision; but perhaps it compares to the system of locks which make it possible for ships to travel from the Atlantic to the Pacific Ocean through the Panama Canal. The locks may seem, to the untutored mind, an awkward, cumbersome, and thoroughly unnatural device. But the engineers who contrived the system had a difficult engineering problem to solve, namely the conveyance of ships from one level to another, over extensive terrain of differing levels of altitude. The means they used exactly and excellently serve that end.

Similarly in the realm of consciousness. Consciousness, like the water of the Panama Canal, flows in a continuous stream; yet in order to facilitate passage of the vessel of individuality, it is expedient that locks be dropped and water level be altered so as to separate one segment of the passage from another segment. This is the reincarnationist's answer to those who object to reincarnation on the memory issue.

In addition to the instances of phobias and recurrent dreams, there are in the Cayce files a number of other interesting mental aberrations. Hallucinations, for example, are in several cases attributed to the abnormal recall of past incarnations. In one instance the reading stated that there had been the inadvertent opening of one of the inner centers or *chakras* of the body, thereby causing the flow of the *Kundalini* force and giving rise to hallucinatory impressions. (Cayce was here using terms of Hindu psychology—the *chakras* being the seven "wheels" or vortices of energy through which the more non-physical part of man is, presumably, expressed through the physical body; *Kundalini* referring to a force presumably situated at the base of the spine which is intimately associated with the sex force and the creative power generally.)

Serious mental illness was in many cases attributed by the readings to a purely physical cause, and some remarkable cures were accomplished through purely physical means. One case of this type has already been referred to in Chapter 2: the case of the girl who returned to sanity on the removal of an impacted tooth. Another striking case is that of a postal employee who became disagreeable, mororse, and increasingly violent. His family persuaded him to go to a hospital for a checkup. Medical examiners pronounced his condition to be manic-depressive psychosis and he was committed to a mental institution. A Cayce reading was requested by the man's wife. The reading indicated that a fall on the ice many years ago had resulted in a spinal derangement in the coccyx area which had in turn reacted on the whole nervous system. Specific osteopathic adjustments were recommended in connection with some electrical treatments. The family succeeded in having these treatments administered and in six weeks the man was pronounced normal and released from the hospital. No karmic cause was indicated; if the fall on the ice had a karmic source, no mention of it was made. In any event, a purely physical treatment resulted in a cure.

In several cases, however, mental disease was ascribed by the reading to possession by discarnate entities. Since ancient times it has been believed that some forms of mental derangement are due to possession by evil spirits. Students of the Christian Bible will recall that Christ is said to have caused evil spirits to depart from a demented man; and Catholics will point to the fact that the rites of exorcising spirits are still practiced by Catholic priests.

This whole idea is, of course, completely alien to the views of modern psychiatrists, who naturally regard the idea as an outworn superstition. Once it is admitted, however, that identity can persist beyond death, there is no logical reason why such identities, of an evil nature, could not maliciously attempt to possess themselves of, or otherwise influence, the body and personality of a living person.

In the few cases of obsession which appeared in the Cayce files, the recommended cure usually included electrical treatments of some type ("outside influences cannot stand the high vibration") and prayer and meditation. In one case the subject followed the recommendation closely and freed herself in several months' time of the whispering voices which had disturbed her. In another case, the subject did not follow the reading's prescription except with respect to one detail, that of diet; no improvement took place. Apparently there was a karmic cause operative in the first case at least: the entity had in a past life used occult means to control others.

All of these cases point, perhaps, to new horizons of understanding in the tragic field of mental abnormality. In general, of course, the greatest significance that the Cayce data holds for psychiatry and psychoanalysis lies in its expansion of the boundaries of the unconscious mind. In the few examples of mental abnormalities cited here there is apparent only the negative aspects of its content. However, it must always be remembered that the unconscious is more than a mere dark cellar of fears and horrors. It is a memory reservoir, to be sure, but a reservoir of both the good and the bad. The Cayce readings, in fact, call it the "memory of the soul-mind" in contradistinction to that of the body-mind. Though within this memory there are undoubtedly deterrent factors, there are also factors of beneficent usefulness. Through the unconscious, for example, one can communicate with all

121

other unconscious minds, and thus acquire knowledge unavailable through sense impressions.

If the reincarnation principle ever gains scientific acceptance, one of the primary concerns of psychologists should be the clarification and expansion of the whole idea of the unconscious, and a formulation of the proper techniques whereby the conscious mind may not only redeem its negative but also avail itself of its positive aspects

Chapter XIII

Marriage and the Destiny of Woman

ONE of the most intimate and difficult of human relationships is that of marriage. Infinitely rewarding at its best, unspeakably oppressive at its worst, marriage offers the uttermost extremes of human happiness and human bondage—with all the lesser degrees of felicity and restraint in between.

From the point of view of law, marriage is a contract, a civil institution. From the point of view of psychiatry, it is a theater of sexual and emotional urges. The church regards it as a sacrament. Psychology sees it as a problem in behavior and adjustment. The cynic sees it as a trap for fools.

According to the enlarged and more comprehensive point of view provided by the reincarnation principle, each of these definitions is accurate, but partial. The psychologist, Link, defines marriage as a "step by which two imperfect individuals unite their forces in the struggle for happiness." If by the struggle for happiness is also understood the struggle for self-perfection (without which no true happiness can exist) the definition will come fairly close to the point of view of the ancient wisdom. A formulation of marriage from this expanded point of view might be that marriage is the opportunity for two imperfect individuals to help each other discharge their respective karmic debts, forge new qualities of soul, and advance in spiritual understanding and strength.

The Cayce readings frequently affirm that no major human relationship is the result of chance. Marriage would seem to be an exemplification of this fact in its highest degree. No marriage is a start on a clean slate. It is an episode in a serial story begun long before. In one way or another, the readings indicate, the parties have been related to each other in other

123

lives. The readings having to do with present marriage relationships as sequels to the past have a singular dramatic interest.

Marriage is seen by the Cayce readings as the natural human state:

Yes, it is well for the entity to be married; this is the natural life for an entity in the earth.

Q. Would marriage at this time be advisable?
A. It's advisable at any time if you find the right person! This depends upon the bond of purpose.

A home is seen to be a reflection of the ultimate harmonious state toward which we all are striving:

Do make the home your career, for this is the greatest career any soul can make in the earth. To a few it is given to have both a career and a home, but the greatest of all careers is the home, and those who shun it shall have much yet to answer for. For this is the nearest emblem of what each soul hopes eventually to obtain, a heavenly home. Then make your home as a shadow of a heavenly home.

For the home where there is unity of purpose in the companionship is the nearest pattern in the earth of man's relationship with his Maker. For it is ever creative in purpose, with personalities coordinated for a cause, an ideal.

These, of course, are not new ideas. The point of view of the readings is, however, both liberal and modern with respect to practical details and with respect to the position and destiny of woman.

It is interesting to note that woman's equality with man and her complete right to self-determination are taken for granted. It is nowhere stated in those exact terms in the readings; but it is implicit throughout. This underlying point of view appears perhaps most clearly in readings where questions of a choice between marriage and a career are involved. It becomes very clear that the fascist and totalitarian concept that woman's destiny is the home and children and nothing else finds no acceptance in the Cayce clairvoyance.

As in the phsycial readings, where no single school of treatment is applied, no single course of action is universally applicable with regard to marriage. The underlying psychological and spiritual principles are always the same; but their translation into action may be different in every case. Some women are told to marry; some are told—emphatically—to have a career. Some are told to have a career first and then marry. Others are told to combine the two at the same time; others still, to choose between the two—they cannot serve two masters.

A young girl of eighteen—shy, timid, unhappy—wondered what to do with her future. Her life reading was insistent that before she think of marriage she become active in some work having to do with the helping of children. "If the entity seeks to better itself in wedlock, it will be sorely disappointed unless first it contributes something to the social and material welfare of children." The reading went on to specify that work with teen-age girls, as in camp counseling or the like, would be one possible outlet.

A practiced psychologist will admit the soundness of this advice from the purely psychological point of view. Teaching, working with people younger and more inexperienced than oneself, is an excellent way of extraverting a personality. The necessity of leading others induces a self-assurance that might forever be lacking otherwise. Marriage can well be a disaster if an inappropriate mate is chosen out of the desperation of an introvert's loneliness. Even if the mate chosen is an appropriate one, failure is always possible if one of the partners is not sufficiently well-integrated to face the adjustment problems and strains of marriage. In this case, then, education in social work and a career *before* marriage was seen to be the proper course.

In another case, a gifted girl was told to combine a career with marriage—but warned that she should not marry at all unless she found exactly the right mate. A variety of past-life specializations had made her very versatile; she was an accomplished sculptress, weaver, and worker in pottery. In addition she was gifted as a teacher, singer, and eurythmicist. With such a heritage she was fitted in this life to become a leader and teacher in the spiritual sense, and the reading, after pointing this out, went on to say: "We find that there should be a combination of the home and a career—but dependent on the type of husband chosen by the entity. For unless there is one who is in *complete* accord, and who would contribute to the helpfulness of the entity herself, we find that there will be dissensions and disappointments to one so highly evolved, such as to leave harmful scars on the inner self."

125

In interesting contrast to this instance is the case of a gifted and beautiful young actress who, when she fell in love, wondered if it would be possible to combine marriage with her career. Her reading gave her a very pointed negative answer. "The entity has the qualifications to make a success of either of these careers—marriage or the stage. It is not possible for her to make a success of both. She must decide the matter for herself."

It becomes clear, after close study of these readings, that recommendations were always made on the basis of what would lead to spiritual growth. If a woman were seeking a career for selfish reasons—fame, money, clothes, dominance, position, self-glorification—the source of information was aware of that motive and directed her toward homemaking instead.

This advice was given not out of sentimental or traditional notions concerning the sanctity of the home or woman's place in it. It was based instead on the view that motive and purpose are the criteria for the judgment of any course of action, that a selfish course of action is always inferior to a selfless one, and that the responsibilities of a home and marriage are by their very nature more conducive to selflessness than the self-seeking rewards of some careers.

Hence homemaking and childrearing are recommended to many women—even though gifted in other ways—because such may be the best possible discipline for the attainment of the particular spiritual qualities they need, the best possible check on the conscious or unconscious selfishness with which they would pursue a career. On the other hand, other women who are gifted may be genuinely desirous of using their gifts for the service of humanity. To such a woman, a home, husband, and family may hinder the fullest expression of her gifts. Hence she is urged to marry late in life, or—if temperamentally possible—to combine the home with a career. The ultimate purpose, both of the married and the non-married state, is spiritual development; and both men and women—being equally spirits—are entitled to equal opportunities to whatever state may best serve the purpose of that development.

The right to self-determination is seen by Cayce not only as a social right, but also as a cosmic one. In metaphysical terms, this is known as freedom of will; and many a bitter argument has been waged over it throughout the centuries.

One of the most important features of the reincarnation principle is its affirmation of free-will. An error commonly made by people who accept karma and rebirth is to assume that all of life is predetermined. The consequences of such a belief are psychologically paralyzing and spiritually demoralizing. The inertia and passivity of the Hindu, who has in large part accepted a fatalistic interpretation of karma, exemplifies the danger of such a position.

It is necessary to realize that every sneeze, every mosquito bite, every evening's meal, was not cosmically and karmically determined ages ago. Most of the details of our lives are completely subject to our thought and will *now*. In fact, every event of our lives, whether it be a major event like marriage or a minor event like buying an ice-cream soda, is, in the last analysis, self-determined. The restrictions placed upon us now are a result of our mistakes in self-determination in the past. They merely *seem* like external agents to us because we have forgotten our own past actions, and the range of our vision is too tiny to see their intimate connection with our present circumstances. Through a proper understanding, then, of the reincarnation principle, the ancient dilemma of free will versus determinism is resolved. Man has freedom of will as a dog on a leash has it; that is to say, the dog is completely free to do as he wills within the radius of the leash. Karma determines the length of each man's leash; within that radius, he is free.

This issue of free will comes forcibly to the student's attention as he surveys the readings on marriage, and especially the readings in which people ask questions about whom they should marry. Again and again the readings indicate that marriage ties are of a karmic nature; that is to say, the partners of a marriage are old acquaintances, forgot, who have met again to work out some mutual karmic debt. We are led to reflect then, that when people say "Haven't I met you somewhere before?" they are not merely using an adroit (if timeworn) opening for a flirtation; they are stating a possible cosmic fact.

However, it is clear that in marriage relationships as in everything else, man has freedom of will and power of choice. It is also clear that even where a karmic tie exists between people, and shows itself as a powerful attraction between them, marriage in the present is not always advisable or necessary. Two brief examples of questions and answers may serve to illustrate the point.

Q. Should I marry the boy who is now courting me?
A. There is a karmic influence in this association. But it is not for the best that you marry him.

Q. Would marriage with F. S. be best for our mutual development?

A. It might be made so; but, as we find, there are others with whom there may be brought about a better mutual development. These others are specially from relationships in the Egyptian period. But the choice should be made by the entity. You *do* have some karma to be worked out with F. S. But as husband and wife would be a hard way to meet it.

The inadvisability of marriage, even in cases where a karmic tie exists, may be explainable in several ways. First, the individuals may have other lessons to learn this time, more important than the relationship problem in question. Another possibility is that one or both of the individuals may be spiritually insolvent—that is, not prepared to meet the problem as yet. Still another possibility is that the marriage being contemplated is too extreme a penalty for the delinquency, or the punishment does not fit the crime. And finally, perhaps the spiritual lesson to be learned can better be learned singly than together.

The readings do not often specify the exact reason why marriage is or is not advisable in each case. Even in the instances where marriage is regarded as being appropriate, the decision whether or not to undertake it is left entirely up to the individual. The readings, following the best guidance practice, seldom make an outright decision for the counselee.

This basic attitude is seen clearly in the following case, wherein two young people inquire whether or not they should marry. The reading told them that they had had two experiences together, one in Persia and one in Egypt. This accounted for their strong mutual attraction. With regard to their marrying, the reading was noncommittal. It said: "If there is a coordination of ideals and purposes, this can be made a beautiful experience."

In the question period the girl asked: "Is there anyone else with whom we could each be as happy, or happier, in marriage, than with each other?" The answer came: "Oh, we might name twenty-five or thirty such, if you choose to make it so! Marriage is what you make it! There is an experience to be worked out here, if you want to do it now. Since you have to do it sooner or later, you might as well do it now—if you want to. . . ."

In a few instances the information is flatly emphatic, one way or the other, as here:

Q. Is it advisable for me to marry the man to whom I am now engaged?
A. *No!*

In the majority of cases, however, it is insistent on the individual's complete privilege and responsibility of choice. But at the same time it usually specifies the criterion by which the choice should be made. A man asks: "Would R. W. be my proper mate?" and is told: "This must be your choice, not ours. Is there not only a mental and physical, but also a spiritual attraction between you? Does spirit answer spirit, purpose answer purpose? Have you the same ideal? If you haven't, be careful!"

The information was even more explicit on this point in the following instance where a woman asked which of four men she should marry. The reading replied:

This depends on what you set as your ideal. All of these four people have been associated with you in the past—some as helpers, some as hinderers. To say to you that you should keep away from this one or be joined together with that one would place you in a false position, and place them in a false position also.

The choice must be made by *you*, as directions are taken for a life of service. Know that all men are free willed.

From passages such as these one can deduce the principle of choice by which a marriage partner should be selected. It is probably safe to say that the majority of marriages are entered into because of an irresistible physical attraction. By the view of the Cayce readings, one should be well mated not only physically but also mentally and spiritually. A successful marriage must stand upon this equilateral basis as upon a tripod; if any of the three aspects is slighted, the marriage is crippled as a consequence. The ideals of each person must be at least roughly equivalent to the ideals of the other in all of these three realms; else danger and disaster are in the offing. A thoughtless entry into marriage, slighting these important considerations of choice, is an invitation to trouble.

One must be on one's guard, then, when one begins to feel an irresistible fascination for a person of the opposite sex . . . one must be on one's guard, that is, provided that one has sufficient forethought to wish a sexual attachment to develop into a successful marriage, and provided that one is not in the mood for setting off the tinder of an explosive karmic situation.

Chapter XIV

.The Lonely Ones

IN ANY consideration of marriage from the long-range point of view of reincarnation, the question inevitably arises as to why a given lifetime does not include marriage for some men and women. Even though they are reasonably attractive physically, and temperamentally normal, some people seem never to have the opportunity to marry. Is there a karmic explanation for this, one wonders, in the Cayce readings?

The French have a brilliant epigram on the subject of the married and the non-married state: "Marriage is like a besieged fortress: those who are outside want to get in; those who are inside want to get out." Cynical though it may seem, there is much truth in this observation. Marriage has brought so much psychological misery to so many people that it seems almost surprising that other people should still consider the married state a desirable one, that they should still be able to disregard its many threats to peace of mind and see only its promises of felicity. And yet—despite the common knowledge that marriage has its very real difficulties—the unmarried generally have a sense of having been cheated of something precious—a sense of frustration and failure.

The sexual element of this situation, of course, is an important one; and the frustration of non-marriage, in "civilized" countries at least, has been the equivalent of total or comparative sexual starvation for the woman, if not for the man. In primitive societies this is not the case. But in our present form of Western society, the single state represents a kind of frustration, and even carries with it a kind of disesteem. This is especially so in the case of the unmarried woman; and the cases that follow are all of women because

131

in the Cayce files they were more frequently concerned about the matter than men, and their cases more conspicuous.

Alone. There is something desolate in the word, something unspeakably sad. Just as "for the last time" is perhaps the saddest phrase in the language for lovers, so "I am lonely" is perhaps the saddest of all sentences to have to utter with regard to oneself. Without spiritual illumination, aloneness after love, or aloneness never having known love, is one of the most sterile, most thwarting of all human conditions.

The major life problem of the woman whose case is described below has been a constant sense of aloneness. She is a social secretary in New York City—a Norwegian woman of poise and considerable physical attractiveness. She was forty-seven at the time of her first reading from Cayce. She had at that time been married twice; the first husband died shortly after marriage. She married again—this time to a man much older than herself, and the marriage was so unhappy that she soon obtained a divorce. She had no children. All the members of her family had died; she literally had no one. Her position as social secretary brought her into contact with people, but it was a superficial contact. She would have liked to remarry, but the opportunity somehow did not present itself. She was alone.

The questions she asked in her application for a reading reveal her sense of isolation and bewilderment. "Why have I always been so alone?" she asked. "Is there any particular reason why I shouldn't find companionship in marriage? Why am I such a misfit?" The reading disclosed that there was indeed a reason for her loneliness. Two lifetimes back, in Norway, she had initiated her present psychological situation by a tragic misstep: suicide.

She was at that time the mother of two small children, and the wife of a man who for some undisclosed reason had fallen into disgrace with the community. After the birth of her second child she became despondent and destroyed herself in the nearby fjord. "Thus we find the influence arising in the present as periods of melancholia, and as a loneliness which is almost unbearable at times."

The karmic pattern in this case seems to be quite clear. At a time of disgrace she took her own life, thus depriving her husband and children of the love and care they needed. Her lack of appreciation of family bonds, her lack of sense of honor and responsibility with respect to them, brought about the situation in which she now finds herself. Only through the lack of things does one learn to appreciate their worth.

It is a thought-provoking situation. It illustrates not only the soundness of the Catholic Church's prohibition of suicide as a serious sin, but also the truth of the fact that for every act, for every indifference, for every neglect, for every disparagement or misuse of the gift of life, we are held finally accountable.

The next case of loneliness presents the same basic pattern, though details differ markedly. It concerns a woman of English descent who teaches kindergarten but who has always longed to be married. She was the only child of middle-aged parents, both of whom died when she was very young. She was reared in a staid and conservative manner by two elderly aunts. As a result she has had great difficulty in adjusting to other people of her own age. Throughout her life she has felt lonely and set apart from others, and she has developed marked introvert tendencies.

There was one love affair in her life, but the attraction was purely a physical one. As the psychological incompatibility became more and more apparent, the incident closed. Since then her life has seemed to her to be frustrated and empty. She enjoys her work and is professionally successful; she is efficient, competent, intelligent. At recurring intervals, however she is engulfed by a depression which lasts for several weeks and then gradually subsides. During these fits of depression she has often contemplated suicide. One would never imagine her to be subject to such a profound dejection, as she is an attractive woman with a positive manner.

According to her reading the outstanding event in her history was suicide in the Persian period, four lifetimes back, when Bedouin tribes made a raid on her country. At that time she was a daughter of the ruler, and was one of those taken hostage by a Bedouin sheik when the raid was made. Afterward she was transferred to the man next in charge, by whom she had a child. Soon after the birth of this child—a girl—she committed suicide. The daughter was thus left to the tender mercies of the warlike people among whom she lived, and fared very badly until she was picked up in an emaciated condition by a traveling religious teacher and brought back to health.

The reading indicates that the mother committed suicide only because she so fiercely resented being subject to another's will; and "the entity lost through this experience, to the low dreg of taking its life only to satisfy itself—not in self-defense or in defense of principle or of country." Further details the reading does not give; but one reads between the lines here and senses that she was proud, haughty, arrogant, self-willed, and that she destroyed herself rather than suffer humiliation to her ego.

In view of her present temperament—a marked independence of manner, which seems almost as brusque, and self-sufficient as that of any man—it seems likely that the psychological sin of her Persian life is the very thing that casts up a barrier between herself and men in the present. It is a certain lack of pliancy, a refusal to renounce her self-determination, which perhaps frightens men away from her now.

Curiously enough, she has, in this life, always longed for a child. Had it not been for the difficulties raised by one of the elderly guardian aunts, she long ago would have adopted a baby girl. Another curious carry-over is the fact that she has frequently thought of suicide. Since obtaining her reading, which gave her a reasonable explanation for her situation, she no longer considers suicide as a way out, knowing that what she does not meet now she will have to meet at another time.

In another one of her readings she was told, however, that she could still expect marriage in this incarnation, but later in life; that she should meanwhile try to make herself helpful in every way possible to all those with whom she came in contact. When she asked how soon she might expect this happy consummation, she was told, "When you have proved yourself it will come about." She was given clearly to understand, in several places, that this is a testing period for her. When she asked, "Why have the last five years of my life been so entirely devoid of all contact with men?" she was told, "It has been a testing period of that which is your basic purpose for this incarnation."

Here, then, are two cases where suicide involving the abandonment of a child has resulted karmically in loneliness and the lack of a husband. There is a third case in the files, that of a Texas music teacher, who finds herself in the same situation for the identical reason—suicide, committed while a member of the French court.

We are not entitled to generalize, of course, on the basis of only three cases, as to the general karmic consequences of self-destruction. It is Manly Hall's opinion (*Reincarnation: The Cycle of Necessity*) that its usual karmic result is that a future personality will die under conditions where the desire for life will be the greatest. We have no case in the Cayce files to corroborate this view; but it is a reasonable one. (There are several other cases in the Cayce files where suicide has been committed in the past, but none where any karmic result was apparent in the present. It is possible that in these cases the karmic effect will become apparent only in later lives.)

Loneliness in the present and the inability to get married can arise from a variety of other causes, however. The following case, for example illustrates a totally different karmic origin.

One is reminded, in studying this case, of Oscar Wilde's epigram: "There are only two tragedies in life: one is not to get what you want; the other is to get what you want." The basic reason for this strange paradox lies in man's poor judgment—in what the Hindus call *avidya,* or ignorance. The fairy stories in which a character is offered three wishes by a fairy godmother frequently show him making foolish wishes, the consequences of which he must afterward abide by. Stories such as these are deeply symbolic of two facts: first, that most men do not really know what they want in life; and second, that much of man's suffering arises from the foolish choices he himself makes—choices arising out of poor judgment, limited or materialistic point of view, mistaken selfishness, or short-sighted self-interest.

The following case is an example of a decision made as far back as Atlantis, the consequence of which is still being felt in the present. The case concerns a woman of about forty years. Her figure seems stocky and heavy-set, but this is largely due to lack of exercise and faulty posture. Her face is severely innocent of makeup, her hair virgin of any permanent. Her dress is determinedly unfeminine; all her clothes are selected on the basis of utility and economy rather than with any idea of enchancing her appearance. In the hands of a beautician, a figure conditioner, and a dress counselor she could emerge into a beautiful mature woman; the features of her face are regular and good, and she has, through religious conviction more than anything else, developed an outgoing and charming manner.

She has had only an eighth-grade education and has earned her living principally in factories and in jobs of a manual or mechanical nature. On a psychological test measuring values (the Allport-Vernon Scale, based on the Spranger Value Types) she scored highest on the religious and social values, as was to be expected, since her principal interests in life are the reading of religious books and in being active in some form of social service. However, she leads a solitary and lonely life. None of the members of her family shares her religious outlook. There has been little romance in her life.

From the point of view of a psychologist, this woman presents a fairly clear-cut case of what is called the "masculine protest," or the refusal to accept the role of woman. This protest is apparent in her almost belligerently feminist, and unfeminine, attitude. It is apparent also in her almost puritanic refusal to make any efforts at self-adornment or any efforts towards the attraction of men. The psychological mechanism of this attitude is interesting and is well explained by orthodox psychology. But the explanation of orthodox psychology seems incomplete. Why should she have been born, we ask, to the bodily and psychological "heredity" and "environment" that "predisposed" her to having a masculine protest in the first place? Her past life history supplies the answer.

In the first life back she was a near relative of John the Baptist, and consequently grew up in an atmosphere of religious fervor. This was the basis for her religious bent in the present. Before that she was—in the male sex—a worker in wood and metals in a still earlier Palestine period, which seems to have led to her mechanical, practical outlook in the present. Before that she was a woman of high rank in Atlantis; an unhappy love affair brought her great mental anguish and confusion. As a result, "the entity determined that it would never again in material experiences love those that could disappoint and cause heartache." And here we have the starting point of the determination to be free of the ensnarements and hazards of love.

Her present lonely and unmarried state is, then, not karma in the retributive sense. We see no action and reaction here, as we did in the suicide cases related above. We see rather the Continuity Principle in operation, with respect to the force of desire. She once made a decision, struck an attitude with regard to her fellowmen and her relations with them. With typical Atlantean intensity she determined that *never again* would she permit her affections to be involved with other people, and especially with the opposite sex. The decision was made not out of spiritual and loving renunciation; it was made out of the ego-inspired desire not to be humiliated after giving affection. In the interim she has never seen reason to change her attitude. So now she must abide by all the logical and psychological conclusions of her decision, to its last reduction to absurdity, until she changes her mind and her will with regard to it.

Whether or not she may marry in this life the reading does not indicate. But she is at least working in the direction of expressing affection and interest in others. Through the lack of love, she has learned its worth. Through her loneliness, she has seen her sin, the rejection of love, objectified.

136

The next case concerns a woman who has been strongly suspected of being homosexual. While it is never explicitly stated in the Cayce readings, it seems highly presumable that in some cases homosexuality is due to a recent change in sex, and the almost insurmountably strong carryover of opposite-sex traits.

The woman in this case was born in England, but came at an early age to America. At the time of her reading, she was practicing her profession in a large city of the United States. In appearance and manner she is extremely masculine. Her voice is deep like a man's. She wears tailored, manlike clothes, uses masculine gestures and stances, and wears her hair extremely short. The suspicion widely held among her friends that she is homosexual rests on observation of these characteristics, together with the fact that for many years she lived with a woman who was extremely feminine both in appearance and manner. They were inseparable companions, and the arrangement had all the earmarks of a homosexual attachment.

Two immediately preceding lives are the most significant in connection with her present personality. In the second life back she was in England during the Crusades. She was one of the many thousands of women who were left behind by their husbands, and who were faced with the necessity of struggling for themselves. This typical Crusade experience has left its psychological imprint on many people. Some women reacted to their abandonment and solitude in one way, some in another.

The woman in this case reacted with a vigor and generalship unusual in her sex. Apparently she suffered a good many hardships, recognized the plight of other women similarly situated, roused herself to activity, and organized the women into some kind of communal plan for their mutual protection. "And ever since the entity has had little confidence in man, especially of those zealous of activity in unsettled fields. The tendencies to hold grudges, to be suspicious, to question the activity of others, arise from that sojourn."

It was in this incarnation that certain masculine, aggressive, positive qualities emerged in her psyche. We assume that this was their initial appearance (at least in this cycle) because in the previous incarnation she was in Palestine as a woman, and the reading makes no mention of masculine tendencies. By the end of the Crusade period, these masculine traits had become so pronounced that in her next life she incarnated as a man. Again born in England, she was one of those adventurous men who came to America with Hardcastle shortly after the arrival of John Smith. Her name then was James Buhanana; she was a free-booter and free-thinker, and traveled widely through the eastern coastal states. Later she went with other adventurers into the interior.

We find her now a manlike spirit in a woman's body—a body which is itself almost like a man's. If in point of fact she is actually homosexual (exact information on this point is unavailable) the case is doubly interesting. But even if she is not, the situation is highly charged with psychological significance of a very valuable sort. For it brings us face to face with the immensely important principle of polarity.*

The psychologist Jung has dealt at some length with the fact that each individual is both male and female, with one of the two predominating in his psyche. Just as the physical body contains rudimentary sex organs of the opposite sex as well as its own, similarly the psyche of the human being has undeveloped faculties, faculties held in abeyance as it were, that belong more properly to the opposite sex. This psychological fact, arrived at by Jung through long years of clinical observation, fits in very well with the position the Cayce readings take as to the origin and development of man.

Briefly, that position is this. All human spirits were created sexless and divine. But the principles of polarity, or sex, was one of the architectonic principles of the universe. And when the spirits became entangled in matter they did so in many ways in relation to the laws of polarity. At first they were androgynous, containing both sexes within themselves. Then they became bisexed. The early centuries of Atlantean history contain many strange examples of grotesque forms created out of the blundering use of the sexual power. The present bisexual division is only a phase in our development, which is probably tending toward the androgynous on a spiritual level.

Each of the two polarities, male and female, has its typical qualities. In our culture epoch at least, the typically male and typically female attributes can be distinguished as follows: strength, aggressiveness, positiveness, dominance, harshness—these are male; submissiveness, passivity, gentleness, kindness—these are female.

Suppose now that a spirit, through successive identifications with a male body or a female body in the same culture epoch,

* The Cayce readings nowhere use the word "polarity" or make explicit statement of the principle. It is adduced here by the writer as interpretation of the facts of the Cayce readings, and will be found to harmonize with all the data therein, as well as with the facts and principles of the ancient Hermetic wisdom.

has developed one set of these qualities so highly that he is in danger of becoming one-sided. This is a very real danger, both to himself and to the rest of the world. We have an excellent example of it in the philosophy and conduct of the Nazis. The Nazi superman ideal was not superman so much as it was super*male*. It exalted the male polarity characteristics of strength, power, aggressiveness, dominance, harshness, and self-seeking. These qualities have their place and their necessity; but when untempered by feminine qualities of love and self-sacrifice they become cruelty, lust, and ego madness. The flagrant and terrible evidences of this the world has already seen.

Maleness is incomplete in itself. Its overemphasis results in evil. Hence the necessity of complementing it by the female polarity virtues. This complementation takes place to a degree through marriage, through union of opposites. Each partner of the union is modified and tempered somewhat by the other. But the modification is still incomplete. Through the span of one lifetime a predominantly male psyche is very inadequately tempered by his mate to female virtues, and vice versa. But successive incarnations that provide for alternation between male and female bodies afford the necessary mutually corrective experiences. Thus once again the reincarnation principle is seen to be the necessary new dimension in psychology; only through repeated rebirths is the completeness of the psyche made possible. Only in this way can dominance and submissiveness be fused into the perfect poise of the potent, initiating spirit who is at the same time acquiescent to the will of God.

We have an interesting example of this attempted correction of the psyche through alteration of the body's sex in the case we have just considered. The entity had developed through two incarnations—first as woman, then as man—the positive, male qualities. She had done so at the expense of gentleness, beauty, forgiveness, tolerance, patience. To have been born again in a male body might only have aggravated still further an already exaggerated tendency. Birth in a female body, carrying over all the male qualities which she had developed so disproportionately, was an attempted psychological corrective. The imbalance of her development was made all the more evident through the contrast of inner with outer, of quality with body, and the bodily role expected of her by society. Her lack of feminine qualities should have in this way become conspicuous and therefore uncomfortable; the attention of the indwelling ego should have been drawn to the need for a corrective balance. Masculine women and feminine men, therefore, who permit themselves to become homosexual are perhaps taking the line of least resistance by reverting to a previous state of existence; perhaps they are refusing to learn the lesson of equilibration which their body is trying to teach them.

There are numerous other cases in the Cayce files of women who have mannish tendencies traceable to recent previous incarnations as men. Although the presence of masculine traits due to a recent male incarnation does not necessarily preclude marriage, it does seem to render it more difficult or more unlikely, and it frequently seems to preclude the ability to have children. Many women who had difficulty in bearing children, or could not have them at all, were told that this was due to their recent change in sex.

No matter what the karmic cause for loneliness, however —whether it be suicide, the determination not to love, or the overemphasis of opposite-sex qualities from an other-sexed incarnation—it must be recognized that the unmarried state is, like any other, an opportunity for inner cultivation and self-transformation. "Let us cultivate our garden," said Candide, at the end of many variegated adventures. And men and woman alike can apply this wisdom to themselves, when they find themselves seemingly trapped in a barren cell of loneliness.

In order to have companionship, one must be worthy of it. In order to have friends, one must be friendly; in order to have love, one must give love. By cultivating within themselves that which will make them worthy of what they desire, the lonely ones will more quickly realize the happy consummation of love.

Chapter XV

Some Problems of Marriage

ONCE the choice of the mate has been made, the partners are committed to a definite karmic combination, a definite psychic interaction. A thorough study of the Cayce readings that have to do with marriage leads to general notions as to the significance of the marriage choice with relation to both the past and future. In terms of a dramatic analogy, one might express this situation as follows.

By their decision to marry, a man and woman have unknowingly agreed to co-star once again with a particular fellow player, with whom there have been one or more previous joint experiences. They have thereby evoked a special stage setting for the drama of their present lives. This stage setting may, in fact, consist of two or three successive sets: remotely, in the furthest background, there may be a laboratory in Atlantis, gleaming with instruments of power and precision; then, more closely forward, a goat-herd's cottage huddled underneath a mountain crag in Greece; and finally, close in the foreground, an elegant drawing room of the age of Louis the Sixteenth.

Now they pick up the threads of the drama enacted between them in the glittering and sophisticated court in France. Rivalry, intrigue, betrayal, and treachery may have been the crescendo of events in the acts just preceding—climaxed in France by an irresistible hate and murder. Or perhaps the episodes had grown successively less violent over the ages; perhaps the subtler forms of psychological cruelty—arrogance, selfishness, sarcasm, indifference—had been the latest elements of conflict.

But whatever their dramatic precedents, the two protago-

141

nists of this new performance have at every moment the power to alter the progress of the plot. The stage is set, but the lines are not written. Like the celebrated Italian commedia dell'arte, in which the setting and a general sketchy outline were previously agreed on by the company, but the actors improvised their lines and created the situations and resolutions as they went along, the actors of this new play are at every moment free to alter the free-flowing course of the plot, and thereby redeem the weakness of the previous acts.

Or, to depart from the analogy with the drama, it might be said that each person has freedom of will and choice with regard to the marriage partner as with regard to everything else, but that the act of making a choice is like the act of boarding a bus; once on the bus, one is committed to a certain specific route and a certain general direction, which differs from the direction and route one would have followed had one entrusted oneself to another bus. Moreover, the interior circumstances of the bus may not be completely to one's liking. The driver may be rude and unpleasant, the atmosphere stuffy, the windows hermetically sealed, and one's seat-partner objectionably talkative. There may be a variety of unforeseen circumstances for which one had not bargained when one decided on the Highland Park rather than the Dexter Road bus. But the attitude one maintains and one's general conduct throughout the length of the drive are determinable by the self, and for one's attitude and conduct, no matter what the circumstances, one is ultimately answerable.

There are a number of specific cases of marriage karmically explained in the Cayce readings.

No Greek Nemesis was more relentless, no Greek tragedy more terrible in its awful justice, than the progress of destiny in the strange case to be considered now. The woman in this case was a very beautiful girl of twenty-three when she married her husband. Lovely brown eyes, beautiful dark brown hair which waved loosely around her face, and a beautiful figure conspired to give her the appearance of an actress. Even at the age of forty-one, when she obtained her life reading from Cayce, she had the stunning type of beauty that makes heads turn in restaurants. Her fashionable and wealthy friends would have been intrigued indeed to know the inner story of her life.

In the eighteen-year interim since her marriage to a well-known and highly successful businessman, she had lived through a most difficult and emotionally thwarting experience. Her husband was completely incapable of the sexual relationship. To some women, perhaps, those who feel no need for and no pleasure in sex, such a situation might not seem tragic. But to a woman such as this one—sensual, affectionate —it was a tragedy indeed. Annulment of the marriage or divorce might have ended the difficulty simply enough; but this woman could not bring herself to take either of these steps. She loved her husband; she could not bear to hurt him.

There was a period in the first few years when she entered desperately into a variety of liaisons with other men—not out of desire to be unfaithful to her husband, but out of sheer physical and emotional necessity. Gradually, however, she overcame even that impulse, largely through taking up the study of theosophy and the practice of meditation. Life had gone on in this strange mold for eighteen years when the crisis came. A former suitor of hers came back into her life. "From the moment we met again," she writes to Mr. Cayce, "the flame came back to him in its full intensity, and I responded too. I am trying to release us, but I find my health going down as it was before I took up my studies . . . I would not hesitate to have a liaison with him if he were not married. I would not leave my husband for a number of reasons which you may see, and also he has evolved into a very beautiful character. . . .

"Perhaps my desire for this man is not love, but due to the peculiar circumstances of my married life. However, he also is a fine person. He loved me from childhood and I did not know it (his mother told me that). He did not let me know until he was able to support a wife. It was too late then, for I had just returned home to announce my engagement to my husband. Peculiar circumstances all along, which spell karma to me, seem to have dogged our three lives.

"I did see him intimately at intervals, because, for one reason, he was going to pieces. Another, I thought it would cure him of his desire—a sort of psychological subconscious cleaning . . . I broke it off for I did not wish to 'two-time' his wife. I know his wife and I like her. I don't want to disturb her. Society is against it and from her point of view it would be wrong if she knew it. I don't want to hurt anyone. The man does not dislike her, I believe, though she gets everything she wishes by making fun of him or nagging over weeks at a stretch. She does not hesitate to belittle him in public, but she does have some good qualities. She cannot have children. . . . My husband knows I am asking you for physical help, but he does not know the situation."

Here, then, is the woman's own statement of her life

problem.* It is dramatic enough, even as it stands, but the life reading, and its revelations of the past antecedents of her problem, inspire a sense of awe, almost, at the singularly appropriate punishment which two erring souls are meeting.

We must go back two lifetimes ago in France, at the time of the Crusades. Here we find the wife in the name of Suzanne Merceilieu, married once again to her present husband. Monsieur Merceilieu was one of those adventurous men whose imagination was caught by the crusaders' cause. And, like many another man of religious zealousness, his personal life was in a compartment quite separate from the professions and principles of his religious faith. It was of supreme importance to him that the tomb of the Saviour be rescued from the possession of the Infidel; to apply to his own relationship with his wife the major principle of love which the Saviour taught had never apparently entered his mind.

And so when he left his wife to go to preserve Christendom from the Infidel, there was one other thing he wanted preserved in his absence—namely, his wife's chastity. And, fearing that religious zeal might not inspire her with the same heroic abnegation that it inspired in him, and that instead of embracing Christianity for consolation she would embrace the remaining male Christians instead, he saw to it very carefully that no such consolations would be possible.

There is an ingenious device called a chastity belt, or girdle of chastity, known in Europe as early as the second half of the twelfth century, and known also to have been used as recently as 1934 in France and 1931 in New York City when its forced adoption was a major element in two legal trials. It consisted of an arrangement of metal and leather, or metal and velvet, which was provided with a lock and key and which was carefully adjusted to a woman's body so that no sexual relations were possible in the absence of the owner of

* A false impression might be got from this letter. It might be assumed that people who obtained life readings from Cayce previously gave him full accounts of their situation, thus providing him with material upon which he might elaborate in his sleeping state. A few overwrought persons, like the woman mentioned here and the subject of one of the following cases, did write at great length concerning the tragedy of their lives previous to obtaining the reading. But this was the exception, not the rule. Persons applying for a reading were requested to give only their name, birthdate, and place of birth. Most persons applying for a reading gave little or no information other than that indicated in the application blank; if they did discuss some of the features of their situation, it was usually in very general terms.

the key. In such a fashion did Monsieur Merceilieu assure himself that Madame Merceilieu would remain true to him.

The exact words of the reading are: "The entity was among those doubted by the companion and was forced to wear a stay that prevented liaison with others." The use of the word *force* leads us to believe that Madame Merceilieu did not much like the idea, even to begin with; the next sentences show us that she resented it all the more strongly afterward, and "determined to be free, some time, some where, and to get even. . . . Being forced to remain in a state of chastity caused the entity to form detrimental determinations. That this has become a portion of the entity's present experience, then, is only the meeting of self."

Let us analyze now the retributive justice here involved. The man who used mechanical means to restrain his wife is rewarded by being rendered physically incapable of the sex relationship. There could be no more appropriate punishment. On first glance, it seems unjust that the woman who was the object of this cruelty should twice be subject to a lifetime of sexual frustration. But only superficially does it seem unjust. For sin does not consist of external acts merely. It consists of intentions, motives, states of mind, attitudes of soul. This woman was unjustly restrained. Her reaction to this mistrust in her and the brutal form it took was one of vindictiveness and hate. No overt action (so far as we know) gave expression to that hatred and that thirst for revenge; but the determination for revenge was there none the less.

We have seen once before how any decision made by the soul will persist over the centuries. This soul's determination to "get even" was rewarded with full opportunity to do so. This time she was superbly beautiful, infinitely desirable. She found herself married to the man who had wronged her in a previous life—with full opportunity to madden him with jealousy, humiliate him before his friends, or crush him with divorce. What more could she ask for? What more perfect setting for full, triumphant, exultant revenge? The situation seems almost like a fulfillment of an elaborately malevolent fantasy revenge of her once infuriated and rancorous self.

In the meantime, however, she had grown spiritually. She could no longer bring herself to be unkind to anyone. Her letters betray her sensitivity throughout. She could have had a liaison with her returned lover—a liaison which could easily have been kept secret from her husband—but she could not bear to hurt the man's wife, who might more easily have discovered it. She refrained. Her physical and emotional health demanded some form of sex-expression; but she loved her

145

husband. She did not divorce him. She sacrificed her physical desires, her beauty, her youth, to her sense of loyalty and devotion.

In the cryptic and deeply meaningful phrase of the reading, she was "meeting herself," meeting her own ancient determination in the situation of her life. And she has redeemed that self she met. She has passed the test which she herself had set for herself six centuries ago. "Vengeance is mine; I will repay, saith the Lord." "For it must needs be that offences come; but woe to that man by whom the offence cometh!" Both these biblical statements express the fact that karmic law can be relied on to punish any offender; that man himself must not vindictively take punishment into his own hands, nor vow to get revenge. (This does not necessarily mean that society has no right to protect itself against the criminal. Condemnation of an offender against the civil law is a considered, social act, undertaken for the greatest good of the greatest number. It abides by the laws agreed on; it is not done out of the emotional impulse of vindictiveness. Ideally, at least, society's administration of its laws is an impersonal application of justice, and as such is a reflection in the human realm of the laws of karma in the cosmic realm.)

One other instance occurs in the Cayce files of a marital tragedy due to the enforced use of the chastity belt during a Crusade incarnation of the husband and wife concerned. In this case the karmic reaction is somewhat different. The husband was, according to the wife's account, very patient, understanding, and gentle. Yet after almost eight years of marriage, the thirty-two-year-old wife continued to have a terrible fear of the sexual relationship. This of itself understandably created a very difficult situation; it was further complicated by the almost idolatrous attraction of the wife toward a male friend, an Italian opera star.

The sexual difficulty was explained in the reading by the fact that the husband, in their Crusade incarnation, had restrained her with a chastity belt. It is quite clear how he, in having a wife who fears him sexually, is reaping the consequences of his action. The fact that the wife is suffering from all the maladjustments attendant on her abnormal fear is also a karmic consequence. Her reaction to her Crusading husband for her restraint was one of hate. And hatred forges bonds. In the words of the reading: "There are doubts and fears in the present arising from latent hate. The condition created then is to be met in the present by understanding. For if you would be forgiven, you must forgive."

The attraction to the opera singer was accounted for by another life experience. He had been her lover once in Indo-China. In answer to her question: "How shall I handle the situation?" the reading says: "Meet it according to what you choose as your ideal."

The element of fear appears once again in another case where the karmic cause is entirely different. From the point of view of the personal suffering involved, the story of this case is almost overwhelmingly tragic; from the point of view of psychiatric analysis, however, the case offers excellent material for the study of the inter-relationship between karma, heredity, and environment. The woman writes in 1926:

> I am almost on the eve of insanity and suicide—the most miserable woman on earth and a dope fiend. All my life my mother, who had suffered living deaths with the birth of six children, talked so much to me about pregnancy that when I married eighteen years ago I was so scared of pregnancy that I now am living away from a dear sweet husband because I cannot bear to have him in my sight or near me. I have prayed and tried psychology, psychiatry, Christian Science, and Unity, and all to no avail. Do you think there is any hope for me? I wanted children and *loved* my husband but was scared of sexual intercourse and now am worse than ever and, as I say, ready for suicide which I had planned this week when I learned about your work.

The reading went back two lifetimes in explaining this woman's tragic situation. First of all it showed that she had been a vain, selfish, materialistic, pleasure-seeking woman in the French court. Her life was a gay one, but it sowed the seeds for the tragedy of the succeeding life as an early settler in America, when she became the mother of six children and saw all of them burned to death. "The entity lived in fear the remaining days of that life. She felt wrath and a lack of confidence in the divine for not having protected her and the children. This brings into the entity's present life the dread of bearing children, and all the consequences of that dread." (It seems likely that she was vibratorily attracted to her present mother by virtue of their common emotional problem: fear. The mother's reiteration of the horrors of pregnancy served only to reinforce the dread already in the child's unconscious.)

The tragedy in Colonial times is understandable, because we know that only through the loss of material certainties does man turn to spiritual things. But in the process of meeting one set of karmic conditions she had unwittingly created another. To have lost six children must have been agony indeed, even to a selfish woman. But the test was not passed successfully. Of the two possible reactions to her situation—loving acquiescence and resentful fear—she chose the latter. Of the possible mental interpretations—"This tragedy is the will of an inscrutable but just God," or "This tragedy is the injustice of a cruel God," or "The senseless sport of a godless universe"—she chose the latter interpretation.

And so there was one central lesson that this woman still needed to learn. That lesson was simply this: *perfect love casteth out fear*. She needed to depart from her selfish and materialistic concept of life; she needed to learn so great a love for the man who was her mate, so great a love for the unborn souls who might choose her as mother, so great a love and reverence for the divine principle of creativity within her, that material fears could not make themselves felt.

Unfortunately modern psychology has not for the most part acknowledged the power of love. Love, to the majority of analysts, is at most an expression of libido; since Watson's brilliant experiments in dropping and stroking babies, psychologists admit it to be one of the three legitimate human emotions. But as a positive force in the universe, as an essential aspect of the Divine Source, and consequently an essential quality of all fragments thereof which we are, as the sovereign solvent of all human ills, love has yet to be officially recognized. Perhaps it is because psychologists are shy about using the word. We can understand their reticence (if reticence it is) because should the word "love" become as bandied about as "service" has already, it would soon acquire the same overtones of commercial insincerity and pseudo-nobility with which "service" has already become polluted.

One other case that is interesting from the point of view of sexual adjustment and psychoanalytic treatment is that of a husband and wife who were professional people, practicing their profession together. They had both been under psychoanalytic treatment for almost two years at the time of their Cayce reading. The husband was a pronounced introvert; the wife had had three nervous breakdowns, from the last of which she was not expected to recover. The wife was fifty-one at the time of the reading; the husband, fifty-four. Their only child had died in infancy.

The marital inharmony between them was intense. The analyst who was treating their case heard of Cayce's work and wrote for a reading on both of them. He requested not a life reading, but a mental-spiritual analysis. As a result we have no data on the former lives of either, except for a single but highly significant detail that appeared in the reading of the wife.

The question was asked in the wife's reading: "Why does the entity take life more seriously than the average person?" The answer came: "Because she took it more seriously in other experiences." Then followed the question: "How did the entity's inferiority complex originate?" The answer was: "From the fear and dislike of men. You cannot take the vows of celibacy and keep them, and then lightly turn around and try to gratify the appetites of one who is not easily satisfied."

Here we have a highly important clue to the wife's inability to achieve a satisfactory sexual adjustment. In a previous life she had in all probability been a nun; it is understandable that a person who for a long time deliberately restrained the sexual nature for reason of principle should find it difficult, even under a changed marital status, to be spontaneous and natural in the expression of it. This is psychologically credible in the span of one lifetime; it is equally in the span of two.

It would surely be stretching a point to conclude that all frigid women were celibates in a previous existence. There are undoubtedly many reasons, both organic and non-organic, both karmic and non-karmic, for frigidity in women. But it is possible that in some cases unresponsiveness is traceable to a situation such as this one.

It is worth noting that the psychoanalyst in this case had suspected an Oedipus complex as an explanation for the neurosis of the husband. He was told in no uncertain terms by the reading that this was not the case.

Q. Psychoanalytically speaking, what is the entity's emotional age?
A. About two months.
Q. Is there an Oedipus complex in the entity's psychology?
A. Read what has already been given. You are looking only for material explanations.
Q. What are the reasons that the entity has not found happiness in his marriage?

149

A. *He is seeking the gratification only of himself.*

Selfishness, then, was the basic difficulty. In fact, in all the tragic cases of marital disharmony in the Cayce readings, it is apparent that, immediately or remotely, selfishness is the root of the difficulty. This is a fact of much suggestive importance. To be sure, the term "selfishness" may seem too naïve a term for the modern mind; perhaps a new expression, such as "the Zeus complex," or possibly the "SSQ" (Self-Satisfaction Quantum) will need to be coined before selfishness attains the status of a scientific, laboratory-tested vice.

It is, however, somewhat refreshing to find the readings employing a word so simple and so universally understandable (by virtue, perhaps, of being so universally applicable). *"Selfishness is the basic sin"* is a continuous refrain of the Cayce readings. And starting from that simple statement, one can cut through mountains of psychological jargon and elaboration, and emerge with a crystal-clear hierarchy of human values and a crystal-clear philosophy of therapy.

"Love does not possess!" exclaims a Cayce reading, in epigrammatic vein. "Love *is*."

Marriage usually begins in the illusion of love as possession. Its vicissitudes and sorrows are intended only that we shall learn the truth of love as *being*.

Chapter XVI

Infidelity and Divorce

IN ALL countries where monogamy is the rule, infidelity is a fairly widespread marital problem. Perhaps the basic explanation for its frequency is a biological one, aptly summarized in these anonymous lines:

> *Higamus, pigamus,*
> *Men are polygamous;*
> *Hogamus, pogamous,*
> *Women, monogamous*

In addition to biological factors, there are, of course, psychological and social factors that contribute to marital infidelity. But if the reincarnationist view is accepted it naturally becomes a matter of interest to investigate the problem of infidelity for possible karmic origins. The Cayce files contain three outstanding cases in which karma seems to be the basic determinant.

The first case is that of a woman, mother of two children, whose husband had been having an affair for some eight years with another woman; the wife had been aware of the situation only within the last two years of that period. She asked in her reading why she needed to suffer this distressing experience, and was told: "Because of your own unfaithfulness in the experience before this."

The second case is that of a woman who, during her French court experience, had been shamelessly unfaithful. She was now meeting the same situation with her present husband, who had been her principal paramour in her earlier incarnation.

151

The third case is that of a woman whose husband began, in their first year of marriage, to drink to excess and to have one affair after another; on several occasions he actually went so far as to bring another woman into the home. Through all this the wife remained faithful and continued to live with him in the intermissions between other women, only to be rewarded by becoming herself venereally diseased. The reading attributed the karmic origin for this woman's tragic situation to her immediately preceding incarnation. She was the illegitimate daughter, in that life, of one of Commodore Perry's sailors and a Japanese girl. Possibly because of her unorthodox origin she felt herself to be an outcast, and on reaching maturity gave herself with abandon to a life of sensual pleasure. She soon became a source of infection to the many men with whom she consorted. "And far-reaching were those influences," said the reading, "even to the meeting of it in the present experience."

In short, such cases would indicate that the infidelity of the mate sometimes occurs through karmic necessity. On the basis of these instances it cannot be assumed, of course, that *all* cases of infidelity are karmic. John's unfaithfulness to Mary may be due to the fact that Mary deserves this treatment because of her unfaithfulness to Claudius in ancient Rome, but on the other hand his philandering may stem from Mary's failings in the present; the infidelity may be no more than a contemporary reaction to a contemporary instigation —a case of quick karma. The touchstone for judging whether such a situation is karmic is probably, in the absence of clairvoyant vision of the past, to determine whether there appears to be adequate contemporary provocation.

According to karmic law, if one has been flagrantly unfaithful in the past, one deserves to be treated with flagrant infidelity in the present. Only in such a manner do loyalty and consideration become a part of the character. It is because of this educative necessity that the readings so frequently counseled against divorce: If a spiritual lesson is to be learned through a difficult marriage, there is little point in running away from it because sooner or later one must acquire the spiritual strength to meet it.

By no means, however, do the readings take a prohibitive attitude toward divorce—in many instances they definitely approve of it. The criteria by which the right or wrong of such an action was judged seem to be twofold; the obligation to the children and the obligation to each other. Cases where divorce was distinctly advised were invariably those in which there were no children, or, if there were, where the children would benefit from the divorce; those in which the karmic lesson of the marriage had been learned, or those in which one of the partners of the marriage had so badly met the situation as to be dragging the other down.

A typical case is that of a New Jersey woman of forty-nine who had no children and whose marriage was inharmonious. She was told that she should cultivate her exceptional abilities as a teacher, and that she should leave her husband. The reading went as follows:

Yes, it is well for the entity to be wedded; this is the natural life for an entity in the earth. But when a relationship exists that prevents the purposes for which the entity entered, and this becomes apparent, and there is no altering of it, it is better that there be a disassociation.

Know deep within yourself that you must be about the business that you entered the earth to complete. You are getting a late start, but you may yet accomplish much in the instruction of young girls. . . .

A contrasting example is the case of a woman who was twenty years older than her husband. There was a serious incompatibility between them; he drank excessively, and was abusive and irrational in behavior to her and to her son. No karmic explanation of the situation was given, but divorce was not advised. The reading said:

Disappointments and differences have arisen between you. Do not withdraw, but rather let your attitude be one of loving indifference. Do not be mindful of the slights and slurs; know that indeed, as you sow, so shall you reap; and this is true of your relationship with him as well as his with you. Do to him, under *any* circumstances, as you would have him do to you.

It is presumable in this case that some karmic lesson still needed to be learned, or some karmic obligation fulfilled.

In absence of clairvoyant knowledge of the past-life facts and merits of each case, the point at which withdrawal from marriage bonds may rightfully be made is admittedly difficult to discover. One strong argument in favor of the Catholic indissolubility of marriage is that it holds errant human beings to a task they might otherwise be tempted to escape from out of too facile a self-justification.

Although the Cayce readings' recommendation of divorce is too frequent to indicate sympathy with absolute divorce prohibition, the standards of self-evaluation which they set up are so high and so well founded philosophically that their ultimate effect would undoubtedly be to decrease rather than increase divorce.

Marriage as an institution is, by the reincarnationist view, less sacrosanct than many people think. If society wishes to make marriage indissoluble, well and good; if not, again well and good. Cosmic law will not be thwarted by either system—if man fails to meet an obligation in one existence, he will irrevocably be called to task in another. The outer forms which man sets up are almost as arbitrary and almost as unimportant as the rules he devises for gin rummy. In the last analysis it matters very little what rules are set up for any game, because through the forms and conventions of all of them it is skill and honesty in playing which are their intrinsic value.

On the other hand, marriage is *more* serious than many people think. The obligations which are so lightly disregarded by thousands of people every year are not merely meaningless sociological conventions; they have their true binding force in the corporate nature of humanity, of which each of us is as a living cell. A cosmic law of equilibrium is continuously operating, and whatever selfishness we manifest there is no better crucible for its dissolution than marriage. We must therefore learn to accept its difficulties and frustrations in a sacrificial spirit, realizing that our lesser self is on trial that our great Self may be born.

Knowing that our marriage partner has come to us through ancient bonds of attraction; knowing that not chance but purposeful intention of the overself has guided us to even the most cheerless of situations; knowing that within disharmony is opportunity for advancement through selflessness, we see divorce to be almost a deprivation. Conversely, recognizing that no institution should enslave people into unhealthy, miasmic, contorted relationships, and that selfless love should not be cast before the swine of unregenerate selfishness, we see divorce to be as sound and sane and decent a procedure as the dissolution of any other legal contract.

We return again to moderation, balance, the golden

154

mean. They are virtues to be sought not only by individuals in their quest for spiritual perfection; they are to be sought also by society in its efforts to create the forms through which individuals may express themselves.

Chapter XVII

Parents and Children

For many centuries the family has been more or less a sovereignty, presided over by the father—or, in some civilizations the mother. Such sovereignties still exist; in fact, they preponderate. From the materialistic point of view, indeed, children can be regarded as the property of the parents. They were created through the sacrifice and the labor of the mother; they were maintained through the toil and sacrifice of the father. The parent is materially stronger, more mature, and more powerful than the children—therefore it is his right to rule.

In spiritual reality, however, there is no absolute superiority of parent over child. All living creatures are equal members of a vast spiritual community. Spiritually, parents do not own their children; they do not even create them. They merely evoke them. A mysterious process goes on inside their bodies which enables them to unite with a mate for an instant and call into play equally mysterious processes which result in the preparation and birth of a body.

This body becomes the dwelling place for another spiritual being like ourselves. Temporarily he is speechless and helpless; the responsibility we feel and the care we endow upon him are worthwhile experiences. They are conducive to sacrifice and love; they lead to tenderness and attachment of the deepest sort. And this is as it should be, so long as it does not develop possessiveness and domination in one of their many forms.

Kahlil Gibran has stated the case well in *The Prophet*. He says:

Your children are not your children. They are the sons
and daughters of life's longing for itself.
They come through you but not from you.
And though they are with you yet they belong not to
you.
You are the bows from which your children as living ar-
rows are sent forth.
Let your bending in the Archer's hand be for gladness.
For even as He loves the arrow that flies so He loves
also the bow that is stable.

Parents should have a sense neither of domineering superiority nor of envious inferiority toward their children; and this
equipoise of loving detachment, which is the only fitting attitude of parents toward creatures in their charge, is possible
only through recognition of that central spiritual truth that all
men, all spirits, were created equal. Parents are, to use a favorite expression of the Cayce readings, the "channels"
through which life flows and through which souls are given
the opportunity of incarnating. People are enjoined therefore
to enter the marriage relationship with a sense of the sacred-
ness of what they are doing. The point of view is explicitly
sexual here; that is to say, Cayce's view coincides with the
Hindu view that sexuality is in itself a divine and sacred
thing.

Old-line Christion theology has unfortunately put a psychological blight on sex as being intrinsically sinful. Through
a tragic misinterpretation of the symbolism of the Book of
Genesis, all mankind is considered to have descended from
the "original sin" of Adam and Eve. Though the marriage
ceremony legitimizes sexual relationships, it has been held
that children are conceived in sin. Such twisted notions with
reference to the natural God-given functions of the human
body are far-reaching in psychological effect, giving rise to
suppressions, guilt feelings, and deep-seated conflicts of the
most serious and crippling sort. The alternative, however, is
not free love or the uninhibited expression of sexual desire.
The alternative is the full understanding that the creative
power of sex is a divine prerogative. "The love of and for a
pure body," says a reading, "is the most sacred experience in
an entity's earthly sojourn."

This point of view is stressed in many readings, and is notably found in instances where a woman asks about the possibility of having children. The request was usually made for a
physical reading in such cases; the woman wanted to know
what preparation to make for conception and birth. Physical

advice was given in abundant detail. Nothing of unusual nature appeared in these readings, except that osteopathic treatments be given throughout the period of pregnancy to insure a greater pliancy of the body. The suggestions as to diet, exercise, and personal care were of the same general nature as might be prescribed by and competent physician, with the peculiar advantage of clairvoyant insight into the specialized needs of each particular body.

However, the readings laid equal, if not greater, stress on the importance of mental and spiritual preparation, since the attitude of the parent would attract like-minded incoming entities:

> The entity should realize that the preparation of the mind and spirit is creative in nature and is as necessary as purely physical preparation, if not more so.

In a reading for a woman of thirty-six who asked if she might still hope to have a child, Cayce said:

> Make of yourself a better channel, physically, mentally, and spiritually. People are too prone to look upon conception as a purely physical condition.
>
> Remember how Hannah prepared herself, and Mary. There are many cases recorded, and there are many others of which nothing is known, and yet there was a long preparation.

Another reading said:

> It has been given as an opportunity to man through coition to create a channel through which the Creator may give to man the opportunity of seeing His handiwork. Be watchful, then, of your attitude and that of your mate in creating this opportunity; for the character of the incoming entity depends in part upon the attitude of the parents.

It also becomes apparent in these readings that no parent-child relationship can be regarded as a chance relationship. Almost always there have been previous-life connections with one parent or the other; in the comparatively few instances where no such past-life relationship existed with either parent, the family situation provided an environmental opportunity that coincided with the child's psychological needs. The Cayce files showed that some children had a karmic tie with one par-

158

ent, but no previous relationship with the other. In such cases there was a marked tendency toward indifference between the child and the parent who were related for the first time. The following typical cases illustrate the variety of possible past relationships between parents and children.

A mother and son between whom there was a close bond of affection had been mother and son before; a father and son who likewise were very close had stood in the relationship of older brother to younger brother in a previous life; a mother and daughter who did not get along together had had no previous relationship; a mother-daughter combination in which the daughter was very indifferent to the mother was accounted for by the reading as a previous sister-sister relationship in which there had been a serious disagreement ("You quarreled then and haven't made up yet"); a father and daughter had previously been together as husband and wife; a mother and daughter between whom there was marked antagonism had been rival for the same position and the same man in a previous life; a mother-son relationship in which the son attempted to dominate the mother was traced back to a previous experience where their positions were exactly reversed, as daughter-father.

These cases suggest that numerous principles are operative in the attraction of child to parent. Like the threads in an expertly directed puppet show, however, these principles are to a large degree hidden from us; the Cayce material is highly suggestive, but does not afford sufficient detail to make a genuinely systematic statement of law.

While it is true that like attracts like, it would seem to be equally true that, for various karmic reasons, ancient antagonists and temperamental opposites are often drawn together. A marked instance of temperamental disparity is to be seen in the case of a child who was five years old when a life reading was taken on him. He was characterized as selfish, unwilling to acknowledge his error when in the wrong, and indifferent. His outlook was, in its impersonality and its dedication to purely intellectual values, essentially that of a research scientist. In the previous incarnation he had devoted himself to steam as an instrument of power. Before that he had worked with chemical explosives; before that he had been absorbed in mechanics; before that he had been an electrical engineer in Atlantis.

Four lifetimes of such intensive dedication to pure science provides an interesting illustration of a persistence of "value," in Spranger's sense of the term. Here is clearly enough a Theoretical Type, but he had become overbalanced in the direction of the truth value at the expense of the love, beauty, and unity values of life, which are equally valid; his attitude toward others was one of detachment and cold indifference. The reading further stated that he would be most successful in this life in anything dealing with electrical or steam engineering, and involving mathematics. The characterization proved to be accurate in every respect. He is today a successful electrical engineer; his traits of character are essentially what one might expect from the background attributed to him, although some modifications seems to have taken place by virtue of his family environment.

One might have expected, if like attracts like, that he would have been born into a scientific environment—that his father might be an engineer and his mother, possibly, an exteacher of mathematics. He was born instead into a family of impractical idealists. The value type of the father was distinctly social or religious; the mother, though an introvert, was drawn into the social-service activities of her zealous husband. The boy's older brother was also an idealist, whose principal concern in life was helping other people.

The boy's appearance in this family would not, so far as can be determined, be called karmic in the strict sense of the term. At the same time there would seem to be some corrective principle operating here—the correction of an unhealthy over-emphasis. It almost seems as if the entity were aware of his limitations of outlook and chose to enter an environment that would expand that outlook to include more humanistic values.

The boy was thrown into continuous contact with people whose principal purpose in life was helping other people. His down-to-earth sense of reality often brought the rest of the family into a healthy restraint; on the other hand their outlook was a daily reminder to him of the existence of other values besides his own. While this experience has not brought about a complete change in his basic life value—the pursuit of pure science—yet it has had some effect on his personality in that it has made him less selfish and more social. Thus the corrective purpose of his parental choice would seem to have been fulfilled, at least in part.

That incoming entities have a certain freedom of choice with regard to parents is fairly well established in the Cayce data. There is some evidence to show that with the less highly evolved there is less scope of choice; but in general, choice of parentage would seem to be the soul's prerogative. It is not easily understandable why an unborn entity should deliberately choose a slum environment, degenerate parents, an ill-equipped body, or any other unfavorable circumstance. Superfically, such a choice would seem to be psychologically implausible; but more deeply analyzed, there is no real psychological contradiction.

The situation is comparable to that of a man who suddenly realizes he is becoming too fat. Some restriction on the part of his insurance company, or a refusal on the part of a woman, or difficulty in fitting himself in clothes may suddenly make him aware of his bulk. So he determines to lose weight, selects a suitable reducing studio, calls for an appointment, registers, and undertakes a course of reducing treatments. Six months later he emerges with a reduced waistline and a healthier heart action, his purpose accomplished. Apparently souls are in a position to do much the same thing. The deliberate decision to accept an unpleasant situation is not an inconceivable human act; people frequently choose some unpleasantness when they can see it to be a means to an end.

Curiously enough, this freedom of choice seems to have some bearing on the matter of infant mortality. In a general way, according to the readings, the soul can foresee at birth the type of earth situation in which it will become involved by virtue of its choice of parents; because of the freedom of human will, however, not all future events can be foreseen. As a consequence, the soul may discover, after it has made its choice and been born, that the parents are not living up to the expectations which they seemed to promise before the time of its birth. Realizing then that its own inner purpose for incarnation may be frustrated by the altered circumstance, the soul will withdraw.

A case in point is that of a young woman who was told that in her previous life she had died very young. She had taken incarnation with those particular parents principally because of an attraction to the mother; not long after her birth, however, the father began to drink and to become negligent and abusive. Disappointed, the young soul made the decision not to live, and after a short illness common to early childhood, it returned to the realms from which it had come.

The reading indicates very pointedly that withdrawals such as this are a common phenomenon. If this is to be believed, then infant deaths can be compared—in some instances at least—to the discreet departure of a theatergoer at the end of an unprepossessing first act. In some instances this may, as in the case above cited, reflect on the conduct of the parents; but in some cases it may merely reflect the mistaken judgment of the incoming entity.

Sometimes the death of a very young infant may be interpreted as a necessary experience of grief for the parents: the child has appeared only briefly, in a sacrificial spirit, to help them experience the healing agony they need for soul growth. An obscure novel of the last century uses this type of sacrificial act as its theme. In this story, a young woman has a father who is materialistic, arrogant, and proud of his possessions and the beauty of his children. The daughter loves him but can do nothing to spiritualize his values. She dies in an accident, and returns not long afterward to the same parents as a crippled child—purposely taking on this type of body and experience out of love for the father and the desire to bring him an anguish that would purify him. This was pure fiction, to be sure; but it suggests what may sometimes happen when an entity wishes to perform an educative service of love to two people who need to experience sorrow in order to grow. The Cayce readings hint that such may sometimes be the case.

Another interesting point—and one which is not merely implied but flatly asserted many times in the Cayce data—is that the moment of conception does not coincide with the entrance of the soul. The readings frequently counsel expectant mothers to watch their thoughts during the period of pregnancy, inasmuch as the character of their thoughts to some degree determines the type of entity attracted to them. The following extract illustrates this point of view:

Q. What mental attitude should I keep during the coming months?

A. It depends upon the type of entity you desire. If you wish a musical, artistic entity, then think about music, beauty, art. Do you wish it to be purely mechanical? In that case, think about mechanics—work with such things. And don't think this won't have its effect! Here is something that every mother should know. The attitude held during the period of pregnancy has much to do with the character of the soul that would choose to enter through this channel.

Moreover, it would seem from the Cayce data that the soul can enter the body shortly before birth, shortly after birth, or at the moment of birth. As much as twenty-four hours can elapse after an infant is born before the soul makes entry, and in some cases there are even last-minute changes with regard to the entity which will enter. It may at first glance seem inconsistent with the basic reincarnationist point of view to believe that a body can exist without its animating soul; however, there is here no necessary inconsistency. The body is called by the Theosophists the "vehicle" of the soul. Just as it is perfectly conceivable—to use an analogy suggested by the term—that an automobile chassis should be completed, its ignition turned on, and its motor running, even though the driver has not yet entered the car, similarly it is conceivable that a body can be structurally complete and its organic life processes already functioning, without the presence of the dweller who is to animate it.

To reason by analogy is, of course, not always a valid or conclusive procedure; but we are led to speculate in this manner only because we are confronted again and again in the Cayce readings with such curious assertions as this and have so insufficient a knowledge of the hidden processes of life that we are unable to account for them with scientific precision. Someone once asked Cayce the inevitable question: "What keeps the physical body alive until the soul enters?" The answer was cryptic, not to say obscure. "Spirit! For the spirit of matter, its source, is God."

Further clairvoyant research on this, and many other points, is needed. When such research is used, following up the varied implications of the Cayce data on childhood, child-parent relationships, and birth, we shall undoubtedly find ourselves in possession of a whole new science of eugenics, child psychology, and race improvement. Birth is far less of an accident than it might seem; childhood far less of a parenthesis. In this, as in so many other areas, the Cayce readings are exciting by virtue of the new horizons of inquiry they point to.

Chapter XVIII

Karmic Family Entanglements

AMONG the multitude of sorrows that befall men and women is the anguish of having brought into the world a defective child. Materially, it is a problem in extra care and expense; socially, it constitutes a kind of unspoken stigma; spiritually, it is a source of questioning the ways of God to men, and of deep anxiety for the welfare of the child.

To such parents the reincarnation principle can be a source of reassurance and courage. In the first place, it is evident on this principle that any abnormality is probably of karmic origin. There are a few instances in the Cayce files where a birth injury was pronounced to be non-karmic (a further discussion of this point will be found in the chapter on karma), but on the whole, birth deformities are highly indicative of some past-life transgression. Secondly, the connection between parent and afflicted child is almost always of karmic origin also. Again and again, in readings taken on children suffering with mongolian idiocy, deafness, water on the brain, and many other tragic afflictions, one finds the phrase: "This is karma, for both the parent and the child."

One of the most striking examples of this type of karmic bond is to be seen in the case of a Jewish girl of twelve who had suffered since early childhood with epilepsy—an affliction which is not only embarrassing at the time of seizure, but also productive of a deep-seated personality blight. According to the reading, this family triad of father, mother, and child was previously associated together in America at the time of the Revolution, in exactly the same relationship. The parents found it financially advantageous to throw in their lot with England rather than with the Colonists, and they made it their concern to gather information that would be of value to the Crown. The daughter was beautiful; she was reckless; she was clever. Such talents in combination were very convenient to the purposes of the parents; instead of restraining her, they prompted the daughter to turn her natural instincts for enticement to profitable political use.

Although the reading does not tell what the end of this singularly interesting drama was, it points out the consequences in the present lifetime; and we are led to reflect, in considering them, that if the mills of the gods grind slowly, they grind exceeding small. The life reading on the girl begins:

> The parents of this entity should parallel their past experiences through their own life readings in order to discover their opportunities and their obligations toward her.
>
> Each soul who sees the present hardships of this entity should realize that indeed *each soul meets itself;* and God is not mocked; and whatever a soul sows, that shall it reap.
>
> For the self-aggrandizements and self-indulgences of the past now find their expression in a physical condition of one who is reaping its own whirlwind. . . .
>
> Those who are now responsible for the entrance of the entity into this material plane were those who were then largely responsible for her failure to exercise due self-control, and, in fact, they allowed it for the sake of greater material gains. Consequently, they too are meeting in the present much that may be overcome in this experience.

In short, the daughter is meeting her former indiscretions of sexual excess in her present physical affliction. It is only fitting that the parents be charged with the care of one for whose waywardness they were largely responsible.

A second interesting case is that of a New York girl who was born blind. This little girl—an attractive child, to judge by her photographs—had some light sensitivity, but was unable to distinguish the forms of objects. A physical reading was requested by the mother; but as no life reading was taken on the child, we do not know the karmic cause of her affliction. However, the mother obtained a life reading on herself, and the reason for her obligation to the child was made clear.

It appears that the mother had been a teacher in her past life. And, to quote the reading, "the entity took advantage of

165

a situation that brought turmoil to a mother. And though the entity rose to a place in the hearts and minds of many—man looks on the outward appearance; God looks on the heart. In this present affliction you and your husband are meeting your own selves. For you once placed selfish purposes before God's laws."

We can only conjecture as to the exact nature of this dramatic intrigue, in which it would seem that the father was also involved. All that we know specifically is that a teacher exploited a mother to her own self-interest and at the expense of the mother's peace of mind. It seems likely that there are two distinct streams of destiny here. The woman who was exploited had herself some physical karma to meet in the form of blindness, probably from some antecedent life. The present life was selected for its expiation; and the present mother was chosen as the channel of entrance in order to be given an opportunity to meet her own personal karmic obligation.

A third interesting case is one of mongolian idiocy. Here again very little detail is supplied, but it seems clear that the mother's mockery of afflicted persons during an incarnation in Palestine was the karmic cause of attracting a defective child to herself in the present.

Another case concerns a premature infant born with the uncommon affliction known as "waterhead." The mother died a few days after having given birth, and the young, widower father placed the child in a Catholic home. When she was four years old he requested a physical reading on her. He writes: "She is very intelligent, understands everything, knows people by name, and can carry on a fairly nice conversation. She cannot walk, because of the weight of her head, and she must be careful how she holds it."

No life reading was taken on the little girl, and therefore there is no indication of the karmic nature of her affliction. However, the father had a life reading on himself in which he asked his previous relationship to the child. The answer was, briefly and sharply: "In the experience before this you could have helped and you didn't. You'd better help in the present." Unfortunately, there is not sufficient data in the body of the reading to establish the exact nature of his sin of omission. All we know of his last life is that he was a trader in Fort Dearborn, and that he "gained mentally and materially, and lost spiritually."

One inference suggests itself very strongly in connection with this case—namely, that indifference to human suffering causes destiny to place it upon our own doorstep. A human being may not be so callous as to commit a positive act of cruelty against another; yet he may be, like the souls whom Dante puts in Limbo, no more actively good than he is actively bad. Such an attitude in the presence of pain is not, perhaps, sufficiently active a sin to result in future physical deformity of his own. But he must somehow become sensitized; he must somehow learn concern for the afflicted ones of the earth; he must, in short, develop sympathy. And what better means could there be, since he himself does not merit affliction, than that he should become the parent of an afflicted child. Through the agony of watching the helpless ineptitude of his own offspring, he is given the opportunity to understand the agony of parents of afflicted ones, and the meaning of human pain.

If, after two successively more intimate opportunities to learn active charity he still remains indifferent, possibly the sin of omission will have assumed large enough proportions to generate affliction within his own body—and in the next life he may be born in some way afflicted himself. Such a sequence of events is nowhere stated explicitly in the readings, but it is strongly suggested in this and many other instances.

Cases such as the ones cited above show how karmic debts exist between parent and child; there can also be bonds of a karmic nature between child and child of the same family. In the Cayce files a curious case of sister-sister antagonism illustrates this point.

The relationship of the two girls in point had been marked since early childhood by jealousy, suspicion, and hate; quarrels flared continually between them, and on the slightest provocation. No such antagonism existed among the other brothers and sisters in this family of five children. From the Freudian point of view, the hostility between the two sisters would perhaps be explained on the basis of some infantile jealousy for the possession of the father. According to the Cayce clairvoyance, there was, as a matter of fact, deep-seated jealousy of a sexual nature on the part of one of the two women; but it was occasioned not by the present-life father, but rather by the past-life husband of the older girl.

In order to keep the personages of this rather complicated relationship clear, we had better give names to the three persons concerned, in their present-life relationship: Lou is the younger sister; Alice, the older sister; and Tom, the husband of Lou. When Lou asked in her life reading for an explanation of her previous relationship to her husband and sister (with both of whom she was having difficulties at the time) she was told of the following little drama.

The three had known each other well in the late Colonial

167

period in Virginia. Tom was then the husband of Alice. Lou, a sort of mothering angel in the community, had nursed Tom back to health at a time when his wife was for some unspecified reason separated from him. Lou's motives had been purely those of a sister of charity, but her kindness established a bond of understanding between herself and Tom which Alice resented bitterly when she discovered it. The unfounded resentment and jealousy soon developed into hate; and these corroding emotions cut so deep in the psyche of the embittered woman as to remain there even after the passage of centuries.

Rationally speaking, there was no need for Alice in the present life to hate her younger sister or to bully her. But deep in the unconscious recesses of her mind was the pattern of hatred. And in Lou, all the mechanisms of defense and retaliation were alerted by the unconscious also. Unwittingly they began to reenact the emotional drama of the past; unconsciously they became embattled females because once before they had had apparent reason for battle.

A second case of sibling bonds of a karmic nature concerns two English-born children who, during World War II, were cared for by an American woman who at the time was directing her own progressive school in a New England state. The boy was ten, the girl five, at the time of adoption. Their guardian, who was familiar with child psychology, both academically and through a lifetime of practical experience in educating children, became concerned over the marked hostility between the brother and sister. Apparently the brother was the principal aggressor. "He is extremely bright," the woman wrote in one of her letters, "but such a pathetic child —like a dog at bay, and using Nazi methods." She asked for a life reading on both children.

The reading disclosed the highly interesting fact that the two children were formerly members of opposing clans in an old and fiercely fought Scottish feud. Here again the animosity persisted like an undercurrent to the stream of consciousness, such that several centuries later the current of hate was still so strong as to give rise to antagonism between a ten-year-old boy and a five-year-old girl.

These two instances are sufficient to illustrate the principle involved, and to suggest both to individuals tortured by inexplicable animosities between themselves and their siblings, and to analysts confronted by such problems among their clients, a possible source of the difficulty. To be sure, there is good reason in any family for antagonism among members merely on the basis of contemporary irritations. The chemistry of temperament is such that incompatible elements which would merely be sources of indifference or mild dislike in casual encounters become insufferable and even explosive when in the crucible of intimate family life.

The critic of the reincarnationist view might point to this fact on one side and to the Law of Parsimony ("The simplest explanation is the best") on the other, saying that there is no necessity for postulating reincarnation to explain family hatreds when the facts are well explained as they now stand. To this objection most reincarnationists would fully agree were it not for their loss of faith in the Law of Parsimony as commonly interpreted. It undoubtedly serves and has served a useful purpose in keeping man's speculations about the universe in sobering restraint; but the expanded vision of the universe afforded by new discoveries in science, let alone the theoretical horizons of the reincarnationist principle, throws a glaring searchlight on the assumption that the "simplest" explanation must be correct, and shows that it may be a revelation of the simplicity of man's mind rather than an accurate reference to the simplicity of operations of the universe. What is now conceived to be "simple" may in the light of new facts prove to be merely fragmentary.

If the general reasonability of the whole reincarnation principle is accepted, the arguable details fall naturally into place. Though contemporary reason admittedly can be found for any antagonism between human beings, it is at the same time conceivable that the basis for the antagonism was laid many centuries ago.

It must be remembered, of course, that the uncovering of a past-life cause for antagonism does not of itself dissolve it. If the partners in the yoke of hatred do not wish to remain harnessed together, life after life, they must make a conscious, deliberate, and patient attempt to substitute love for hate, and kindness for animosity.

This admonition holds true not only of antagonisms that occur between members of the same family; it holds true of all antagonisms and all situational ties that bind us with individuals anywhere. In the last analysis, the constant transposition of role which we experience with regard to the family should show us that we are members, in ultimate reality, of no single family. We are members, rather, of the one great family of the human race; we should learn to live constantly in the awareness of that truth.

Chapter XIX

Past-Life Origins of Vocational Competence

Immortality—endless existence of the soul in a future state.
The Funk and Wagnalls New Standard Encyclopedia

IMMORTALITY is commonly conceived of in Christian theology as extending in only one direction—toward the future. In the light of new conceptions of timelessness afforded by fourth-dimensional physics, such a view seems somehow incomplete. Apart even from scientific speculations, and considering the matter only from the viewpoint of religious faith, it would seem that spirit must be essentially timeless and that consequently if the soul is deathless it must also be birthless. If it is to exist eternally in the future it must also have existed eternally in the past. The biological episode we delimit by the terms "birth," "life," and "death," must then be merely an appearance, so to speak, a projection, of the eternal non-material soul.

This view, though it has been largely rejected by modern Christian theology, was acknowledged by early Gnostic Christianity. A number of modern poets have given expression to the idea, the most quoted among them probably being Wordsworth in his "Intimations of Immortality." Wordsworth's feeling that our birth is but a sleep and a forgetting was, in the light of the ancient wisdom, thoroughly well-founded. His conviction that the soul that rises with us has elsewhere had its setting and cometh from afar has been aptly quoted by hundreds of believers in pre-existence. When he says, however, that "trailing clouds of glory do we come," a reincarnationist would wish he had spoken with a little less romanticism and a little more psychological realism. In an ultimate sense it is true of course that the soul comes originally from Divinity and therefore shares—forgetfully—in its pristine purity and splendor; and in the super-sensuous realm of the over-soul there may indeed be a divine radiance and beauty. The psychological facts of the matter, however, would seem to be, more prosaically and also more modestly and more inspiringly, that we do not come trailing clouds of glory so much as we come trailing a very substantial cargo of accumulated abilities and disabilities, defects and capacities, weaknesses and strengths.

Nowhere does the exactitude of the balance forwarded become more apparent than in the life readings that deal predominantly with vocational guidance. It has already been seen in the readings how the Continuity Principle operates so as to bring forward attitudes, interests, and qualities of character. It becomes apparent that the same principle operates with respect to human abilities and thus becomes an important factor in human occupational life.

A typical example from the readings can be seen in the past-life experiences of a fashionable beauty specialist of New York City. Her establishment is a luxurious salon devoted to figure reconditioning, hairstyling, and personality improvement; she herself is a very attractive and elegant woman. Three past lives were given in her life reading, only two of which seem to have a direct bearing on the vocational bent of the present. The first was in the French court, at the time of Louis XV, where she wielded much power over the court and over the ruler. Here she learned diplomacy and coquetry and much about the niceties of conduct, carriage, and personal adornment. Previous to that she had been, in Rome, among the first of the nobility to embrace Christianity; before that she had been in Egypt, about 13,000 B.C., where she was active in the temple service. Here she learned to cultivate a beautiful body through dancing, music, and art, and learned also how to prepare lotions, ointments, and powders for body beautification.

Experiences in the French court can frequently be noted in the readings to have an effect similar to the one apparent here; that is, they are generally conducive to a worldly, sophisticated outlook, and a talent for the niceties of social life. The woman's Egyptian temple experience requires some explanation. It seems that there were two principal temples in this particular Egyptian period. One of them was called the Temple Beautiful and the other the Temple of Sacrifice. Descriptions of them are to be found scattered through dozens of readings, and from all these piecemeal descriptions we can

171

form a fairly comprehensive notion of what they were like.

The Temple Beautiful was in the nature of a school or university; unlike most universities, however, this one took as its central concern not merely the cultivation of the intellect, but the expansion of the total human personality. All the arts and sciences were applied to the achieving of beauty of soul and beauty of body in its students, who were thus prepared to become active sources of influence in their own and other countries. The fact that it was called a temple suggests its religious or spiritual orientation; the fact that it contained seven centers or focal points of disciplinary training, corresponding to the seven *chakras* or inner organs of man, suggests that the curriculum and the architecture were planned on a basis of thorough occult knowledge.

Vocational guidance on a spiritual basis was one of the many functions of the Temple Beautiful, and many persons now interested in vocational counseling, personality development, or personality integration through art or religion are found to have been active there either as teachers or students. In many respects there is a very striking resemblance between this ancient Egyptian wisdom school and the magnificent conception of Boris Bogoslovsky in his remarkable book on education, *The Ideal School.*

The Temple of Sacrifice was more in the nature of a hospital, where electrical techniques (learned apparently from the Atlanteans) were used to perform surgical operations, and electrical frequencies were used to heal many conditions and minimize bodily deformities. The ideal of bodily perfection and racial improvement was the guiding principle here, and again the word temple suggests a spiritual orientation.

Turning now to the past-life occupations of a successful osteopathic physician, we find the following history. Four past lives were given, of which three provided tributaries to the vocational stream. First, he was a physician in early America, well acquainted with the Indians; from this contact he acquired his interest in natural remedies and herbal medication. (It can be frequently noted in the readings that people who have had previous close contact with the American Indians, or were themselves once American Indians, tend to love nature and wild life, to have an interest in handicrafts, and to lean toward natural methods of living and healing.) In his second life back he was a supervisor of baths and massages in the early Christian era; in the third life back he was in Persia, following an unspecified vocation; and in the fourth previous life, he was in Egypt in 13,000 B.C., as an embalmer.

This experience may have given him some acquaintance with the inner structure of the human body and with the effects of various herbs, spices, and other preparations on human flesh.

In another case, that of a Hollywood artist and color director in motion pictures, the reading describes the subject as a man who in three past lives pursued an artistic vocation. Four lives were given in all: as an interior decorator in late Colonial America, when the first mansions were being built; second, as an army officer, a Cossack, in Russia; third, as a decorator for the queen in Indo-China; fourth, as an interior decorator in the Temple Beautiful in Egypt. One gathers the impression as one reads of his Cossack incarnation that much of his verve, alertness, and perception of detail comes from this experience, when he loved to dress magnificently and make his personality felt. Thus many of the temperamental qualities that give dash and life to his work seem to have had their origin in an experience when occupationally he had no connection with art whatsoever. The more technical aspects of his proficiency arose from the three specifically artistic lifetimes.

A successful New York composer and arranger likewise had a past career of variegated but related experiences. He was, first, a teacher in early New York, responsible for establishing the first song and music classes as part of the daily curriculum of the schools; second, a German wood carver who made musical instruments; third, a buffoon to King Nebuchadnezzar in Chaldea; fourth, an Atlantean who went into Egypt and became active in the music of the temple worship. This man's present concern with the form, finish, and perfection of tone in musical instruments apparently stems from the wood-carver experience; his sense of fun and quickness of wit from the experience as court jester; his musical ability proper from two experiences as a musician.

Sometimes a man's hobby is found to be a throwback to a former incarnation. There is the case, for example, of a bank president who since boyhood has had a passion for sports of all kinds, but especially for baseball. When the pastor of the Baptist Church to which he belonged expressed vigorous disapproval of playing ball on Sunday, the banker promptly resigned from the church—a forthright example of religious integrity that has had illustrious precedents both before and after the time of Henry VIII.

Banking became this man's profession and the source of his affluence; his spare time, however, he devoted to the operation of a baseball club which has since become a training ground for the big leagues. It is interesting to note his past

173

occupational experiences: first, as an early settler who was concerned with importing and exporting goods; second, as a Roman who managed the state games of the arena; third, as a nomad leader in Persia who founded certain places of exchange; fourth, as a keeper of the treasury in Egypt. It will be noted that three of these lives had a direct contributory influence on his present profession of banking; the second one back, as manager of the Roman arenas, undoubtedly gave him much of the managerial ability that has stood him in good stead as bank president but also was the source of his impelling interest in outdoor competitive sport. The circumstances of his life were such that only as a hobby could he indulge this urge.

In another case, that of a food inspector in the Navy, the life reading explains the man's hobby rather than his profession of purchasing and inspecting food. All his life this man has had a consuming interest in stones and gems; he founded a gem exchange and has always been closely associated with gem cutters and collectors. Since retirement from the Navy, he has devoted all his time to this interest—further stimulated to do so by the strange encouragement given him by his Cayce reading. His past lives were given as follows: first, as a trader in trinkets and firewater with the Indians in Ohio; second, as a merchant in Persia, who traveled by caravan and dealt in the linens of Egypt, the pearls of Persia, the opal, firestone, and lapis lazuli of Indo-China, and the diamonds and rubies of the Cities of Gold; third, as a Hittite in the Holy Land who provided the precious stones used in the garments of the priests.

There are two points of special interest in this case. First, a basic principle of selection used by the readings is very markedly apparent—namely, the lives given were chosen by the criterion of *usefulness* to the subject. This man—who was near the retirement age at the time of his reading—was not given an account of those lives which had prepared him primarily for his work in the Navy; he was given rather an account of those lives which had a bearing on his hobby because in the field of gems there was still much constructive work that he could do.

He was told that, despite his long and ancient familiarity with gems he had never fully understood their true value. He had seen them as objects of beauty, as items worthy of collection or sale, and even as religious symbols when he provided them for the garments of the priests; but he had never seen their true significance. And this brings us to the second point of special interest in this reading, namely the disclosure that

174

gems have certain curative or stimulative properties by virtue of the vibrations which compose them.

There are many instances in the Cayce files, dated earlier than 1944 when this man's reading was given, of individuals who had been told to wear certain stones, gems, or metals for the sake of the vibratory influence they would have. In no case did the suggested stone correspond with the traditional birthstone of the calendar month. The exact principle of suitability escapes discovery, but the explanation was several times given that each stone and each element has its own atomic energy; the very elements of the body are atomic in nature also. The appropriateness of stone to individual must be determinable only through clairvoyant sight or through instruments not yet devised for that purpose.

This case, however, is the only one wherein an individual was advised to study the subject; and though the suggestion might, ten years ago, have seemed astonishing—indeed, fantastically absurd—our acquaintance now with atomic energy makes it credible at least. It should be noted, incidentally, that these allusions to the atomic energy of stones had been coming through the Cayce readings for almost twenty years before the scientific discovery of atomic power. The man in this case became profoundly interested in the matter and has since concentrated all his efforts along the lines of research sketchily outlined by the readings.

There are several other unusual departures made by the readings in the field of occupational counsel, on the basis of past-life experiences. One has to do with the designing of what the readings called "life seals"; the other has to do with electrotherapy. Both of these are described as revivals of the ancient art and science of Atlantis and Egypt.

The priests and priestesses who instructed in the Temple Beautiful in Egypt, either through clairvoyant perception or through analyses comparable to those made by contemporary psychology, were able to determine what life work was most appropriate for each student in view of his karmic problems and karmic gifts. The vocational choice made by the student on this basis determined the course of training he would receive. (These courses included training in dietetics, in its body-building, therapeutic, and regenerative aspects; physical culture; the art and science of dress; teaching, healing; spiritual ministry; music; art; oratory; arts and crafts; and meditation, including the use of music and odors.)

When the final decision was made as to the proper field of specialization, a "life seal" was made for the student by a

175

person trained in the art. This was a symbolic picture which represented the entity's past pattern of development and which served as a reminder to him of the purposes of his existence. This life seal or plaque consisted usually of a circle divided into three or four equal parts, each section containing a scene, image, or symbol signalizing a past incarnation in which the student had acquired some urge, talent, or strength of soul, or it represented some talent or strength of soul which he yet needed to acquire. The contemplation of these seals served to awaken or educe from the innermost self of each student the faculties latent there; it served also to awaken comprehension of his relationship to the creative force of the universe. The readings maintained that when the Hall of Records in Egypt would be discovered and opened, some time in the late twentieth century, some of these plaques would be brought to light.

A certain young woman was told that she had been active in the Temple Beautiful in three capacities: in providing the music used to raise bodily vibrations for meditating and healing; in devising body-beautifying diets; and in designing the life seals just described. She was told that she could be vocationally successful this time either as a nutritionist or as a musician; she was told further that, through the practice of meditation, she would be able to tap the same level of superconscious mind which enabled her in Egypt to see the history of a soul and chart its spiritual life goals in symbolic design. This girl has put both suggestions into practice. She has successfully made music her profession; she has also, through meditation, cultivated the ability to sense the proper elements for the life seal—an ability which she uses only in a noncommercial manner.

A third unusual departure in occupations is to be found in the frequent recommendation that persons take up a study of electrotherapy in combination either with chemistry, hydrotherapy, or music. Electrotherapy is, of course, already fairly common in our civilization. Its significance is seen in an unaccustomed light, however, as the readings recommend it as a career to several people on the basis of their Atlantean or Egyptian experiences.

It seems that in 10,000 B.C., at the time of the last of three cataclysmic destructions of Atlantis, a great many Atlanteans took refuge in Egypt. They brought with them, of course, their highly advanced knowledge of art and science; and though they were unable for various reasons to recreate their high-powered civilization, a remnant of their science became fused with the culture of Egypt. All the cases wherein some form of electrotherapy is recommended as a profession have in common, then, this interesting feature: they suggest a field of work which is relatively new to the civilization of the present, but well known to the ancients. The knowledge of this science has been lost to history but remains dormant in the unconscious memory of individuals who were in incarnation then, and active in that field.

In most cases of a passionate interest in flying, electronics, television, hypnotism, telepathy, atomic energy, and so forth, the basis for it is seen in the fact that this was the individual's occupation in Atlantis. By way of generalization from the readings it seems safe to say that in any instance of extraordinary interest or high success in a vocational field, there has been one or more previous incarnation spent in the practice of the same occupation, or closely related occupations.

The qualification "closely related" is necessary because of a number of cases of outstanding success in an occupation where there apparently was no previous experience in the same field. For example, a very successful woman writer whose articles appear in the most fashionable and popular women's magazines of America had four past incarnations, only one of which seemed concerned with writing, and that merely in a non-professional way. They were as follows: first, as an actress, a barnstormer, in early America; second, as a Christian who reported to other Christians the activities in Antioch; third, as a mother and homemaker in Palestine; fourth, as a teacher in the Temple Beautiful and an emissary to the "Gobi land."

This woman's writing style is simple, straightforward, and vivid. The reading attributes her abilities as a storyteller and entertaining reporter to her barnstorming experiences; her insight into mother-child relationships to the Palestine experience; her intuitive faculties to the Egyptian experience. The exact nature of her "reporting" activities in Antioch is not made clear, though the probability is that it was a matter of writing letters. Her narrative simplicity probably stems from that experience, though the reading does not comment on it.

Of course, as we know, not all previous lives were given in the readings, consequently we do not know whether the woman ever had an incarnation as a professional writer. However, judging from the four that were given, we would conclude that her various writing gifts stemmed rather from four different fields of activity, and that this was the first time she combined them into the profession of writing.

Many other cases lead to the conclusion that a new departure in vocational pursuits is by no means inimical to success, provided that the interest has been soundly founded in the past and certain related faculties have been developed. For example, there is the case of a man of thirty-one who, though already married, decided to take up the study of medicine. For some reason not made clear in his correspondence he had not studied medicine as a youth, even though his father was a doctor and he presumably had the opportunity and incentive to do so.

He obtained a reading from Cayce and was particularly anxious to know if his decision to study medicine at this late date was a wise one, and if it promised success. The reading emphatically reassured him on this score, and pointed out that his determination to become a physician had arisen during the American Revolution. His rank then was that of orderly and messenger, but apparently his sympathetic nature and gifts as a counselor induced his superior officer to entrust him with certain morale-building activities among the men. It was at this period that his yearning to be a physician arose. Apparently he was filled with pity at the physical suffering he witnessed, and wished that he had the knowledge to relieve it.

It is interesting to note that the entity chose a doctor for his present parent so that his own entrance into the medical profession might be facilitated. The reason for this delayed decision to study medicine is not made clear, though an early marriage may have been the cause of it; there may have been a tremendous karmic attraction, arising from some other incarnation, between himself and the girl, and with impetuous forgetfulness of other goals he may have obeyed the urge and married. There are other possibilities to account for the situation, of course; but the important point here is that the reading gave him assurance of success in a field which he was entering for the first time.

To sum up, then, analysis of the past-life origins of vocational competence indicates that such competence seems to have some basis in one or more past lives spent in the same or closely related fields. An ardently pursued hobby often gives indication of the fact that in some previous life it was the individual's vocation. Many apparently new professions are in reality the reappearance of ancient Atlantean and Egyptian arts and sciences. Some people seem to be attempt-

178

ing a new vocational field for the first time in their soul history. If an interest has been thoroughly developed in the past, and certain related abilities have been already cultivated, success in the field is entirely possible.

Chapter XX

A Philosophy of Vocational Choice

THE vocational histories in the Cayce files raise many questions in the mind of the thoughtful investigator. First of all there is the problem of beginnings—a problem which troubles most reincarnationists as they try to push back to the first emergence of the soul from God. What initially set off one soul in one occupational direction and another soul in another? If the spirits of men originally emanated from Divinity as equal and undifferentiated, why then should one start off in the direction of agriculture, another in trading, a third in textiles, a fourth in music, and a fifth in mathematics? Was there some minute element of individuality in each which led to the diversity of human activities that they chose —and if so, what determined that individuality?

Although the Cayce files provide no clear-cut answer to this question, they do furnish fairly satisfactory information with respect to another question that suggests itself—namely: what later causes a soul to change from one occupation to another? There are examples of many such changes in the Cayce filies, and an analysis of the pertinent data indicates that the transition can be accounted for by either of two basic factors: desire or karmic law.

In several previously cited cases, desire has been seen to be a force equal in strength to karma. It seems clear that a soul can begin to experience desire for a new talent or quality of being through contact with a person who expresses such a talent or quality. According to Cayce, many individuals who witnessed the ministry of Jesus in teaching and helping the sick and afflicted became inspired through a kind of contagion to wish to do likewise. The force of this desire carried them through several successive lifetimes in an effort to acquire a teaching or healing gift. Sometimes the desire takes form not primarily through the influence of an inspiring personality, but rather through an uncomfortable sense of inability in a stiuation requiring gifts that the person does not have. However aroused, desire would appear to be an important determinant of the soul's destiny. It gradually gathers momentum and takes more and more specific form and direction; finally, through the choice of suitable parents and a suitable environment, the soul is enabled to begin to perfect a new facet of its nature.

Perhaps it takes several lifetimes, as in the case of introversion and extraversion, fully to achieve a transition from one occupational proficiency to another under the impetus of desire. If this inference is correct, it should be an encouraging thought to people who feel themselves to be mediocre in their profession. Perhaps their mediocrity, by comparison with the excellence of others, is due to the fact that this is only their first or second attempt in an untried field.

In addition to desire, karma seems to be an important factor determining vocational change. It is obvious that the maturation of a crippling physical karma would interrupt the progress, let us say, of a successful career as a dancer, already of several lives' standing. In impeding the free expression of the one vocation, such an affliction would of necessity induce change to another, and possibly reawaken some other talent long-since buried.

The case of the girl lamed with tuberculosis of the hip joint described in Chapter V is just such an instance. For a long time after this girl was stricken, she wondered what occupation she should follow to be socially useful. She was told to study the harp; told also that she would have a natural gift for it because she had specialized in stringed instruments in an early Egyptian incarnation. The girl followed this advice, and, in fact, discovered that she had a distinct talent for the instrument, though it had never occurred to her to study it before. She has since given numerous concerts together with her sister, and though she has not achieved fame, she has at least realized a profession that keeps her happy and busy. The immediately preceding lives had been spent in other occupations, so it is clear that a physical karma here acted to interrupt one vocational sequence and to initiate, or revive, another sequence.

Another question that occurs is this: how many different occupations must a soul experience before his evolution (with respect to this planetary system) can be said to be complete?

It seems obvious that for a well-rounded development every soul must have worked at many different things; it seems highly unlikely that anyone could graduate from the solar system having reached perfection in art and having total ignorance of mechanics and medicine and sociology. It is conceivable that the Cosmic Board of Regents requires a certain number of credits in all these fields; but by what curricular arrangements all the courses for so large a student body are processed is another question.

Whatever the basic plan may be, this much at least seems clear: that there is a close inter-involvement in many cases between vocational problems and spiritual ones. That is to say, a vocational difficulty in many cases seems to be subordinate to some defect of character which needs to be corrected. A case in point is that of a forty-eight-year-old bachelor who, because of certain personality difficulties, found his profession of real-estate agent increasingly distasteful. He obtained a reading from Cayce for the purpose of discovering what change of occupation to make and was told that in the previous life he had been a teacher whose nature was imperious and dictatorial. This harsh rigidity of character had been carried over into the present and formed the basis of his difficulties in making easy social adjustments. The reading counseled him to remain in his occupation even though it was uncongenial; "for, while it is not always easy, you are learning a needed lesson."

There are many similar cases in the files and a reading of them recalls a reflection of Tolstoi. He remarked that the circumstances of life are very much like the scaffolding of a building. The purpose of these wooden platforms is merely to serve as an external skeleton through which the labor of inner construction can be carried on. But the outer framework has no ultimate importance in itself and no permanence. As soon as the building is completed, the scaffolding is removed. Perhaps vocations can be understood in this light —as the matrix through which some aspect of man's spiritual growth takes place.

Perhaps, on the other hand, vocations are not always subservient to the growth of some moral quality. Perhaps they are in themselves intrinsically necessary as realms of matter which need to be mastered by the spirit. Perhaps in each realm of activity man is learning to understand and master matter in one area of manifestation, learning to understand and work with the principles of life as they express themselves in one circle of the cosmic concentric circles. Perhaps this mastery—of medicine, music, agriculture, art—is essential to his becoming ultimately a co-creator with God, a poised, pure, and potent spirit, a harmless, radiant, loving and creative center of expression, capable himself of generating forms and lives and worlds.

Such a cosmic perspective as this is exciting. When we return to the tangible exigencies of daily life, however, we are still faced with the very practical question: How can persons who do not know their vocational past, and who have no clairvoyant insight into the central spiritual lesson of their lives, make a wise vocational choice? An individual professionally interested in this problem once requested a research reading from Cayce on the subject. The question was asked whether a psychological test could be devised that would serve to make systematic exploration into the past-life urges and thus give vocational guidance to persons whose previous incarnations were not specifically known. The answer indicated that an astrological chart would be helpful in many cases, but that since astrology as now generally practiced does not take into account previous earth incarnations, interspersed between astrological sojourns, the data would be to a large degree unreliable. "For," says the reading, "in much of the populace, the proper vocation is dependent upon what the individuals have done with their astrological urges during the earth incarnations. In some cases it is in keeping with the horoscope; in others it is only partially so, in others still it is diametrically opposed, because of the earth activities."

This information is of considerable interest and, if taken seriously, could lead to fruitful scrutiny of certain unexplored areas of astrological science. But until these areas have been charted we are left facing the same basic problem: i.e., our inability, without clairvoyant sight, to know each individual's past incarnations, and our consequent inability to steer him to a vocational choice appropriate to his latent abilities.

Bewilderment with respect to vocational choice is extremely widespread. Like an actual physical handicap, however, this indecision may have an educative purpose; it may be necessary for the closer scrutiny of the meaning of life and of work, and a more spiritual grasp upon the meaning of selfhood in relation to other selfhoods. While some entities seem to enter the earth plane with so clear-cut a vocational purpose as to manifest itself at an early age, others may be in some transitional stage which requires reformulation of concepts. Therefore they need to undergo a period of doubt and confusion, for these are always the necessary preludes to clarity and strength. This explanation for vocational bewilderment seems highly presumable from all the available evidence;

though the Cayce readings here, as elsewhere, are not explicit.

In one respect, however, the information gleaned from the Cayce data has an unmistakable value: It is suggestive both of new directions for psychological research and of new attitudes in the approach to a vocational problem. Somebody once asked an Irishman if he knew how to play the violin. "I don't know," was the Irishman's reply, "I've never tried it." This brash answer is not so absurd as it may appear. It was made out of pure untutored wit, but a study of the Cayce readings would seem to show that it contains at the same time the distilled essence of unconscious wisdom. For no man knows what gifts lie dormant in the secret storerooms of his mind.

It is a curious fact that in banks all over the country there are millions of dollars in saving accounts whose owners in most cases have forgotten their existence. After accounts have been inactive for a certain period of time, the bank authorities make an effort to trace the depositors through their last-known address. If this effort fails, the bank is obliged to place the amount of deposit in what is known as a "dormant ledger." This is perhaps a startling fact, especially in a nation of people whose interest in money is notorious, and yet it is a true one. These dormant accounts represent a situation which is apparently comparable to the life situation of man.

The Cayce files reveal many instances where a faculty or talent had apparently lain, long forgotten, in the subconscious vaults of memory. The reading served to draw the person's attention to that faculty; the individual's effort to reawaken it resulted, in a surprising number of cases, in a genuine vocational competence. The facility of acquisition here constitutes an inferential argument for previous life experience along those lines. The knowledge of this fact can give all of us a sense of having a reserve force in our subconscious, much as if we had been told of a forgotten savings account in the town of our childhood. Even in a general sort of way this should be a helpful idea; to be of any practical value, however, for the choice of a vocation, the information needs to be more particularized. If clairvoyant help such as Cayce's is available to us, we are fortunate; if not, it should be possible for us to tap the deeper layers of memory, through suggestion, hypnosis, or meditation, in order to discover in what fields our previous abilities lay.

Another mode of discovering and releasing our unknown faculties would seem to be through the practice of pursuing hobbies. Any impelling interest very probably streams from activity in a previous lifetime: an extravagant interest in things Spanish argues an incarnation in Spain; in things Chinese, an incarnation in China. The cultivation of such interests through a class in the Spanish language or a lecture course on China might serve to stir the deep unconscious memory and reawaken faculties acquired in that lifetime. It might also lead us to people with whom we have had previous connections in the same lifetime from which our common nostalgic interest springs. It is through people, principally, that the course of our life is changed. The meeting with persons with whom we have had ancient karmic ties may completely revolutionize our lives by opening up spheres of activity which otherwise would have been closed to us.

Bewilderment with respect to vocational choice can be occasioned not only by paucity of gifts, but also by versatility. It appears that some people have had so many incarnations in so many fields, and have through intense application acquired so great a competence in each, that they are torn between one and the other. Many a gifted young man or woman is tortured by the sense of indecision and aimlessness, despite the wealth of his gifts.

The logical first step in vocational choice is, of course, to take inventory of one's abilities, be they many or few, and make a choice among the strongest of them. This is the very sensible answer of psychologists, who have devised exact measuring scales by which to gauge human talents. The Cayce readings, though they do not speak with numerical precision in such matters, subscribe to the same view as vocational psychologists, and usually indicate in highlighted form the individual's outstanding abilities.

In cases of vocational uncertainty, however, or in cases where a special admonition seemed necessary, the readings' underlying philosophy of vocational choice becomes apparent. Three concepts are repeated so frequently as to suggest themselves as the core of this philosophy. The first of these concepts is this: *Determine your ideal, your inner life goal, and seek to accomplish it.*

The formulation of ideals is an integral part of the whole Cayce philosophy of adjustment; it has special pertinence, however, with respect to vocational self-direction. The readings are insistent that one should be explicit about one's ideals; as an aid to concrete thinking they repeatedly suggest taking a piece of paper, making three columns headed Physical, Mental, and Spiritual, and writing beneath them the highest goal to which one aspires in that department of being. Here are some typical quotations:

In analyzing yourself and your ideal, do not merely carry them in your mind, but put them down on paper. Write "Physical," draw a line, write "Mental," draw a line, write "Spiritual." Put under each, beginning with the spiritual (for all that is in mind must first come from a spiritual concept), what is your spiritual concept of the ideal, whether it be Jesus, Buddha, mind, material, God or whatever is the word which indicates to you your spiritual ideals.

Then under the mental heading write the ideal mental attitude which arises from your spiritual concept, in relationship to yourself, your home, your friends, your neighbors, your enemies, to things and conditions.

What is your material ideal then? . . . In this way an individual analyzes himself. Then set about to apply the knowledge you have attained.

The beginning is to determine your ideals. Set them down in black and white. Take yourself in hand and draw a picture. You're a pretty good engineer and good at drawing pictures of other things. Did you ever try a picture of yourself? How far do you actually span from what you would like to be, or from what you would like others to think you are? What is your mental ideal? Remember that in the material plane, mind is the builder.

In short, the readings recognize that our ideals must of necessity be various, by that true integrity of being and true self-direction are possible only through the clear-cut formulation of goals. From this conceptual realm our vocational choice should stem.

The second concept of the Cayce philosophy of vocational choice is this: *Strive to be of service to others.* How can I best be of service to humanity? should be, finally, the guiding principle of all persons as they make their vocational choice. Ultimately all of us must learn to see ourselves as cells in the body, not of a militant State, but of humanity itself. "Service to others is the highest service to God," is a frequent refrain of the readings. "He that would be the greatest among you will be the servant of all," is another.

That the readings consider this to be the final ideal, toward which all our temporary ideals must tend, erasure after erasure, is very explicitly seen in the following statement:

For there is only one ideal, and that is to make the Creative Energy of the Universe (called by many names) your ideal; and to make your body, your mind, and your soul an active force for service to that Energy and to your fellowmen.

As a necessary corollary to this theorem is the proposition that financial security, fame, and success in the worldly sense should be secondary to the goal of service, and that they will follow it as the wheel follows the ox. A thirteen-year-old boy who had a variety of gifts from which to select, asked: "Which of my aptitudes should I follow for the greatest success in adult life, financially?" He was told: "Forget the financial angle and consider rather which is the best outlet for the greatest contribution you can make toward making the world a better place in which to live. Efforts should never be expended purely for mercenary reasons. Pecuniary gains should come as a result of the entity's using his abilities in the direction of being helpful."

Another individual asked: "In what field of endeavor am I most likely to succeed financially?" He was given this reply: "Leave off the 'financially.' Let the financial be the result of honest, sincere desire to be and live so that others may know the way also. Good gives the increase." An exporter and importer was told: "Then let your watchword be: service to my fellowman, that those whom I contact may use my steps as a ladder to assist *them*, and I not using *them* as stepping-stones. Let fame and fortune (for both are sure to come as results) be a *result* of a life well spent and service well rendered, rather than using others as stepping-stones to fame and fortune."

One is reminded of the story told of the great architect, Sir Christopher Wren. It is said that one day he was passing the site of the great new cathedral of London for which he had made the design. Building was already in progress, and, curious to know how the workers regarded the task in which they were engaged, he stopped several of them in turn and asked them all the same question: "What are you doing?" The first man looked up and remarked, shortly, "I'm laying bricks." The second said, "I'm earning a few shillings." The third replied, "I'm helping to build a great cathedral." It is toward the attitude of the third man, who had in view not the physical task nor the monetary reward, but the conceptual goal of beauty and well-being for all men, that the Cayce readings seek to lead those who are attempting to make a vocational choice.

187

The third basic concept in the Cayce vocational philosophy is this: *Use that in hand; start where you are.* This may seem like advice so obvious as to be unnecessary; and yet, like many other obvious truth, it is under the necessity of being restated because of the human tendency to disregard simple, near-by facts when complex and distant ones are so much more intriguing.

Many people, once they have caught the vision of service to humanity, become enveloped either in a haze of vague idealism or in a flurry of anxious zeal. Their new perspective on life's purpose may catch them in the middle of a worldly career from which there is no practicable way of extricating themselves; their responsibilities to a family or financial barriers which prohibit the acquisition of specialized training seemingly exclude them from fulfilling their newly conceived sense of mission. It is people such as these that the readings frequently find it necessary to remind of the fact that *one can only use what one has at hand.* A journey of a thousand miles begins with one step; that step must be taken from the point at which one now stands.

The following illustrative extracts are typical. A woman of forty-nine asks: "What is my true life work?" and is told: "Encouraging the weak and the faint; giving strength and courage to those who have faltered." "How may I get into this work?" she asks next. "Do *today* the things your hands find to do!" she is told. "What do you see in store for me and where would it be best for me to fulfill my destiny?" she persists. "What have you in hand today?" the reading reiterates. "Use that which you have where you are. Let Him guide your ways. Put yourself into His hands. You be the channel; don't tell Him where you would like to work or labor or serve or be served! Say, rather, 'Lord, I am yours. Use me as you see fit.'"

Another woman is preoccupied with the same matter. She is sixty-one, the wife of a former consul to one of the north European countries, with a long and varied life of travel in the Orient and much artistic and religious study behind her. "Please give a detailed account as to how I can best serve humanity," she asks. The answer given her is substantially the same. "In those ways that open to you day by day. It isn't always the individual that plans to accomplish some great deed that does the most. It is the one who meets the opportunities and privileges which are accorded it day by day. As such opportunities are used, there are better ways opened. For what we use in the way of helpfulness to others, increases in itself." "Begin where you *are!*" another person is told. "Be what you should be *where you are!* and when you have proven yourself, He will give you better ways!"

This philosophy of practical economy—known to every capable housewife who must make the most of what she has to work with—is applicable not only to persons who suddenly have discovered that they wish to be of service to humanity; it is applicable also to all persons who long for great achievement of any kind. It seems, in fact, that the readings' endless insistence on *using that in hand* and *starting where you are* is an effort to counteract two tendencies in human nature: the paralysis of short-view ignorance, and the paralysis of long-view knowledge.

Many a man knows exactly what accomplishment in art or science or politics he would like to achieve, but—because of a mistaken, materialistic myopia—becomes discouraged and inactive; his goal seems impossible of attainment. Out of his ignorance of the continuity of life and of effort, he does not realize that time is unimportant and that what is begun in one life often finds fruition in the next. By the illusory restrictions of time, it may be admittedly impossible for him to become a great musician in the present lifetime; but if he permits this thought to paralyze his will to such an extent that he drops music completely, he thereby puts himself at a standstill and leaves just that much undone for other incarnations. If, however, he applied the long-view wisdom compressed into the admonition *use that in hand; start where you are,* his paralysis is dissolved and his energies liberated in the proper direction.

On the other hand there are many persons who become intellectually excited at the tremendous vista of progress opened up to them by the reincarnation principle, yet do not translate this mental enthusiasm into daily practical conduct. Many Theosophists and Anthroposophists become so engrossed in the study of the cosmic laws under which spiritual evolution operates that they forget that their own spiritual progress is not automatically taken care of through the knowledge of the laws thereof. They are much like a man who is so engrossed in studying a road map that he never starts on a trip. Abstractions have become so much their life-blood that when it comes to performing some actual transmutation of character or some useful service to mankind, they are conspicuous by their intellectual absence. It is not only Theosophists and Anthroposophists who are guilty

189

of this frailty, of course; even before the time of Hamlet, in-action has notoriously been the sin of philosophers.

In the three principles which seem to be the core of the Cayce vocational philosophy, we find that the unobstructed cosmic outlook on human destiny of the readings is complete-ly balanced by down-to-earth common sense. There is, of course, no reason why the knowledge of reincarnation should unhinge anyone's mental equilibrium; on the contrary, there is every reason why it should render his every decision saner and sounder because it is made in accordance with an ethical and cosmic frame of reference. It is true that the first ac-quaintance with the reincarnation idea and its vast expansion of horizons is sometimes so inflating that it leads people to begin soaring without the necessary ballast of common sense. A study of the Cayce philosophy of vocations should correct any misconception on this score, and demonstrate that no matter how all-embracing one's concept of human destiny be-comes, the fact still remains that self-perfection is a slow, daily, inch-by-inch process.

Moreover, one is constantly reminded by the Cayce read-ings that whatever one's circumstances may be, they are com-pletely appropriate to one's inner stage of unfoldment. Even though they may seem to be an obstacle to the practice of one's true vocation in life, one must recognize them as step-ping-stones rather than stumbling-stones. The only way to change outer circumstances is through the patient alteration of one's self upon the resistant material of those circum-stances, such as to be worthy of better ones. Says one read-ing:

Know this: that whatever situation you find yourself in, it is what is necessary for your development. An entity must apply in its associations from day to day a word here and a word there, one today, another to-morrow and the next day, with the understanding that from such activities in word and deed, self-development will come.

Little by little, brick upon brick, is the structure built. By words of mouth, by little acts day by day, an individ-ual gives expression to its discernment and builds surely towards a complete expression of its knowledge, of its latent abilities, and of its true purpose. When an entity has prepared itself through constant forward movement towards service, the necessary circumstances for change will come about so that he may see the next step, the next opportunity.

Build, then, with that in hand, little by little, line upon line. Haste not and be not over-anxious; for is not the whole of the building of His making? . . .

Chapter XXI

Implications of the Data on Human Abilities

THE implications of the Cayce data on human abilities and their continuous development from life to life are of considerable practical importance. For one thing, they offer one a sense of the illimitable possibilities for expansion that lie before one, dependent on individual efforts.

We have already spoken of the dormant ability-accounts which can be drawn upon to the extent of one amount or another. Naturally the resources which each individual commands are entirely dependent upon the amount of effort previously deposited, so to speak, in the bank of life. It is obvious that this system must work forwards as well as backwards. Just as we are assured of an exact present reckoning with regard to the past, similarly we are assured of an exact future reckoning with regard to the present. Whatever time and energy and thought and attention we put into the acquisition of a talent now, shall stand on our account book to our credit in the future.

All over the world there are thousands of wistful, obscure people who pursue some youthful dream despite their certain knowledge that they will never fully achieve it. If they are regarded from the ordinary point of view, there is something infinitely sad about their futility; but their pathos becomes less pathetic when we regard them in the light of the karmic Continuity Principle.

An old man's loving efforts to make flowers grow may not bring him dahlia prizes or national recognition in the horticulture magazines; yet he is laying the foundations for botanical and horticultural knowledge now that some day, in some future life, may make him the plant wizard of his age. A middle-aged woman's fuzzy attempts at art serve not only as a never-failing subject for the wit of her family and friends; they serve also as a basis for a competency that may some day enable her to paint the Sistine Chapel of a future epoch. The teacher who patiently gives piano lessons year in and year out, plodding dimly along, with all hopes of a concert career long withered and dead, may be still walking if only she knew it the path that leads to world applause and fame. The beat of the metronome is building into her subconscious an exact sense of rhythm; the yearly repetition of velocity studies, finger exercises, preludes, sonatinas, inventions, and fugues is cutting deep harmonic grooves in her musical memory. Another life or two or three and perhaps she will be the virtuoso of her day, amazing her contemporaries with her instinctive powers of invention and improvisation, her extraordinary sense of time.

In short, according to the reincarnation concept, *no effort is ever wasted.* If karma works with impartial exactitude to penalize us for evil conduct, it works with equally impartial exactitude to reward us for constructive effort. The realization of this very important fact can so polarize our consciousness as to make despair virtually impossible. At every instant we are creating our own future and dictating the terms of that future. It shall be positive or negative, depending entirely on whether we at this instant are making positive, constructive efforts, or are being negative through capitulating to the error of the apparent.

This concept has several important corollaries. First of all it leads clearly to the proposition that the concluding portion of life, known as "old age," need not be a period characterized by resignation, inactivity, and a feeling of general uselessness. "Old age," as we commonly think of it, is a superstition. In the Egypt of 10,000 B.C. the common life expectancy was, according to the Cayce readings, far over one hundred years, and knowledge of the principles of proper diet and proper thought habits made senility of much later and much less marked appearance. Modern scientific evidence is accumulating to confirm this seemingly exaggerated report. Our experimental laboratories are already making revolutionary discoveries in the effects of food on health, strength, and longevity, and undoubtedly it will soon be demonstrated that the marks of decrepitude are due in large part to faulty eating, living, and thinking habits, and also in large part (from the discoveries of psychosomatic medicine in mind-body relationships) to the psychological expectancy of uselessness, to a sense of having reached a limit, of having been supplanted in life by youth.

This attitude of mind is due to what may be called the horizontal view of life—or the habit of comparing oneself with others on the horizontal level of space and time. But by the reincarnation principle the only true view of life is the vertical one. Comparisons with those younger than ourselves are not only odious; they are unnecessary. For all of us in reality are striving to surpass only ourselves. In a certain sense our progress is not relative to other people; it is relative only to ourselves and to God.

A full realization that this is so cannot but release us from all anxiety with regard to those who find themselves at a different and presumably more advantageous point in the immediate life cycle than our own. Competition is no more than an illusion of the materialistic. In spiritual reality, we are in competition with no one but our own lesser self.

Although the exact structure that society will assume in future years cannot be foreseen, it seems likely that the custom of retirement from active wage-earning at a certain age will persist at least until knowledge about youth preservation is far more highly advanced. In any case, no matter what the social arrangements, a person of advancing years should by no means regard himself as being put on the shelf along with the moth balls and last winter's blankets. He should, on the contrary, tranquilly devote his time to the cultivation of new faculties and new talents, or the study of things which the pressures of family responsibilities or professional duties never permitted him before. He should do this in the confident assurance that he is thereby laying a foundation for the inner wealth of future incarnations. This is one of the several possible interpretations of Jesus' admonition to lay up treasures not on earth, but in heaven—heaven referring to the state of liberated consciousness, and its treasure referring to faculties of mind and spirit.

That this is the point of view of the readings is evident both implicitly and explicitly. We have already seen the case of the man approaching sixty who was told to engage in intensive study of the healing properties of gems. Cases such as this are numerous in the files. A policeman approaching retirement age was told to study chemistry with a view to being useful as a detective. A grandmother of sixty-three was told to be active in helping young people find their place in life. Another grandmother, also sixty-three, was told not only to enlarge her flower business, already established for a good

194

many years, but to cultivate her abilities in writing as well —an idea that had never occurred to her.

Explicitly, the readings frequently discuss our obligation to be constructive to the very end of life. Here are a few typical extracts:

> Be moderate in all things, go not to excess in any, and you will have ninety-eight years of expectancy in this life—that is, if you so live as to deserve it. But what can you give to others? Unless you have something to give, what right have you to be in the way of others? Have something to give and you will live as long as you are worthy.

> Q. How can I best prepare for old age?
> A. By preparing for the present. Let old age only ripen you. For one is always just as young as the heart and the purpose. Keep sweet; keep friendly; keep loving, if you would keep young.

> Q. How can I overcome the fear of advancing old age and of being alone?
> A. By going out and doing something for somebody else; that is, for those not able to do for themselves; making others happy, forgetting yourself entirely. In helping someone else you'll get rid of your fears.

> Q. What hobby do you suggest?
> A. The hobby of helping somebody else. Working out of doors with flowers would also be a good hobby for you; but do plan each day to do a good deed for somebody else who is not able to do things for himself. If it's nothing more than conversation or keeping company with someone who is "shut-in," you will find great help for yourself therein.

The continuity of life, then, assumed so vaguely and unrealistically by the common notions of immortality, becomes by the reincarnation principle psychologically meaningful with regard to human talents and efforts.

A second important corollary to the truth that all talents are self-earned and persist from life to life is the proposition that envy is an unnecessary emotion. When Emerson remarked that there comes a time in every man's education when he realizes that envy is ignorance, he was voicing a truth whose Brahmic force is fully understandable only by the knowledge of reincarnation. Only those can be envious

195

who are ignorant of the fact that what man has done, man can do; what others possess in beauty, ability, love, fame, or wealth, are all possible to me as well, as soon as I have put forth the necessary efforts to deserve them.

In our present level of civilization and spiritual understanding, envy often stimulates to action where other motives fail to function. However, when envy leads to malice, hatred, disparagement, slander, resentment, and all their kindred meannesses, it is evil. Versatility in another is perhaps the most bitterly envied of all things; the man or woman who seeks to prove his worth to the world in more fields than one, and achieves some degree of eminence in all of them is, by geometrical progression, more envied, and by more people, than the man or woman who achieves eminence in only one. He seeks admiration through his versatility, and to some degree he receives it. He gets lip tribute at least; but in men's heart of hearts, he reaps enmity and rancor because he deprives them progressively (as they think) of their own claim to worth.

When it becomes generally known, however, that all talents are within the reach of all of us, then envy should decrease and genuine versatility increase among men. The spiritual order of the universe, unlike certain economic systems, does not demand that a few shall have, at the expense of multitudes who do not. All resources are equally available to all men, provided they use them selflessly and purely.

Moreover, a knowledge of the facts of vocational development should serve not only to decrease the separative sense of envy, but also to increase the unitive sense of appreciation. The fact that other human beings are expressing aspects of our Self which in our present incarnation we are too occupied with other matters to be able to express, is indeed deserving of appreciation. The woman, for example, who is confined by the *dharma* or duty of her present life to housework may yearn in her inmost soul to have been a dancer; there are moments, after witnessing the ballet sequence of a movie, or seeing photographs in the press of dancers caught in exquisite motion, when she bitterly resents the destiny that compels her to cook and dust rather than dance. But if she recalls that after only a few centuries or so—perhaps less— she, too, shall dance, the sting of her envy should dissolve, and she should feel instead a surge of gratitude to the dancers for being her Self in the interim. *Tat twam asi* (Thou art That) is a Hindu aphorism of profound and various applications; one of its more immediate meanings is that in looking on all varieties of human accomplishment we are looking upon externalizations merely of the potencies of our own soul. . . .

A third important corollary to the principle of vocational growth from life to life is the proposition that, like envy, the sense of frustration is to some degree unnecessary. As long as spirit is confined to the world of form, there will, of course, be some sense of frustration; as long as a fragment of divinity inhabits the form of a daisy, it must be a daisy and not a dahlia. A lily may view with longing the vivid coloring of a rose, a rose may pine with passion for the classic lines of a lily. Each, though perfect of its kind, cannot but accept the limitations of its own form.

But, except in poetic fancy, flowers do not wither and die for longing to be other than what they are. Men and women do not usually die of it either, but they suffer; and when the frustration is sufficiently acute, and their mental organization sufficiently sensitive, they can fall into mental and even physical disease because of it.

On the other hand, frustration, like envy, has its important psychological function. If necessity is the mother of invention, we can with equal right say that frustration is the mother of creation. Out of it songs have been written, drugs discovered, continents explored. When Bulwer-Lytton described his utopian country as being without literature—because, since nobody knew frustration of any kind there was no desire to write or to read about the sufferings or satisfactions of others—he was touching on a significant possibility. Frustration, like compression placed upon steam, serves to channelize the energies of man into forms they might otherwise never have taken out of sheer freedom of dispersion. In short, like all other realities of the manifest universe, frustration has its polarity of beneficent and maleficent aspects. Where it compels man to develop new qualities and create new artistic forms, frustration is good; where it causes man to lose inner balance, such that the life force stagnates within him, it is bad. It is this latter, maleficent aspect of frustration that the belief in vocational continuity from life to life serves to counteract.

There is a story told about a snail who, one bitter cold morning in January, started to climb the frozen trunk of a cherry tree. As he slowly moved upward a beetle stuck his head out of a crack in the tree and said, "Hey, buddy, you're wasting your time. There aren't any cherries up there." But snail kept right on going. "There will be when I get there," he said.

Something of the calm, patient, long-view confidence of the snail becomes the inner attribute of the person who is thoroughly persuaded of the principle of vocational continuity. Another pointed illustration of the proper attitude of mind is to be found in an episode in the life of Paganini, the great violinist. For two years, the story goes, he was confined to a debtor's prison. Somehow, while there, he came into possession of an old three-stringed violin; ceaseless practice upon the mutilated instrument was the only way he had of whiling away the time. When he finally emerged from his cell to freedom, and appeared once again on the public platform, he played with a fury and perfection never before attained. He electrified his audience with a virtuosity unmatched before or since. His unheard-of feat—breaking one string of his violin in the midst of a difficult selection, and concluding it on only three strings—originated in those two years of enforced solitude.

Paganini's imprisonment imposed on him a real and unmistakable frustration, but his reaction to it was positive rather than negative. For a long time to come, man will necessarily know frustration through the self-imposed correctives of karma and through the very conditions of manifest existence. But frustration need neither shrink us nor stunt us nor crush us; we can learn to dance even within its fetters and to sing even within its prison walls. Where frustration is inescapable, we can learn to accept it patiently, positively, even joyously, and thus lay the groundwork for our own future victories in civilizations that still slumber in the matrix of time.

Chapter XXII

Personality Dynamics

LIKE the plot of a well-written story, life is interesting because of its conflict. For primitive man, conflict consisted largely in struggle against other men or against the forces of nature. As man advanced on the evolutionary scale, however, his conflicts rose more and more from inner sources. This inner struggle has been described, in various eras, as the opposition between good and evil, between spirit and matter, between reason and passion, between conscience and impulse, or between conscious mind and unconscious mind.

All these descriptions contain truth; they do not, however, explain conflict in the full sense of the reincarnationist point of view. By this view, the primary source of conflict is the mistake a spirit makes when it identifies itself with the level of spiritual density called "matter," through which it must express itself in order to evolve. This false identification leads to self-ish and separative conduct, and this in turn leads to the operation of the retributive aspects of karma. Karmic action objectifies man's evil conduct in such a manner that he himself becomes imprisoned within it; this imprisonment is therefore the first and fundamental source of the mental anguish of man. His struggle against the invisible bars of his self-imposed prison cell constitutes the primary form of inner conflict.

The Cayce readings clearly state that there is still another source of conflict. It must be remembered that karma has two aspects, the retributive and the continuitive. By the latter aspect many incongruous elements or urges can be brought forward from the past at the same time, forming another source of conflict in the inner world of man.

In the Cayce readings, an urge means a strong impulse or desire arising from some past-life experience. For instance, an individual may carry over from one life an urge to musical expression; from another life, the urge to teach. These contradictory impulses give rise to a conflict in his conscious mind in the realm of vocational choice. Shall he be a musician or a teacher? For years he may be torn by an exhausting inner struggle over what to do; the struggle may finally be resolved by a combination of both urges, or the abandonment of both in favor of something else, in line with some newly conceived life goal or in line merely with economic necessity.

A struggle still more difficult than that occasioned by contradictory impulses arises when an urge has been incompletely neutralized. For example: a man may have an urge toward arrogance, derived from some previous life experience in which he possessed arbitrary power over a repressed people. In a succeeding life as a crippled slum child, the arrogance was called to a karmic halt and the contrary attitude of tolerance and sympathy was to some degree induced. The cancelation or neutralization, however, was not complete. As a consequence, there are now two contradictory impulses welling up in consciousness with respect to the same basic trait. Therefore we see in the personality an apparent inconsistency, expressing itself in alternate attitudes of arrogance and tolerance. The individual himself gradually becomes aware of his own inconsistency; if ideas as to the brotherhood of man become active within him, he will more consciously begin the struggle to quell the upsurge of the ancient arrogance. In many people, however, awareness of their own inconsistency is lacking.

This generalization on the incomplete neutralization of urges is made on the basis of both extensive and intensive study of cases in the Cayce files. Innumerable single fragmentary clues support it, and several cases of individuals observed at first-hand over a long period of time in the light of their life reading confirm it. Perhaps the most clear-cut single example is the following case.

There are in this man's personality two basic personality contradictions. The first is a contradiction between the tendency to be at some times seclusive, introvertive, silent, cold, unsocial, studious, other-worldly; and at other times genial, extravertive, expansive, jovial, and sensual. According to the reading, this peculiar discrepancy is due to two distinct streams of experience. An incarnation as a monk in an English abbey gives him his unsocial tendency; a preceding one as a Crusader during the Middle Ages, his joviality. So strange a duality of temperament to some degree alienates people from him; they become hesitant to entrust their confidence to the expansive companion of today who tomorrow may regard them with cold reserve.

The second personality contradiction seems to arise clearly from an incompletely neutralized urge. In one of this man's incarnations his position was that of a ruler in Egypt. An air of patronizing hauteur, of detached and almost contemptuous superiority, had its origin in that experience. But in a succeeding incarnation, he lived in Palestine and came closely under the influence of the carpenter named Jesus. So impressive was the personality of the great teacher that the man acquired from the relationship a strong urge toward social service, and a reasoned conviction as to the brotherhood of man.

In the present life, this latter urge is predominant; he chose for his life task leadership work in the religious and social service field. As an initiator of new modes of bringing light to the populace, his efforts are untiring; as a counselor, he is kindly, helpful, superlatively effective. And yet he is engulfed from time to time with the fierce hauteur of his Egyptian experience, for the urge had been incompletely neutralized by the Palestine and other succeeding life experiences. Becoming aware of its lurking presence, he struggles to suppress it because he knows it to be discordant with his personality ideal. In the course of this struggle he becomes an integrated personality rather than a disintegrated one; and in this manner the front of his unredeemed nature gradually advances in line with his newly conceived goals of self-perfection and service.

An awareness of inconsistency such as this one, a decision as to which personality tendency is the most desirable, and an effort to overcome its antithesis would seem a proper manner of approach to any deep-seated conflict. As we probe into cases such as this, we see more clearly why it was that the readings so insistently repeated the counsel: *first formulate your ideal in life.* At first sight it seems a sensible but rudimentary piece of advice, on a par with the wholesome but ingenuous sentiments of the Campfire Girls. But on mature and searching analysis, we find that the counsel is of primary importance in any adult problem of integration.

Once we have formulated an ideal, we have a compass by which to travel, a means by which to harmonize and transcend whatever contradictory thought vortexes exist in our unconscious mind. The battle may indeed be thought of as being between light and darkness, between spirit and matter, or between good and evil. But in other and more modern terms, the battle is between enlightened consciousness and the unredeemed forces of past unenlightened thought and conduct lying deep in the unconscious.

The ideal as conceived of intuitively by the personality may be an accurate reflection of the basic purpose for which the soul took incarnation—a purpose which might well be called the super-conscious life goal. But sometimes the consciously formulated life goal—though always serving an evolutionary end—may only approximate the super-conscious purpose of the entity as chosen before birth. We might illustrate this generalization with the case of George Eliot, who affords an excellent example of the phenomenon of contradictory urges. Many sympathetic observers noted in this great English writer certain deep-lying contradictions. The following are excerpts from two different biographies:

> George Eliot was half Puritan and half Pagan, and since the two sides never blended in her, she was a prey to perpetual suffering and depression. George Meredith once said of her: "George Eliot had the heart of Sappho. But the face with its long nose, the protruding teeth as of the Apocalyptic horse, betrayed animality." *

> George Eliot . . . a frail looking woman who would sit with her chair drawn close to the fire, and whose winning womanliness of bearing and manners struck everyone who had the privilege of an introduction to her. . . . She had a pleasant laugh and smile, her voice being low and distinct, and intensely sympathetic in quality. . . .

> Besides D'Albert's portrait of George Eliot, we have a drawing by Mr. Burton and another by Mr. Lawrence, the latter taken soon after the publication of *Adam Bede*. In criticizing the latter likeness, a keen observer of human nature remarked that it conveyed no indication of the infinite depth of her observant eye, nor of that cold, subtle, and unconscious cruelty of expression which might occasionally be detected there.†

These observations can be reduced to a hypothesis in rein-

* *Studies in the Mental Development of George Eliot*, by Minory Toyoda, Tokyo, Kenyusha, 1931.
† *George Eliot*, by Mathilde Blind, W. H. Allen and Co., 1888.

carnationist terms. Her "half Puritan and half Pagan" impulses indicate that she may have had one incarnation as a pagan—perhaps a voluptuous Greek *hetaera,* singer, dancer, and mistress to an Athenian statesman—and another as an ascetic—perhaps a monk in a medieval monastery. In the personality as George Eliot, the pagan urge was inhibited by a face and figure which did not permit its free expression. This, plus the environmental influence of being a clergyman's daughter in the Victorian age, could have made the urge to righteousness from her monk experiences predominant, while the voluptuary impulses were held at bay. The "crude animality" of her features may well have been the karmic consequence of beauty misused in her pagan experience.

Nobody who knew the nobility and active kindness of George Eliot's life could possibly accuse her of being cruel; yet, if a keen observer of human nature is to be relied on, a "cold, subtle, and unconscious cruelty of expression" could occasionally be detected within her. The word "unconscious" is significant here; for the reincarnationist interpretation indicates that deep in the unconscious of this eminently kind and noble woman there lay, from some past-life experience, an urge to cold, subtle cruelty—an urge which had almost, but not quite, been transmuted to kindness through the intervening experiences.

The conscious life goal of George Eliot as a personality might well have been "to write books" or "to serve humanity" or "to awaken in other people a sense of moral responsibility." But the life goal of the Overself, of the Eternal Identity, may have been none of these things; the purpose that the entity had in mind in taking incarnation as the homely daughter of a Victorian clergyman may have been to complete the transmutation of cruelty into kindness; or to rectify the sins of sensuality; or to achieve harmonization between monkish intellectuality and a more humanistic sense of values.

The super-conscious life goal, then, is the central and unifying principle of a life, which makes intelligible all the external events and the ostensible purposes of a personality. Should this point of view ever be fully accepted, the art of biography could become more subtle and profound. The biographer would then make it his concern to do more than present an accurate chronicle of a person's life, or a life-like portrait of his ostensible personality; his primary task would be to discover the super-conscious as well as the conscious life goal of the personality. His second task would be to trace the karmic forces converging upon the life by virtue of the entity's having made the choice of goal which it did. A study of the interplay of impulses from various preceding incarnations would serve to explain otherwise irrational components of the subject's character. Naturally, if the biographer is unassisted by clairvoyant faculty, he will need to arrive at these elements intuitively, on the basis of available data on the subject's life. He will need also to have a thorough understanding of karmic principles, such as we have tentatively outlined in preceding pages.

The generalizations made about the biographer and his task would of course hold true also of the psychiatrist, and other persons concerned with the analysis and guidance of the human personality. It is important, however, that a distinction be made between the super-conscious life goal as reincarnationists conceive it, and the unconscious life goal of a personality as generally conceived of by psychoanalysis. In order to make this distinction clear, it might be well to take a hypothetical case by way of example.

Suppose a woman decides to consult an analyst because of a nervous breakdown. Under analysis, the therapist discovers that this woman has all her life desired to dominate other people. She has practiced her tyranny on her husband and her four children under the guise of solicitous love, but now her husband is dead and her four grown children refuse to be dominated. She regards their independent attitude as one of "unfeeling ingratitude"; feels herself to be mistreated, unwanted, lonely, and without any reason for living.

The analyst uncovers some incident of infancy or childhood in which the feeling of insecurity induced her to wish to achieve power through controlling others. After revealing that this had been her unconscious goal throughout her life, he recommends that she cease her efforts to control her children and other people, and devote her life to charities of one kind or another, allowing to all people the same freedom of self-direction that she would wish for herself. For the first time the woman sees her unconscious purpose unmasked; she accepts the doctor's analysis, follows his recommendations, and overcomes the neurosis which had threatened to engulf her.

Now let us view the same case from the point of view of reincarnationist psychology. The primary difference of this interpretation arises from the fact that we recognize deeper-lying causes than those begun in infancy. We infer that this woman had, in a past incarnation, some experience which gave her a tremendous urge for personal power over other people. Either she held an exalted position of authority, and

204

is nostalgically attempting to re-establish the absolutism of her power, or she had a position of inferiority which she so resented that she determined to establish her worth by domination of others. In either case she carried over an urge to tyranny. This is an unconscious urge, an unconscious life goal perhaps, but it is *not* equivalent to the super-conscious, overall, life goal as conceived in the reincarnationist view.

The over-all goal that this woman envisioned before taking incarnation may well have been: *to realize that other persons cannot be regarded as personal possessions or as abject subjects of my will; or to learn the lesson of live and let live.* The rebellion of her children, the overthrow of her tyranny in her little world and the nervous breakdown which it occasioned were events contained within the projected life plan so that she would learn to overcome the powerful urge to domination.

Reincarnationist psychoanalysis differs from ordinary psychoanalysis, then, in proposing that all life experiences conform to a life plan, made before birth, by the Overself, or the Eternal Identity. If the personality is able to learn the lessons affored it by life circumstances *without rebellion*, breakdown is unnecessary; collapse results only so that, in utter bankruptcy, the obstinacy of the personality may be dissolved and conduct be brought into line with the projected life plan of the Overself.

The unconscious life goal as conceived of by psychoanalysis is usually a selfish and material purpose, conceived by the separative personality or ego for its own imagined security or self-preservation, whereas the super-conscious life goal is nonmaterial because it concerns the acquisition of soul qualities and the learning of spiritual lessons. If the personality becomes aware of the inner purpose for which it took incarnation, and the conscious life goal becomes identical with the goal of the superconscious, then progress can be made much more swiftly because the personality puts up less inner resistance to the educative experiences of life.

The existence of deep-lying and sometimes contradictory urges in the unconscious, which we must learn to redeem, is a concept of cardinal important in reincarnationist psychology. This concept has several important implications, and may shed light on several areas of present-day psychology. For one thing, it suggests a possible solution to the important problem of dual and multiple personality.

Dual personality is well known to the general public through the wide diffusion of Stevenson's romantic tale, *Dr.*

Jekyll and Mr. Hyde. What is not so generally known is the fact that not only cases of dual, but cases of triple and multiple personality are frequent in the annals of abnormal psychology, and that, moreover, many of the personality alterations that occur are almost as dramatically different as the difference between Jekyll and Hyde. Leading psychologists in Europe and America have become interested in the problem; but definitive explanation of the phenomenon has never been offered.

There are no instances of this type of abnormality in the Cayce files, and therefore it cannot be said with certitude what the Cayce explanation would have been. However, in view of all the other Cayce data, one of two possibilities might account for the personality change; either possession by one or more discarnate entities, in succession, or an abnormal upsurge of memory of a previous personality of the individual. We infer the former possibility because there are several instances of mental abnormality in the files which Cayce attributed to spirit possession. Although these cases are those of partial and singular possession, there is no evidence against possession being—under certain conditions—total and multiple. The second possibility—i.e., the upsurge of memory from different lives—suggests itself as an extension of the phenomenon of the carry-over of urges from one life to the next.

The second important implication of the concept of past-life urges has to do with what is called in psychology the "specificity of traits." psychologists have found that human traits are specific rather than general. For example, it has been learned that honesty is not an absolute, general quality, but rather a collection of separate traits. "Honesty," to be sure, is a valid ethical concept, but when it becomes translated by human beings into actual conduct, it is not a unitary thing. There is honesty-with-respect-to-money, honesty-with-respect-to-examinations, honesty-with-respect-to-games, honesty-with-respect-to-conversation, honesty-with-respect-to-personal-relations, and any number of separate honesties rather than one absolute honesty in any given human being.

Psychologists explain this specificity of honesty reactions by the fact that a person has been trained to respond to particular situations by his parents and teachers, and has experienced satisfactions or disappointments that have conditioned his future reactions in those same areas. This is a reasonable explanation and it makes intelligible the inconsistencies which exist within us with respect to our qualities.

However, by the reincarnation principle, the specificity of

traits is due not merely to satisfactions or disappointments in a person's formative years, but also to the educative experiences of many past incarnations. It is possible to have learned very thoroughly the lesson of honesty with respect to money—perhaps through an experience of great shame when one's dishonesty was discovered and made public—and not to have learned the lesson of honesty with respect to human relations. It is possible to have learned the lesson of consideration for human life and not to have learned it with respect to animal life.

Such inequalities of character are common to all humanity and can be better understood in the light of reincarnationist psychology. A thoroughly sincere and well-intentioned young man may be deeply concerned, for example, about world peace and universal social justice. He becomes indignant when someone tells him, in the heat of argument, that his nature is basically cruel. He thoroughly disbelieves this accusation and holds his accuser in deepest contempt; but some months later an unusual combination of circumstances serves to make him realize that, in point of fact, there *is* a certain cruelty in his nature of which he had been unaware, and which shows itself as a determined effort to dominate other persons and suppress whatever beliefs give them comfort. This sudden self-knowledge horrifies him; he cannot understand the co-existence of his idealism and benevolence for men in general with his subtly tyrannical and cruel antagonism toward men in particular. He begins to wonder, indeed, if he is "basically" cruel, as his antagonist claimed, and if all his idealistic projects have not been self-deceptive hypocrisies.

Or let us take the case of a wealthy woman who had always considered herself generous. Suddenly she discovers, to her conscience-stricken amazement, that she is generous with respect to material things such as food, clothing, money, or other personal possessions, but that she is very ungenerous with respect to the judgments which she passes on other people's conduct.

Such discoveries as these are common among persons of psychological maturity, and they are very disturbing. They shake self-confidence, cause us to doubt our own integrity, and can go so far as to paralyze effort. Such agonies of introspection are, without doubt, useful stages in our growth. Knowledge, however, tends to dispel anxiety—knowledge that the inequalities of our nature are due to varying experiences in our soul's past. If we accept this knowledge, we can come to regard these inner disparities dispassionately, with the tranquil realization that it is within our power to equalize them—in fact, the painful experiences of life are intended precisely to bring about such an equalization. All qualities must ultimately be learned with respect to all environmental fields of the soul. We cannot expect, however, to do everything at once; it is not without good reason that school is in session five days a week and nine months a year, and it is not without equally good reason that we require many lifetimes to redeem what is unredeemed within us.

Whether these tendencies within us should be called "traits" or "drives," in the terminology of psychology, or "urges," in that of the Cayce readings, is not of primary importance (though the word "urge" is perhaps more vividly descriptive of the propulsive force involved). When the inequality of urges, their mutual antagonism, or their incomplete neutralization is thoroughly understood, both self-understanding and the understanding of others will become immeasurably refined.

One other implication arises from a knowledge of the existence of past-life urges, and this has to do with what might well be called the illusion of innocence. For many centuries men were concerned over the problem of innocence and original sin. Many philosophers were seriously preoccupied about the true nature of an infant—whether inherently good or inherently depraved. Plato regarded the infant's mind as filled with reminiscences of previous states of existence; Locke regarded the infant's mind as a *tabula rasa* or blank page upon which sensations wrote impressions to be conceptualized into ideas. Theologians regarded all infants tainted with the "original sin" of Adam and Eve, which only the proper sacraments could redeem.

By the reincarnationist view, all men are certainly born with an inheritance of sin, but it is original with themselves and not with the allegorical characters of Adam and Eve. Sin arises from the conduct of our anterior selves; it cannot be redeemed by baptism or any other theological ritual. Such rites have their symbolic value and purpose, to be sure, but they cannot be regarded as substitutes for the changes of consciousness which they are intended to symbolize.

Aldous Huxley relates how Peter Claver, the saintly seventeenth-century Spanish monk who gave his life to the service of the inhumanly treated Negroes as they were brought from Africa, often exhorted the slaves to think on their own sins. Such an exhortation would surely seem to be beside the point; "and yet," as Huxley puts it, "Peter Claver was probably right. . . . Right in insisting that whatever circumstances in which he finds himself, a human being always has omissions to make good, commissions whose effects must if possible be neutralized. Right in believing that it is well even for the most brutally sinned against to be reminded of their own shortcomings."

Huxley here touched on a very important issue—namely, that which we have called the illusion of innocence. Most of us consider ourselves more sinned against than sinning, more abused than abusive. All of us believe ourselves to be innocent and good. In part this might be attributed to native creature conceit, but in larger part it is because we have been bathed in the stream of forgetfulness. Our evil past has been hidden from us by the kind economy of nature.

"I have always been good to people," we hear a woman complain, "and yet look how people treat me. Human beings are so ungrateful!" Yes indeed—we might answer—you have been kind in this lifetime because at an early age you realized that you had no beauty and that your only entrance to men's favor was through acts of kindness. But you must realize that this is only a new-fledged virtue on your part. Look at your past life as a beautiful, heartless voluptuary; you are reaping now the effects of what you sowed then. People's treatment of you now does not give proof that humanity is ungrateful; it merely reflects back to you, from the appropriate field, the manner in which you yourself once treated humanity. You have been sowing figs all your life, but harvesting the thistles of last life's sowing. The seasons of life will finally bring to you the figs you are sowing now; meanwhile, accept the thistles as your just harvest, and keep valiantly on in the sowing of figs. . . .

A percipient reader of the human character can see within it just wherein lie the shallows and treacherous depths of which the personality is unaware. In some people one sees latent hate, in others a predatory lust for dominion, in others still, an icy coldness. The personality, self-illuded by its youth, its beauty, its wealth, its intellectual competence, its sensual gratifications, its worldly fortune, or its veneer of conventional courtesy, is innocent of these evils within it; but when the outer security that was its prop is shaken and destroyed, the personality finds itself expressing that which was deeply hidden within it, and meeting situations which compel its redemption.

When a painful experience arises, the personality may be tempted to complain *I* never did anything to deserve this. But his innocence is only an illusion, his logic no more sensible than that of the Frenchman who was tried for murdering his father and mother, confessed his guilt, but begged for mercy on the plea that he was an orphan. In the personality's case he has not confessed his guilt because he honestly is not aware of it, but he is pleading for mercy because he is an orphan—and yet it was his own crime that made him so. Guilty of some evil or some weakness he most assuredly is, else misfortune would not have befallen him. For evil comes to no man unless there is some latent evil within him to which it is vibratorily attracted.

Alteration of character is the educative purpose of the vicissitudes of life—whether these be obvious external calamities like war, pestilence, or flood, or subtle inner tensions and conflicts. When psychology acknowledges the purposive nature of these vicissitudes, on an evolutionary spiral, it will have made a great stride forward.

Likewise, the practitioners of religion, whether they be priest, minister, rabbi, Brahmin, or what, should have a thorough understanding of the agencies of life, both inner and outer, which effect alterations of human character. When men in desperation ask for the meaning of the tragedies of their life, they can console and encourage on a truly scientific basis, giving explanations that have the clarity and precision of an algebraic equation, the grandeur and sweep of a mountain sunset.

Chapter XXIII

Miscellaneous Aspects of Karma

ONE question which people usually ask when they first learn of reincarnation and karma is: "What about heredity?" Almost invariably the known facts about heredity are assumed to be in contradiction with the presumed facts of karma. There is, however, no real contradiction. Cayce once used a very interesting metaphor in this connection. Someone asked, at the end of his reading, "From which side of my family do I inherit most?" The answer was: "You have inherited most from yourself, not from your family! The family is only a river through which the soul flows."

The fact that the laws of heredity play a subordinate role to those of karma can be illustrated by another analogy. Suppose that a native of the African jungle were brought to New York City, where he observed for the first time a theater marquee. He would notice how the little white lights bordering the sign appear to be in constant movement, as if chasing each other; it might almost seem to him as if each globe of light were bumping the next one, and the light transferred, torchlike, from one to the other. In short, it might seem as if the cause for the glow of each light was to be found in the light preceding it. But this is only how the action *appeared;* in reality the principle of causation here lies in an exact, split-second timing of each light such that they flicker on and off in a manner that suggests the desired effect of sequence.

The analogy here is certainly not exact—no analogy ever is —but is sufficiently parallel to suggest how at surface levels there may be an appearance of causality that does not correspond to the deeper actuality of the case. The flow of bodily heredity exists, as the flow of light exists in the theater marquee; but other laws of magnetic attraction are in operation, and their effect is such that a soul gravitates unfailingly to the family group and to the bodily possibilities which best correspond to its own inner requirements.

Heredity, then, and with it other forms of proximate physical causality, are in reality subservient to the magnetic compulsion of the laws of karma. Those who attribute all human tendency to heredity and all human disease to proximate physical causes can, by this view, be compared to the guest at a banquet who turns to thank the servants for the things they bring him at table. To be sure, it *is* the servants who serve him the food; but they do so in response to the bidding of their employer.

Another issue commonly raised in connection with karma is an ethical one. In the case of the blind violinist described in Chapter 4, the karmic origin of his blindness was attributed to his having blinded others with hot irons when he was a member of a barbaric tribe in Persia. The question can well be raised: How can a man be held morally responsible for the customs of his time? Why should a man be penalized merely for performing his social duty?

A French guillotinist, for example, is employed by the state; so is the man who performs electrocutions at Sing-Sing. Can these persons be held personally accountable for the capital-punishment practices of a legal system, such that they need to suffer a karmic penalty for it in some future life? And if the answer to this question is no, then how can the Persian barbarian who blinded the tribal enemies of war be said to differ from them?

These are justifiable questions. A partial answer was indicated in Chapter 11, where it was indicated that it is not the act but the motive, not the letter but the spirit that is a karmic determinant. Moreover, it would seem highly presumable that there is such a thing as social guilt. That is to say, if the practices of a society are evil in an ultimate sense, then all members of that society to some degree partake of that guilt. If in an ultimate ethical sense it is wrong to enslave or kill or maim other human beings—and, according to ancient wisdom, such infringement on the free will of another *is* an absolute evil—then all persons who are members of such a society are culpable; they are passively guilty if not actively so. The guilt becomes progressively greater if they are aware of the moral significance of the custom, yet continue to condone it by not attempting to suppress the wrong. If they are actively engaged in perpetrating the wrong, their guilt becomes proportionately greater.

To blind other persons merely because they happen to be vanquished in tribal warfare is certainly a cruel act. If the man appointed to the job of blinding was himself averse to such cruelty, and performed the task only because it became his obligation to do so as subject of his chieftain, conceivably he would suffer no karmic penalty. But if he did his office— *giving inner consent*—having, that is, within himself a cruelty corresponding to the cruelty of the custom, then he generated a karmic cause.

This issue is admirably treated in the *Bhagavad-Gita*—an excellent and subtle treatise that can be highly recommended to anyone interested in formulating a new ethic of conduct taking as its pivot the karmic concept. (Perhaps the best edition of the *Bhagavad-Gita* for Western readers is the translation by Swami Prabhavananda and Christopher Isherwood, with an introduction by Aldous Huxley.) Its principal message is this: in impersonal detachment from action lies the clue to the non-creation of future karma. Even love must become impersonal love, unattached love, ungrasping love, loving detachment—else it shall forge new bonds in the future.

Had the blind man of the case in point performed his blinding, in ancient Persia, in the sacrificial spirit with which the wise perform all deeds, and without personal satisfaction of his own lust for cruelty and dominance, then no karma could have been created. Hence we can only conclude that, since in actuality he received a karmic consequence, he must have been guilty of being psychologically on the level with the act which the custom of his society impelled him to perform.

In Chapter 19 we observed that the Cayce readings state explicitly that the deformity in some cases of birth injury was not karmic in origin. The point is worth examining more closely, because it is important for the fullest understanding of the karmic concept. Some believers in reincarnation mistakenly assume that, since causation *may* be in the past, therefore *all* causation is in the past; that is to say, they believe that misfortune or illness of the present is the outward token of some past-life sin. This is an erroneous belief. Causation may be either in the immediate past or the remote past; moreover, there are different levels of causation—physical, emotional, mental, ethical.

An additional element to be taken into consideration is the fact that—according to the Cayce readings at least—accidents are perfectly possible, "even in Creation itself." It sometimes happens that a birth injury, or an injury in later life, is purely accidental in the sense that it has no intrinsic relation to causes set up by the individual himself.

Here, for example, is the case of a ten-year-old girl, blind in one eye and totally deaf since infancy. The reading remarks as follows, in the opening sentences of the physical reading taken on the child:

Yes. What a sad condition. And not a result of karma, but an accident, or a lack of proper precaution in cleanliness by the nurse in the early period of the body's present earth experience.

The type of antiseptic used worked upon the sensory organs and brought about inflammation, destroying their activity. . . .

Another case, one of mental abnormality due to a birth injury following the use of high forceps, is commented on as follows:

Yes—yes—we have the body here.

As we find, there may be a great deal of help for this body. This is a bungle of the doctor, not of the soul-entity. Someone must eventually pay, much, for this.

In the condition here, it will require long and patient application, but this should be in a different environment as soon as practical. . . .

Frequently people who had suffered some injury or illness asked whether their condition was karmic or not. Here are a few examples, with direct quotations from the readings.

In a case of hemorrhages, the individual asked: "Is this condition karmic, or is it due to something in my present lifetime?" The answer was: "This condition is due to eating too much of highly seasoned foods."

An individual suffering from noises in the ear asked a similar question, and received this answer: "It is purely physical, not karmic. Remove the stress by the head and neck exercise." (The reference here is to a simple exercise of three movements frequently recommended for the improving of the sight and hearing.)

A man who at the age of fifteen had lost one leg in an accident asked: "Was the loss of my leg a karmic debt, and if so, what?" The answer came: "This was an experience necessary for your better unfoldment. Not in payment of some-

214

thing, but that you might know the truth that might set you free."

Another individual who had suffered an injury to his right hand asked: "Was there a spiritual cause for the accident to my right hand, or was it purely an accident?" The answer: "It was purely an accident—not a spiritual cause."

A reading taken on a man suffering from progressive muscular atrophy begins:

> The condition here is largely prenatal; yet it could not be called the sins of the fathers, nor of the entity itself, but rather that through which patience and consistency might be the lesson for the entity in this experience.
>
> So do not become pessimistic because of the conditions that outwardly appear to be causing the body to become a "shut-in," without the use of anything but the mind. Remember—mind is the builder.

It becomes apparent from cases such as these that some accidents may be truly "accidental" in this sense: that the victim did not himself initiate their cause, on any level of causal sequence. It also becomes apparent that such accidental suffering is the exception rather than the rule, but that it offers the soul an opportunity for growth and the acquisition of new strength.

In fact, the statements made in the two cases cited above very strongly suggest the answer given by Jesus to the disciples who asked him about the blind man, as reported in John 9:1-3. The verses read as follows:

> And as Jesus passed by, he saw a man which was blind from his birth.
>
> And his disciples asked him, saying, "Master, who did sin, this man, or his parents, that he was born blind?"
>
> Jesus answered, "Neither hath this man sinned, nor his parents; but that the works of God should be made manifest in him."

This passage is extremely interesting, from several points of view. The very fact that his disciples should have asked the question, "Who did sin, this man, or his parents, that he was born blind?" indicates the disciples' acquaintance with the idea of the pre-existence of the soul.

Jesus' answer—which sometimes has been quoted as an argument against reincarnation by its opponents—does not

215

admit of an exact interpretation; it seems, indeed, somewhat equivocal.

The Bible is a translation of a translation of a translation of accounts of a remembered series of events.* In passing through the hands of so many scribes, diametric changes of meaning must frequently have taken place. As a result, it is improbable that the Bible as we have it today represents the complete, accurate, original teachings of Christ. Psychological studies in the inaccuracy of human testimony should convince us of the improbability, if nothing else. This passage, then, may be one of the many hundreds of passages whose alteration, deliberate or accidental, alters the statement as originally made.

If, however, the answer to the question about the blind man is a more or less accurate rendering of what Jesus said, then we can only conclude that He was stating much the same thing as Cayce with regard to the loss of a leg and the case of progressive muscular atrophy cited above.

In a preceding chapter we saw the case of a man who for karmic reasons became the father of an abnormal child, yet who had not been actively guilty of cruelty; he had merely been guilty of the negative sin of indifference. We observed that this indirect karmic consequence was possibly the first of several successively more intimate corrective experiences that might come to him in order to sensitize his nature and make him more concerned in the presence of suffering. Conceivably, then, by this interpretation, he could himself suffer some affliction in a future life if he did not vicariously learn the needed lesson through the experience of parenthood; this physical affliction would come to him not because he had inflicted it directly on another, but because he needed a painful educative experience to sensitize a shallow area of his personality.

It is conceivable, further, that the blind man whom Jesus and His disciples met, and the two above-mentioned persons who suffered from a broken leg and progressive muscular atrophy were afflicted for a similar reason. In any case, it must be recognized that whether a life difficulty is karmic or non-karmic in origin, it is always an opportunity for spiritual growth. Karma itself must not be fatalistically interpreted; that is to say, it must not be regarded as blind, inexorable

* For an illuminating discussion of this point, see "The Way of the Translator" by Max Nomad in *The American Mercury,* March, 1945.

force. It does not act with the automatic precision of a machine on which a control button has been pressed.

Karma is a precise law, to be sure; but its purpose is to give the soul an opportunity to bring itself back into alignment with the cosmic truth of being. If the soul therefore becomes aware of its own defects and consciously takes the initiative to bring itself into alignment, whatever ground it displaces in its return movement is that much ground gained from the compulsory effect of karma.

The purpose of karma is to *justify* the soul, using the word justify in the same sense that printers use it when they speak of justifying, or making even with the specifications, a line of type. If one realizes the true intention of karma as being educative or justifying in this sense, one realizes also that it's penalties are not arbitrary or inexorable. Consequently one does not passively accept the penalty, without positive efforts in the direction of learning the spiritual lesson implied in the constriction.

The laws of motion are very instructive in this connection. After a body has been set in motion, it moves along a certain definite line. If another force is brought to bear upon it, differing in direction from its original line of motion, the body will begin to move along another line—one which is the resultant of the two differing impulses. No energy is lost; no law has been violated. One line of force has merely been modified by the application of another line of force. Similarly with karma: its direction can be deflected or modified, and its force diminished, by the initiation of a new line of force—in this case, the new force being right thought and right action. Thus it is seen that a laissez-faire attitude with regard to karma is wholly unnecessary and self-defeating.

This may be apparent enough to a man with regard to himself; but a new ethical subtlety arises when he considers the attitude he should take toward the karmic situation of other people. In Chapter 11 it was demonstrated that recognition of the operation of karma leads inevitably to a certain social dilemma. It was shown how the misuse of authority in past incarnations led in several instances to a situation of poverty and restricted circumstances in the present. If we believe that most tragic afflictions have their origin in a past moral dereliction of one kind or another, what attitude shall we take toward afflicted persons? What attitude are we to take toward the social condition of other people?

Should we say, with scientific logic, "You are suffering what you deserve to suffer, my friend. I cannot interfere with the prosecution of justice," and proceed on our way? Shall

217

we that find sympathy is a sentiment that has outlived its era and charity a virtue outmoded by the rationale of karma?

These questions must not be answered hastily or sentimentally. We know that a vicious murderer will not learn a needed lesson if short-sighted sentimentalists decide that he ought to be paroled after six months of prison. We know that the assignments of the school day cannot be covered if an over-indulgent teacher dismisses school every day three hours early. We know that a child cannot be taught obedience if the fond mother consistently moderates the just penalties laid on him by the father. We know all these things and we know too that the restraints put upon man in the form of disfigurements and misfortune represent in reality the educative intentions of the universe. How, then, can we dare interfere with the operation of a cosmic law?

We see, for example, living in the degradation of unspeakable poverty, the contorted, pitiful victim of a terrible disease; we cannot help feeling, as we regard him, a surge of pity. But if we accept the karmic view of things, we can look upon that sufferer in another light. In imagination we can project ourselves backward, beyond the curtains of the narrow stage of the present, and see the actor of the present in a different role, a different costume, and a different epoch.

On analogy with cases which we have seen in the Cayce files, we can imagine that the contorted spastic of the present, whose limbs twitch so pathetically as he tries to move, was once an arrogant prince in the Czarist days in Russia—tall, strong, virile, lusty, cruel, degenerate. Secure in his possession of untold wealth, coldly indifferent to the privations of the peasants who produce that wealth, insolent in his awareness of his physical strength, sensual and unscrupulous in the satisfaction of his appetites, inhuman in his disregard for the women whom he uses, pitiless in his torture of those who have incurred his disfavor—this is the picture that we see of his former personality. We look about him and we see men whose frames have withered in Siberian wastes to which they have been sent on the prince's despotic whim; we see children whose drawn faces and hollow eyes bespeak the hunger of their peasant-slave existence. And as we see this hideous picture of evil—a picture that could be duplicated in almost any country in the world in the ruthless ages that have precede our own ruthless age—we murmur a wish that someday, somewhere, this man will be called to task for his crimes.

No sooner have we framed the wish than we are returned to the present, and see once again the cripple upon whom we looked with so much pity before. Can we still feel the same unreserved sympathy for him? Can we still—recalling the broken bodies of his victims—say, *Let me help you!*

Suppose the single instance is translated into universal terms—as it eventually must be, if the reincarnation view is accepted at all. We discover, then, a psychological, ethical, and social question of great importance—one that we shall need to face squarely and immediately in our conduct of life. The reader who is a student of sociological systems will recall that the issue has already found one solution in the social philosophy of one nation at least: India. Although the problem only now becomes apparent to us with our young recognition of the reincarnation principle, it has been known to India for centuries.

The masses of people in India have decided the question in favor of non-interference with justice. It is this which accounts in large part for the seeming indifference with which Indians regard the afflicted, and the exclusiveness with which they treat their outcasts.

The caste system of India is based upon the ancient laws of Manu, a great lawgiver and philosopher who, like Plato, stated that society falls naturally into certain necessary hierarchies of occupation. The teaching became a social custom; the custom crystallized into a social order. Tradition and superstition—rife among a population almost 90 per cent illiterate—conspired to make this crystallization hidebound and rigid.

The lowest caste, consisting of those who do the most lowly and menial tasks, became "untouchable" out of the reasoning that if they were born into so low a stratum of society, they must be expiating the arrogance and evil of a former incarnation. Hence the logic of permitting karma to fulfill itself without interference.

Granting the Hindus their first premise that karma attracts us inevitably to the station in life which we deserve, and granting them also their second premise of a hierarchy in society (which is based on an occult truth about the universe also observed by the Catholic Church), we see that their conclusion is logical.

And yet, for all its logic, this solution somehow seems a sad one. By this view, humanity becomes, like Liebnitz's monads, little capsules without windows, each pursuing its own intents and its own orbit in space in self-contained indifference to the progress of other monads.

As one contemplates this dilemma, one is inevitably reminded of that tense, terse poem of Walt Whitman's, entitled, "I Sit and Look out upon All the Sufferings of the World":

I sit and look out upon all the sorrows of the world, and
upon all oppression and shame,
I hear secret convulsive sobs from young men at anguish
with themselves, remorseful after deeds done,
I see in low life the mother misused by her children,
dying, neglected, gaunt, desperate,
I see the wife misused by the husband, I see the treacherous seducer of young women,
I mark the ranklings of jealousy and unrequited love attempted to be hid, I see these sights on the earth.
I see the workings of battle, pestilence, tyranny, I see
martyrs and prisoners,
I observe a famine at sea, I observe the sailors casting
lots who shall be kill'd to preserve the lives of the
rest,
I observe the slights and degradations cast by arrogant
persons upon laborers, the poor, and upon negroes
and the like;
All these—all the meanness and agony without end I sitting look out upon,
See, hear, and am silent.

Whitman was a believer in reincarnation. We know this
from his biography and we know it from the unmistakable
internal evidence of his poems. And we can recognize, in the
sublime detachment and silence of his looking out upon the
world's agony without end, the authentic wisdom of one who
sees the cause within every effect and the effect within every
cause. Inactivity is characteristically the accompaniment of
philosophy—not because of indifference or laziness—but rather because of the capacity to see the necessity that inheres in
the causal chain. This poem of Whitman's seems almost a
manifesto of the wisdom of silent inactivity in the face of the
necessary anguish of man.

And yet we know that Whitman served for several years as
a nurse on the battlefields of the Civil War; all of his strange
and rather solitary life was a generous one of self-giving from
out of his solitude. This poem, then, was expressive not of all
his view of the world, but only part of it. It was a mood; a
mountain-peak perspective; a basic organ-point of tone, perhaps, sounding against the more energetic melody of his daily
life. For his life was not an inactive one with regard to his
suffering fellow men; and this was because he was, to a high
degree, possessed of the great virtue of love.

It is love, in fact, that refutes the logic of non-concern
which seems so intellectually reasonable. This, indeed, is the

central meaning of Christ, whose dedicated career of healing and teaching exemplifies the conviction that no matter what a man's sins may be, one should stretch out a helping hand in his direction. The super-conscious mind of Edgar Cayce surely is not to be placed in the same category with Christ; and yet it, too, exemplified the Christlike spirit of compassionate concern through forty years of effort to help the troubled in mind and the broken in body.

It is this that constitutes one of the most striking integrations of the Cayce readings: reaffirming, in explicit terms, the concept that the scientific sub-structure of life is the karmic law accepted in the Orient, and at the same time reaffirming the spiritual exhortation to love and service which is the keynote of the teaching of Christ.

Regardless of the past-life sins of other men, we must make the effort to help them—knowing that the invisible barriers of karmic law will prevent any infringement upon the minimum essentials of their constriction, and knowing also that indifference toward the suffering of others is in itself a karmically punishable sin on our own part.

In a sense, the outer world and other men are only a proving ground whereon we can learn the virtues of spirit that we need to learn. We ourselves are equally a proving ground whereon other men must learn their virtues. Remembrance of the former fact should prevent grandiose delusions of having unduly helped humanity; remembrance of the latter fact should be conducive to both humility and dignity with regard to ourselves. Our own faults are as painful to others as theirs are to us, but they, too, are learning from our faults as we are learning from theirs.

Another aspect of this subtle matter is the important fact that man's will is *free* and that all of history is not predetermined in minute detail in the fatalistic sense. Our effort to help an afflicted person, then—whether his affliction is physical, economic, social, or psychological—is not only an experience which we need personally in order to perfect ourselves in the virtue of love; it is also an experience which may succeed in altering the other's mental outlook, his consciousness, and thereby the course of his life.

In the last analysis, it must be realized that all karma is mind-created. An error of conduct arises from an error of consciousness; and integral change of conduct can arise only from an integral change of consciousness. Hence the Cayce readings are profoundly correct in stating that mind is the builder, for unless a man changes his mind, and especially

221

his conceptual notion of the Creative Energy and his relation thereto, he can never redeem his negative karma.

We have already quoted the phrase, frequently used by the readings in cases of karmic penalty, *You are meeting yourself*. It is an arresting phrase; it suggests a kind of mirrorlike quality about karma, as if each crucial experience were no more than the strange encounter of oneself with a former replica of oneself. More especially it suggests the following idea, advanced here, be it understood, only speculatively and impressionistically.

The theory of the curvature of space—whatever its present status in scientific circles—is highly consonant with the karmic idea in the following way. If the universe can be regarded as circular in nature, and hence predisposing all cosmic motion to be circular also, then it would almost seem as if the law of karma, as we call it, is only the end result of the circular motion of every act. An act of any kind constitutes a use of energy. The fact of karma may be possible, then, because energy directed by consciousness against an outer object passes directly through that object, like an X-ray piercing a solid, but continues its circular course about the universe until it finally comes back to the initiator, undiminished in force for all its travels.

Thus a man's act of kindness to a cat objectively affects the cat, but the energy of the act continues to travel outward and about until it finally returns to the man as an act of kindness. Similarly an act of cruelty toward another living creature has its objective effect, but continues circularly its own life impulse until it finally returns as an act of cruelty to the originator.

Although this thesis is only a speculative fancy, it can be reconciled to most of the karmic cases we have seen in preceding chapters and perhaps—allowing for variations and subtleties of expression—to all of them. In any case, the idea has a certain suggestive power, as anyone who tries to live by it for a few days will discover. If we will imagine that every act we perform in relation to other persons is starting on a circular journey that will end up by exactly affecting ourselves, we will find that some of our impulses will be chastened and some of our actions ennobled with surprising immediacy.

The karmic concept is an important one because it provides the scientific rationale for the exhortations to goodness which we find in Christianity and all other world religions. Paul Brunton probably does not overstate the case when he says that the safety and survival of Western civilization depends on the restoration of the karmic idea to the thinking of the masses; for a knowledge of karma, properly understood, gives to its possessor a mature approach to life—one that is religious without being superstitious, scientific without being crassly materialistic. The karmic concept gives man both the courage to bear and the courage to dare. He can accept the consequences of his own past actions with dynamic rather than static resignation, knowing that at every moment his is the power to initiate new trains of action and create a new and more abundant destiny.

In the ultimate sense, of course, God created man. But penultimately man is his own creator. Karma represents the boundaries within which man's designing and creating of himself must take place. Karma is the limiter and the disciplinarian; but it is at the same time the liberator and the friend. Knowing this, the Buddhist says, serenely, in all the vicissitudes of life: *I take my refuge in the Law.* And for those who understand the cosmic beneficence of all Law, no matter how seemingly impersonal, these words are fully as moving, fully as consoling, fully as exalting, as the equivalent words of the Christian: *I take my refuge in the Lord.* For the Law is the Lord—and the Lord is the Law.

Chapter XXIV

A Philosophy To Live By

THE postmen who delivered mail to the Cayce home throughout the years were the bearers of some heart-rending pleas for help. In the latter years, letters came from all over the world: from persons in South America, Canada, England; from boys on the battlefields of Europe, or in outposts in the far Pacific, Alaska, and Australia.

It is impossible to read these letters and not be moved to pity. The problems which they outline run the gamut of human misery. One begins to understand, as he reads through a sampling, how Cayce depleted himself giving so many readings. His stature as a humanitarian becomes fully discernible when one realizes that he would not spare himself in the face of all that floodtide of suffering that every day's mail brought to his door.

Some letters came from persons who expressed with many-syllabled competence their educated bewilderment; some from persons who wrote, as one woman did:

> I wonder if it would be posable for me to get a reading about my love life. I seem to be geting very confused. I want to get maried again and have a home and all that should go with it but I am afraid Ill choose the wrong one or maby I shouldn't think of marage again and after all maby no one will realy want me.

They represent all degrees of maturity, from the woman who wrote:

> How can I change my husband and environment so as

to create health, happiness, and a charming personality for myself?

to the young college graduate who said simply:

I want a personal, workable way of life.

But literate or illiterate, rich or poor, educated or not, these people almost unanimously revealed in their letters the bewilderment and perplexity of humanity. Whether shy, introverted, lonely, sick, vocationally frustrated, or unhappily married—all were concerned with the problem of improving their lot in life.

It is no longer possible for such persons to obtain personal counsel on their problems through the clairvoyance of Edgar Cayce, but a study of the recommendations given in comparable cases is helpful in finding a solution for an immediate difficulty. Almost invariably, people were told that the ultimate source of their painful situation *lay within themselves.* This is the first thing, according to the readings, that troubled persons must accept. Every problem is in the last analysis self-caused, and therefore must be self-redeemed.

This may seem a simple precept, but it is frequently difficult to accept. We are inclined to take ourselves for granted, to regard our traits with the same acquiescence as we accept the air we breathe. With rare exceptions, we are inclined to view our own character with complacency; our unconscious instinct is to use our own temperamental constitution as the measuring stick of perfection.

When the realization comes, as the readings indicate it should, that the very fact we find ourselves unhappy or uncomfortable is evidence of something wrong within ourselves, then we are awakened from our complacency. We cease blaming externals; we stop our restless rearrangement of outer things; we turn instead to scrutinize ourselves to discover wherein lies our fault and the lesson we need to learn.

No matter what our difficulty—whether it is loneliness, an uncongenial husband, an idiot child, an inferiority complex, a limited environment—we must realize that only through the transformation of the self can the situation be transcended. Our own attitudes must be changed; our own conduct must be altered. Attitudes cannot be critical, condemnatory, vengeful, proud, indifferent, negative; conduct cannot be selfish, inconsiderate, unsocial. Outer difficulties can only be resolved through educing the appropriate virtues of mind and soul.

The cultivation and transformation of the self, however, can best take place within a systematic concept of the universe and man's relation thereto. Such a systematic concept is implicit in all the Cayce data, and runs like colored strands through the hundreds of life readings given. Lifted from the framework of the individual readings in which they appeared, these strands form a distinct pattern.

This pattern is religious in the sense that it takes the existence of a Creative Power, or God, as its starting point. It is philosophic in the sense that it formulates a definite and systematic outlook on life, the universe, and man's destiny therein. It is psychological in the sense that it provides a concrete approach to the practical problems of the psyche in reacting to the life-situation.

In outline form this pattern seems to be as follows:

> God exists.
> Every soul is a portion of God.
>> (You *are* a soul; you inhabit a body.)
> Life is purposeful.
> Life is continuous.
> All human life operates under law.
>> (Karma; reincarnation.)
> Love fulfills that law.
> The will of man creates his destiny.
> The mind of man has formative power.
> The answer to all problems is within the Self.

In the assurance of the above postulates, man is enjoined as follows:

> Realize first your relationship to the
>> Creative Forces of the Universe, or God.
> Formulate your ideals and purposes in life.
> Strive to achieve those ideals.
> Be active.
> Be patient.
> Be joyous.
> Leave the results to God.
> Do not seek to evade any problem.
> Be a channel of good to other persons.

GOD EXISTS.

The psychoanalytic theory is that God is an infantile fantasy of the human mind. With this view the Cayce readings are in uncompromising disagreement; they are insistent throughout that God *is*. They more frequently speak of the Creative Force—or the Creative Energy—of the Universe rather than of God; and all things considered, their use of this phrase is well suited to the new temper of our age.

We live in an epoch whose genius it has been to liberate more and more of the forces of nature; we discover unimaginable energy at the core of the atom. In a world of such expanded scientific vistas, the term Creative Energy of the Universe as a description of a central, unitary source is perhaps more understandable, with more impact of meaning, than the traditional word, so vulgarized by blasphemy and tarnished by misuse.

All the manifest universe is an expression of the Creative Energy of the Universe; in it we live and move and have our being. We partake of its energy and its divinity, and we must learn to realize our oneness with it.

There are numerous expressions of this concept in the Cayce readings. The following examples are representative.

And what is life? God manifested in the material plane. For it is still in Him that we live and move and have our being. Life is a material manifestation of that universal force or energy that we call God.

Know, as you analyze yourself, that these are unalterable truths: God is, and to Him first you owe all allegiance. Either you work with or against that Divine within.

Whatever electricity is to man, that's what the power of God is.

EVERY SOUL IS A PORTION OF GOD

Each one of us, according to the readings, *is* a soul, a portion of the Divine Energy that brought us into being. We stand in relationship to God, or the Creative Energy of the Universe, as a sunbeam to the sun, or a drop of water to the ocean. We stand in relation to our body as a man to his house or his garment.

A soul is a portion of the Divine Energy, and is as everlasting as that energy itself. Thus, if there is a continued period of activity that is for self-exaltation, then the entity may be said to be separating itself, or losing its relationship. Those however that worship and glorify the First Cause are mindful of the first command to man, in the expression:

227

"Thou shalt have no other Gods before me"—before the I AM of the soul.

Know that you are a soul, and do not merely attain to one.

"Others may do as they may, but as for me and my house, we will serve the living God." Do not interpret this to mean those who may be in your own physical household. Your house is your body—that is the temple of the living God. That is the whole house, made to conform to the will of God.

LIFE IS PURPOSEFUL

Life is not a chance situation, either in an individual or a universal sense. The ultimate purpose of our life is to rejoin God in conscious participation of divinity. We were one with It in the beginning; we departed from It out of ignorant attachment to materiality and out of a sense of separativeness, pride, or selfishness.

The entity was not born merely by chance. For the earth is a causation world; cause and effect are in the earth a natural law. And as each soul enters this material plane, it is to meet or give these truths so that others, too, may gain more knowledge of the purpose for which each soul enters.

You, in the beginning, had companionship with God, losing that companionship by choice of that which would satisfy material desire only. Thus you, as the Master did, enter again and again; you come to fulfill the law, the law that brought your soul into being to be one with Him.

The heritage of each soul is to know itself to be itself, yet one with Creative Forces.

LIFE IS CONTINUOUS

Our rejoining of God as worthy, perfected companions, in full awareness of our divine selfhood, is not accomplished quickly. The perfection of consciousness is a slow growth, whose consummation can be achieved only through aeons of time. In an ultimate sense there is no time, but to our three-dimensional sense there is. By the view that our limitation places on us, we must see that life is continuous.

You don't go to heaven; you grow to heaven!

For life is continuous! There is no halting. We either progress or retrogress.

Life is continuous and only changes in its phases, owing to the state of consciousness or change in the vibratory rate of existence.

What the entity is today is the result of what it has been in days and experiences and ages and aeons past. For life is continuous; and whether it is manifested in materiality or in other realms of consciousness, it is one and the same.

Learn this well: First, the continuity of life. There is no time; it is one time. There is no space; it is one space. There is no force, other than One Force in its various phases.

ALL HUMAN LIFE OPERATES UNDER LAW

Implied in the phrase "continuity of life" is the rhythmic alternation of experience which we, from the earth-view perspective, call reincarnation. Human life operates under laws of reembodiment, and the conditions of this reembodiment are governed by the intricate and unfailing laws of karma.

Know that there are immutable spiritual laws in the earth. Begin with: Like begets like. Whatsoever you sow, you reap. God is not mocked; for as you treat your neighbor, you are going to be treated by the other fellow.

It is not all of life to live, nor all of death to die; for one is the birth of the other when viewed from the whole or the center, and is but the experience of an entity in its transitions to and from that universal center from which all radiation takes place.

Remember, the things you once applied—now you are meeting them! Live with this in mind (and every soul may take heed): You shall pay every whit of what you break of the law of the Lord.

Read the 14th, 15th, 16th, and 17th chapters of John. "In my Father's house are many mansions." Dwell on that, not for an hour, or a minute, but for a day, as you go about your work. Who is your father? What is meant by "mansions"? And that there are many mansions in His house? What house?

It is your body—that is the temple. Many mansions are in

229

that body, many temples. For the body has been again and again in the experience of the earth; they are sometimes mansions, sometimes homes, sometimes huts.

As a corollary to the proposition that human life operates under law is stated the proposition that whatever our present situation may be, it is the effect of causes that we ourselves have set in motion, and is therefore necessary to our growth. Man is what he is because he was what he was.

Know that in whatever state you find yourself—of mind, of body, of physical condition—that is what you have built, and is necessary for your unfoldment.

Don't ever begin to feel sorry for yourself or think that someone has mistreated you. What you sow, you reap. Remember, others will never mistreat you if you never mistreat someone else. It isn't nature, for like begets like.

Do not let periods of abject indifference arise in your present experience. Know that whatever is, is for your own development, if you meet it with the application of creative principles.

Know that in whatever state you find yourself, that, at the moment, is best for you. Do not look back upon what might have been. Rather lift up, look up, now, where you are.

LOVE FULFILLS THE LAW

The law of karma is unfailing in its operation, as is the law of rebirth, until we have become perfect in love. Love fulfills every law.

The children of light first love, for, though I may have the gift of prophecy, though I may speak in unknown tongues, though I give my body to be burned, and have not the spirit of the Son of Man, the Christ consciousness, the Christ Spirit, I am nothing.

Then follow the example of your ideal, who said only to "Love the Lord thy God with all thy heart, thy mind, thy soul; and thy neighbor, thy associates, even thy enemy, as thyself." This is the whole of the law.

THE WILL OF MAN CREATES HIS DESTINY

In this universe of law and order, man is a free-will agent, partaking of the creative power of the great Creative

Force of the Universe, and partaking of its threefold aspects: love, intelligence, and will. It is with man's will that he "sins," or goes contrary to the unitary will of God. It is with his will that he can alter the direction of his soul, and bring it once again into harmony with Universal Will.

Will is that force that is compatible with, or against, the will of the All-Creative Energy. Call it nature, God, or whatnot—it is either with or against! Developing to or from!

Destiny is what a soul does with its will in relationship to the Creative Forces.

Know first that no urge, no influence, is greater than the will of the self to do what it determines to accomplish in any direction—whether physically, mentally, or spiritually.

Know that no urge—astrologically, numerologically, symbolically—surpasses the will of the entity in any experience.

For there is that within self that is creative; and it, that creative force, cooperating with the divine without, will lead to the choice of that which is life. And when the choice is made, then there may be a vision, astrologically and otherwise, of what the end thereof is. But each soul is given the birthright of the ability to choose—under any environment, any circumstance, any experience!

THE MIND OF MAN HAS FORMATIVE POWER

Man, then, is free-willed within the framework of cosmic laws. Penalties are visited on man only if he violates those laws. His will acts as the propulsive force of his destiny; his mind, however, acts as the directive and formative agent. That is why the first step in any program of self-discovery and self-improvement is formulating specifically one's ideals.

Moreover, *mind is the builder.* This refers to the Universal Mind of which each one of our minds is an individuated fragment. Mind, on all planes of existence, creates the pattern from which material things are formed.

For each entity makes a record upon time and space through the activities of that stylus, the mind.

In the flesh and in the spirit, mind is the builder. Thus, as the self has applied the self, so are the patterns of life cut.

231

Thoughts are things; the mind is as concrete as a post or tree.

THE ANSWER TO ALL PROBLEMS IS WITHIN THE SELF

The phrase, *the answer is within,* recurs like a refrain throughout the readings and is apparently intended in several senses. First, the reason for every difficulty is to be found within the self, because by the law of karma all things that happen to us are self-created and self-deserved. Outer circumstances are only the mirror-like reflection of something intimately within ourselves. We meet ourselves in whatever happens to us, consequently an acute self-analysis would give us the clue to whatever befalls us in our circumstances.

Second, there remains in the unconscious mind the memory of all things that have ever happened to us since the beginning of our individuation. Thus there is within us a storehouse of knowledge which is available to us through the stilling of the outer senses and focusing attention within, in the process of meditation.

Third, deep within us is the imprisoned splendor, the divine essence by which we are one with the Creative Energy of the Universe. The solution, then, to every problem, is to turn within to that radiant energy of our divine selfhood.

Study yourself, for in the self one may find the answer to all the problems that may confront you. For the spirit of man, with all its attributes, physical and mental, is a portion of the whole great spirit. Hence the answers are all within the self.

Know this—that all power all healing, all help must come from within.

All that the entity may know of God, or even international relationships—already exists in the consciousness for you to be made aware of. There must be the application to material sources of knowledge, yes; but with faith and trust in universal knowledge. For, as indicated by the great lawgiver: "Think not who will come over the sea that a message may be brought; for lo, it is within your own self. For the mind and the soul are from the beginning."

There, according to the Cayce readings, are the basic truths about man and his relationship to the universe. Far from being remote from the everyday concerns of life and the universal problems of psychological adjustment, these postulates lead naturally to a practical philosophy of living.

First, in the effort to translate these concepts into conduct, one must *realize one's relationship to the Creative Energy of the Universe.* Like a stream, man can rise no higher than his source; whether aware of it or not, he is always acting upon certain assumptions with regard to his origin and his identity. If his assumptions are false—mechanistic, materialistic, atheistic—his life cannot but take on false, distorted aspects.

Man, being the "image of God" in several senses of that much-misunderstood phrase, becomes more truly the microcosmic reflection when he properly sees the macrocosmic original. His concept of his source, and his relation thereto, affect his whole life in all its innermost and outermost remifications. Indeed, his treatment of his body and of his fellow-beings, his use of his time, and the direction of his energy are all ultimately derived from his unexamined assumptions or his formulated concepts as to his identity and his relationship to the universal.

This is the birthright of every soul that manifests in a material plane: to make known to others its concept of its relation to the Creative Forces.

Q. Please advise me how I may be of the most help to my father.
A. The best way to help anybody is to let your life be the reflection of what you think of your God. This makes for a life of service, or the using of life that the Father may be glorified in the earth even as in heaven.

Remember that all is One, and look into yourself if you would understand your neighbor, your friend, your foe. For what you do to your neighbor, your friend, or your foe, is a reflection of what you think of your Creator.
Hold fast to these truths, knowing that your life is an expression of the divine, that your health is an expression of your faith and hope in that divine power within your own self.

After one has sought to realize the identity of his spirit with the Universal Energy and consequently with all other living spirits, which partake equally of it, one should formulate one's ideals, physically, mentally, and spiritually, and seek to achieve them. Activity is of the utmost importance; lip service and intellectual awareness alone are useless. Action is the criterion of sincerity, the measure and method of true growth. *Knowledge not lived is sin* is a constantly recurring theme of the readings.

Know what is your ideal—and be active! Better to do even the wrong thing than to do nothing. Remember, the man given only one talent hid it, and it was he that was questioned, and it was he from whom it was taken.

It is not enough for an entity to have knowledge concerning the law—whether it be karmic law, spiritual law, penal law, social law, or whatnot. The point is, what does the entity do about the knowledge that it has! Is the knowledge used to evade cause and effect, or is it used to coerce other persons into adhering to the thoughts of self? Or is it used to bring help to others in their understanding of the law?

Destiny, or karma, depends upon what the soul has done about what it has become aware of.

Know that every other individual has as much right in the earth as you have yourself, even though he may not be in some respects so far advanced in his learning. For remember —knowledge, or the seeking for the tree of knowledge, is the sin. It is use of what you do know to the glory of God that is righteousness.

Knowledge may not be put on as a cloak, but must be an internal growth toward that which has been determined as an ideal.

If one has fully grasped the meaning of these postulates of existence, one cannot but be patient in whatever enterprise or situation one finds oneself. Patience is not merely a passive thing, therefore; it is active. It is a watchful waiting, a positive rather than a negative virtue. It is the attitude of a soul that knows time and space to be, in a sense, illusory restrictions. When consciousness becomes unfettered by time and space, then is patience made perfect.

Patience is not passive or negative; it is a constructive thing, a positive, activating force. For if one smite you on the cheek, did He say withdraw? No! Rather, turn the other! Be active in your patience; be active in your relationships with your fellowman.

Then begin now to sow the seeds of the spirit in your mental attitudes, and the first of these is patience. *For in patience you possess your soul. In patience you become aware that the body is but a temple, but an outward appearance; that the*
234

mind and soul are that with which you dwell constantly. For each soul is in that process of development to become fully aware of its relationship to its Maker.

Joyousness, also, becomes the attribute of one who knows his identity and knows the law. *Be joyous!* is a command inseparable from *Be good!*

Remember, He is a God of Love, for He is love; a God of happiness, for He is happiness!

Those who walk closer with the Creative Forces should indeed be full of joy, pleasure, peace, and harmony within. For life is a manifestation of God, and the manner of life one lives is an entity's concept of what the entity would like to have its Creator be.

You must give account for every idle word. Not that you are not to be joyous, however. For if you lose the ability to laugh, you lose the ability to be joyous. And the principle of the Christ life is joyous! Remember, He laughed—even on the way to Calvary—not as so often pictured; he laughed. This is what angered them the most.

Cultivate the ability to see the ridiculous, and retain the ability to laugh. For remember, the Master smiled and laughed often, even on the way to Gethsemane.

There should be, together with one's activity, one's patience, and one's joyousness, a certain sense of detachment also. One should not look too closely for results, like a beginning gardener who constantly pulls up the radishes to see if they are growing. Plant, water, and remember that in due time God grants the increase. Do good not for the sake of reaping a reward, but because it is the beautiful, the fitting, the harmonious, the lawful thing to do.

Do not allow yourself to pity yourself or condemn yourself. So live and act, in everything you do, as will bring the very best; and let the consequences of it be in the keeping of Him that gives all good and perfect gifts.

Above all, one must recognize that problems—"if you choose to call them so"—are in reality opportunities. There is little point in evading a difficult situation; sooner or later the necessary strength of soul will need to be evolved, so one might better try to evolve it now.

Know that every soul eventually meets itself. No problem may be run away from. Meet it now!

All well-wrought systems can be compressed and simplified, and the above postulates and counsels of conduct to which they give rise are no exception. Their distilled essence becomes, very simply, the two ancient commandments: *Thou shalt love thy Lord with all thy body, mind, and soul; and thou shalt love thy neighbor as thyself.*

These two commandments may seem theologically platitudinous, but in reality they are a kind of shorthand transcription of the laws of the universe as they affect man according to the Cayce world view. For—if it be granted that a Central Creative Energy exists, and that the purpose of our life is to evolve consciously the perfection that lies latent within us by virtue of our identity with it—if this be granted, then it is clear that the simplest compression of this knowledge into wisdom is: Love the Great Creative Energy, its manifold beauty and its universal beneficent purpose, so that you strive to become one with it and expressive of it, in all departments of your being.

And if it further be granted that karmic, retributive law acts to punish us for whatever infringements we make on the freedom of will and the well-being of other persons as you love your own well-being.

Thus it is seen that the ancient wisdom which teaches the evolution of the soul through successive incarnations and by the laws of karma is in accord with the cardinal teachings of Jesus.

But the era of the usefulness of simplification is past. Man is no longer an infant; he needs the strong food of knowledge —exact, rational, and intelligible. There are many people of the Western world who cannot accept the world view of the Eastern religions, the view reaffirmed by the Cayce readings. And yet, though they cannot accept it without more rigorous scientific evidence than that provided by the Cayce data, they may find it difficult to deny that the reincarnationist view is precise, rational, and intelligible; that it is psychologically credible, ethically sound, and scientifically plausible. To the person who can accept it, reincarnation offers a purpose for living, a pole-star by which to travel, and an assurance that he is not lost in a meaningless chaos of forces over which he has no ultimate control.

Chapter XXV

Conclusion

_____

WE HAVE come a long way, in these pages, from the little incident in a hotel room in Dayton, Ohio, when Edgar Cayce first gave intimation while in clairvoyant hypnosis that reincarnation is a fact in nature. This incident, together with the series of related incidents that followed, may seem a slight substructure on which to erect the psychological and philosophical edifice whose outlines have here been sketched. And yet if one surveys the history of science, one sees that often great and revolutionary discoveries have evolved from unlikely sources. A twitching frog's leg and a piece of moldy bread do not seem propitious starting points for the discovery of the galvanic battery and the wonder drug penicillin; yet such were the origins of their discovery. A swinging lamp in an Italian church led Galileo to the invention of an astronomical pendulum clock; an overflowing bathtub gave Archimedes the clue he needed for the formulation of an important law of hydrostatics.

History affords us innumerable instances of the same general nature. We must, then, acknowledge that truth can be uncovered in humble places; and we must not be too surprised that an uneducated, ungrammatical man, lying unconscious on a couch, should be able to contribute important inferential evidence in support of a revolutionary theory of human life.

Let us now sum up the evidence that testifies to the validity of the life-reading material over and beyond the mass of evidence which incontrovertibly established the validity of his physical clairvoyance. This evidence consists in seven principal facts. They are as follows:

First: Character analyses and descriptions of circumstances were correct, on total strangers, at distances of hundreds of miles and in thousands of instances.

Second: Predictions of vocational abilities and other traits proved accurate in later years not only for adults, but also for newborn children.

Third: Psychological traits were plausibly accounted for by presumable past-life experiences.

Fourth: The data was self-consistent over a period of twenty-two years; that is to say, it agreed with itself, both in basic principle and in minute detail, in hundreds of separate readings taken at different times.

Fifth: Obscure historical details have been verified by consulting recorded history; the names of obscure former personalities have been found in the locality where the reading says they can be found.

Sixth: The readings had a helpful, transforming influence on the lives of persons who received and followed them; this was true psychologically, vocationally, and physically.

Seventh: The philosophical and psychological system which is implicit in and deducible from the readings is coherent, consistent, sufficient to all known facts about mental life, and conducive to the discovery of new explanations for unexplained aspects of mental life. It agrees, moreover, with the ancient and honorable philosophical doctrine that has been taught in India for centuries.

In short, seven strong inferential arguments support the Cayce life readings and the reincarnation principle which they affirm. Although inferential evidence is not necessarily conclusive, it is frequently valid. Even the proof that the world is round is only inferential proof—nobody has actually seen the total spheroid shape of the world; and the existence of the atom is also only inferentially known—no one has actually seen an atom. Yet on the strength of our inferences we successfully circumnavigate the globe and we devise an atomic bomb whose effects are tangible indeed. Surely it is not too preposterous, then, to propose that serious scientific investigation be made of reincarnation on the basis of the inferential evidence that the Cayce readings afford.

Reincarnationists can only hope that those people who are searching for a credible answer to the riddles of existence take the reincarnation principle to heart—that they live with it, act by it, for a while—that they measure themselves and their fellows and the human scene in general by its simple but cosmically significant principles. If at the end of a trial period, as the advertisers say, they are not completely satisfied, they can, at no expense to themselves, return the article to the counter of thought.

It is tempting to exclaim, with the advertisers, that *A trial will convince you;* but it is too well established that no one faith, no matter how sound and scientific its philosophic basis, can satisfy all men, and that there are many who will never accept reincarnation. They will never accept it, that is, until science, the modern messiah, has proclaimed it. It is to be hoped therefore that scientists in the fields of both the psychological and the physical sciences will direct attention to the hypothesis of which the Cayce readings give inferential proof.

Several lines of approach could be used. Laboratory demonstration of reincarnation by scientific method may be a possibility provided that appropriate techniques are used. This is an important stipulation. In order to plumb new strata of reality, new techniques of exploration must of necessity be used.

Hypnosis will undoubtedly prove the most immediately available and most fruitful technique; hypnotic experiments could be conducted on many people to determine whether past-life memories can be invoked. If memories so induced could be objectively checked with historical records and with known facts of the subject's mental life or circumstances, the material would then constitute valid inferential evidence in support of the theory.

A second possibility is the use of trained clairvoyants in collaboration with laboratory experimentation and clinical practice. Once clairvoyance becomes accredited as a faculty of the human mind, its tremendous possibilities as a new technique for obtaining knowledge cannot but be recognized. Persons of percipient powers could work in collaboration with psychological investigators and therapists, the clinical records of the therapy proposed on the basis of presumable past-life causation would of themselves constitute an important body of testimony.

Testimony such as this would be no different from that provided by the Cayce readings, except in one important respect. The Cayce readings were applied with remarkable results in the lives of persons who received them; innumerable written documents attest to their accuracy and their efficacy. But there was no supervision of their administration by trained investigators; no systematic follow-up; no correlative psychiatric or psychological analyses made at the same time the reading was given. If a clairvoyant of powers equal or similar to those of Cayce were to work with the full cooperation of an accredited professional psychological staff, the resultant body of case-study material would have all the evidential force of the Cayce material, but none of its limitations

If reincarnation is indeed the law of life whereby man evolves and becomes perfect—if this is indeed the simple truth about man, the simple key to the riddle of existence and of suffering—then all the theologies and all the psychologies of man will be seen to be like the curiously wavering distortions of the mirrors in an amusement park's Hall of Mirrors; the simple truth will be seen to stand in their midst like the person whose image is so strangely being distorted.

Surely it is worth the attention of serious-minded men to investigate a possibility the establishment of which could be so clarifying, so lifegiving, and so transformative. If indeed the soul of man has many mansions, now, of all times, is the time we need to know that truth. For with that knowledge comes a new nobility and a new courage. With it comes also a new vision—prismatic and wonderful—of the universe; a new understanding—subtler and deeper—of all human life; and a new-tempered resilience for all the manifold perplexities, tragedies, and sorrows of life.